LEGENDERRY™
VAMPIRELLA

A STEAMPUNK ADVENTURE

DYNAMITE®

Nick Barrucci, CEO / Publisher
Juan Collado, President / COO
Joe Rybandt, Senior Editor

Jason Ullmeyer, Design Director
Katie Hidalgo, Graphic Designer
Geoff Harkins, Graphic Designer
Chris Caniano, Digital Associate
Rachel Kilbury, Digital Assistant

Rich Young, Director Business Development
Keith Davidsen, Marketing Manager
Kevin Pearl, Sales Associate

On Visit us online at **www.DYNAMITE.com**
On Twitter **@dynamitecomics**
On Facebook **/Dynamitecomics**
On Tumblr **Dynamitecomics.Tumblr.com**
On YouTube **/Dynamitecomics**

ISBN-10: 1-60690-783-2
ISBN-13: 978-1-60690-783-2
First Printing 10 9 8 7 6 5 4 3 2 1

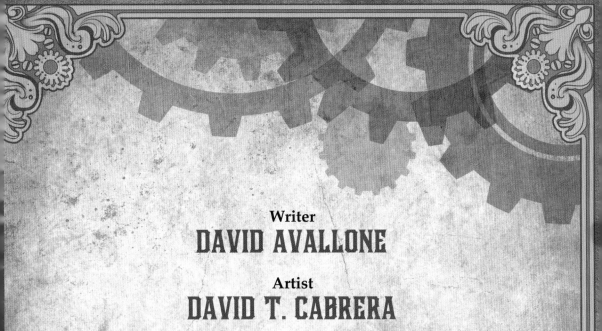

Writer
DAVID AVALLONE

Artist
DAVID T. CABRERA

Colors
ROBBY BEVARD

Letters
DAVE LANPHEAR

Collection cover
JOE BENITEZ and IVAN NUNES

Collection Design
GEOFF HARKINS

Special Thanks To
David Grace, Luke Lieberman, Lisa Kirby, Kim Niemi, Adam Street,
Tony Ezmond, Brendan Burford, Brad Thomte, and Ivan Nunes

This volume collects issues 1-5 of
"Legenderry: Vampirella"
from Dynamite Entertainment.

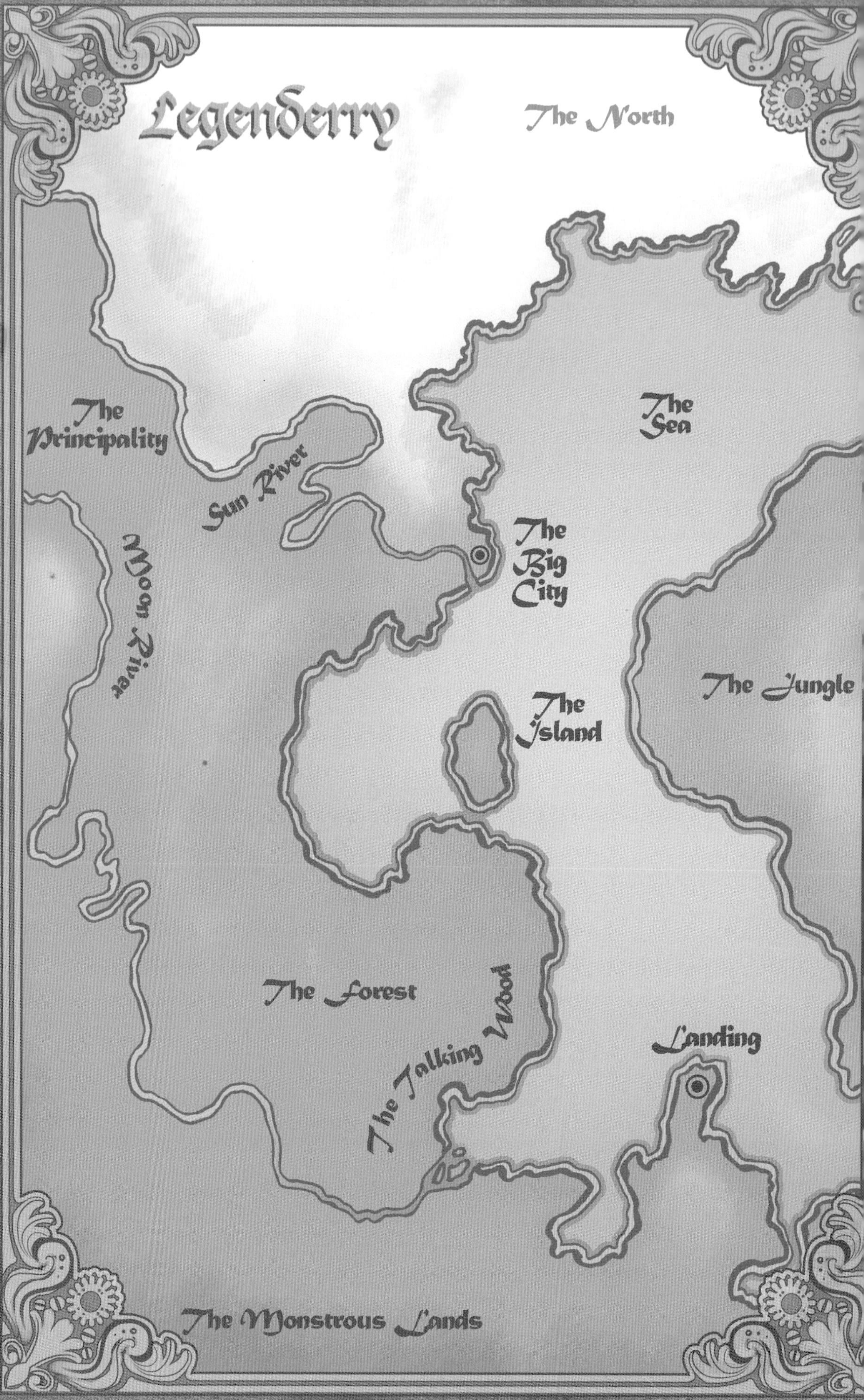
Legenderry
The North
The Principality
Sun River
Moon River
The Sea
The Big City
The Island
The Jungle
The Forest
The Talking Wood
Landing
The Monstrous Lands

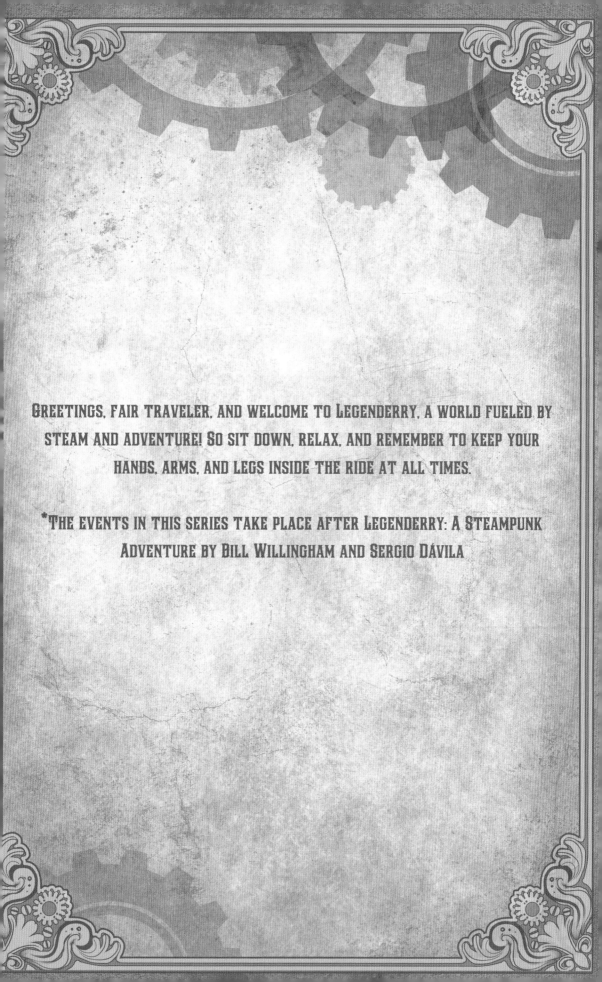

Greetings, fair traveler, and welcome to Legenderry, a world fueled by steam and adventure! So sit down, relax, and remember to keep your hands, arms, and legs inside the ride at all times.

*The events in this series take place after Legenderry: A Steampunk Adventure by Bill Willingham and Sergio Dávila

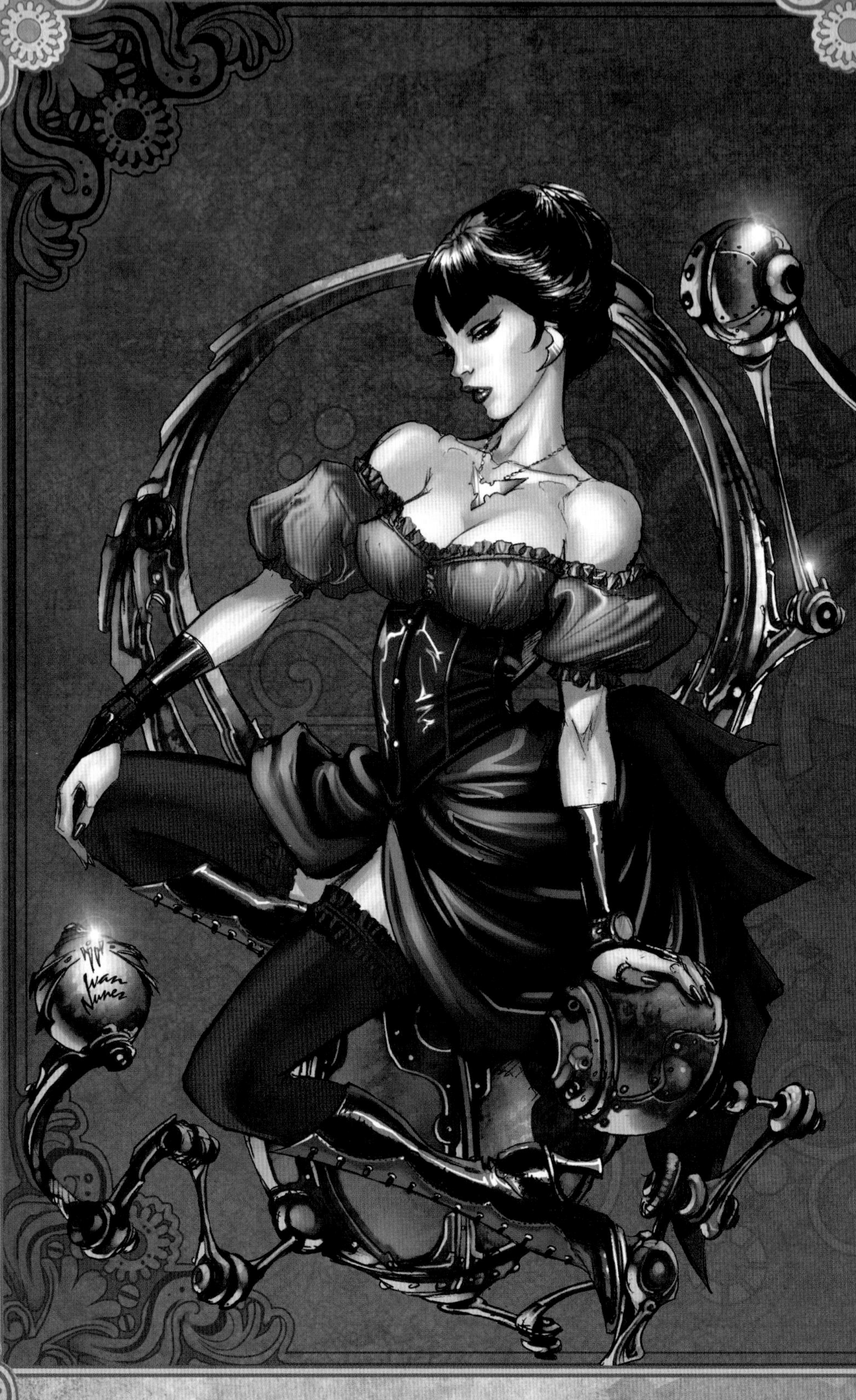

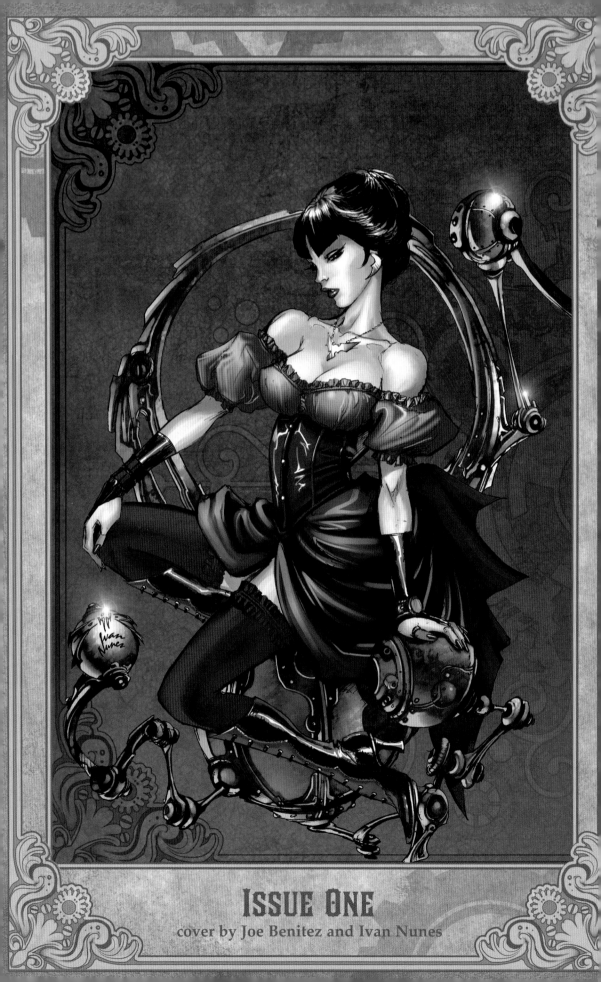

Issue One

cover by Joe Benitez and Ivan Nunes

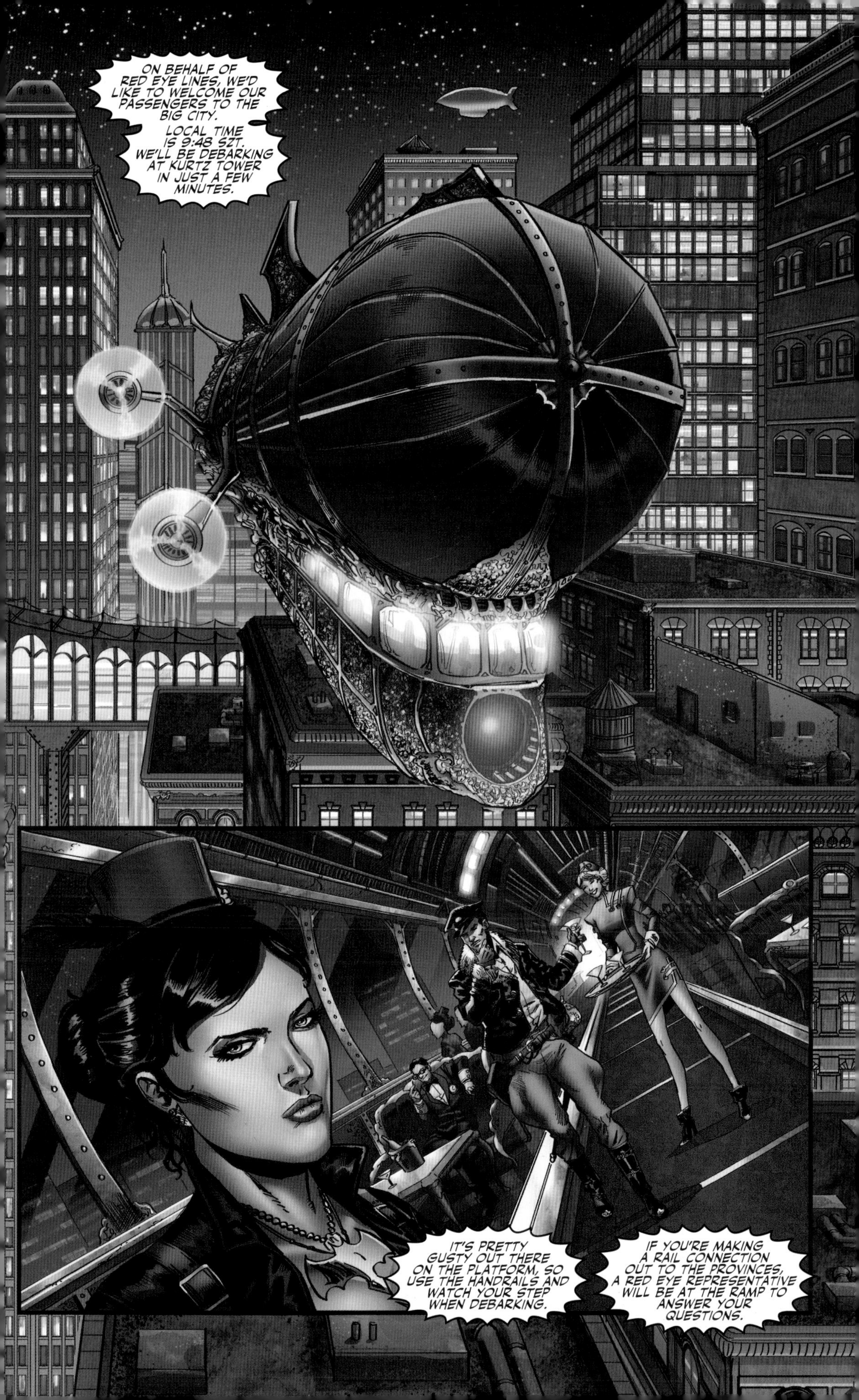
ON BEHALF OF RED EYE LINES, WE'D LIKE TO WELCOME OUR PASSENGERS TO THE BIG CITY.
LOCAL TIME IS 9:48 SZT. WE'LL BE DEBARKING AT KURTZ TOWER IN JUST A FEW MINUTES.
IT'S PRETTY GUSTY OUT THERE ON THE PLATFORM, SO USE THE HANDRAILS AND WATCH YOUR STEP WHEN DEBARKING.
IF YOU'RE MAKING A RAIL CONNECTION OUT TO THE PROVINCES, A RED EYE REPRESENTATIVE WILL BE AT THE RAMP TO ANSWER YOUR QUESTIONS.

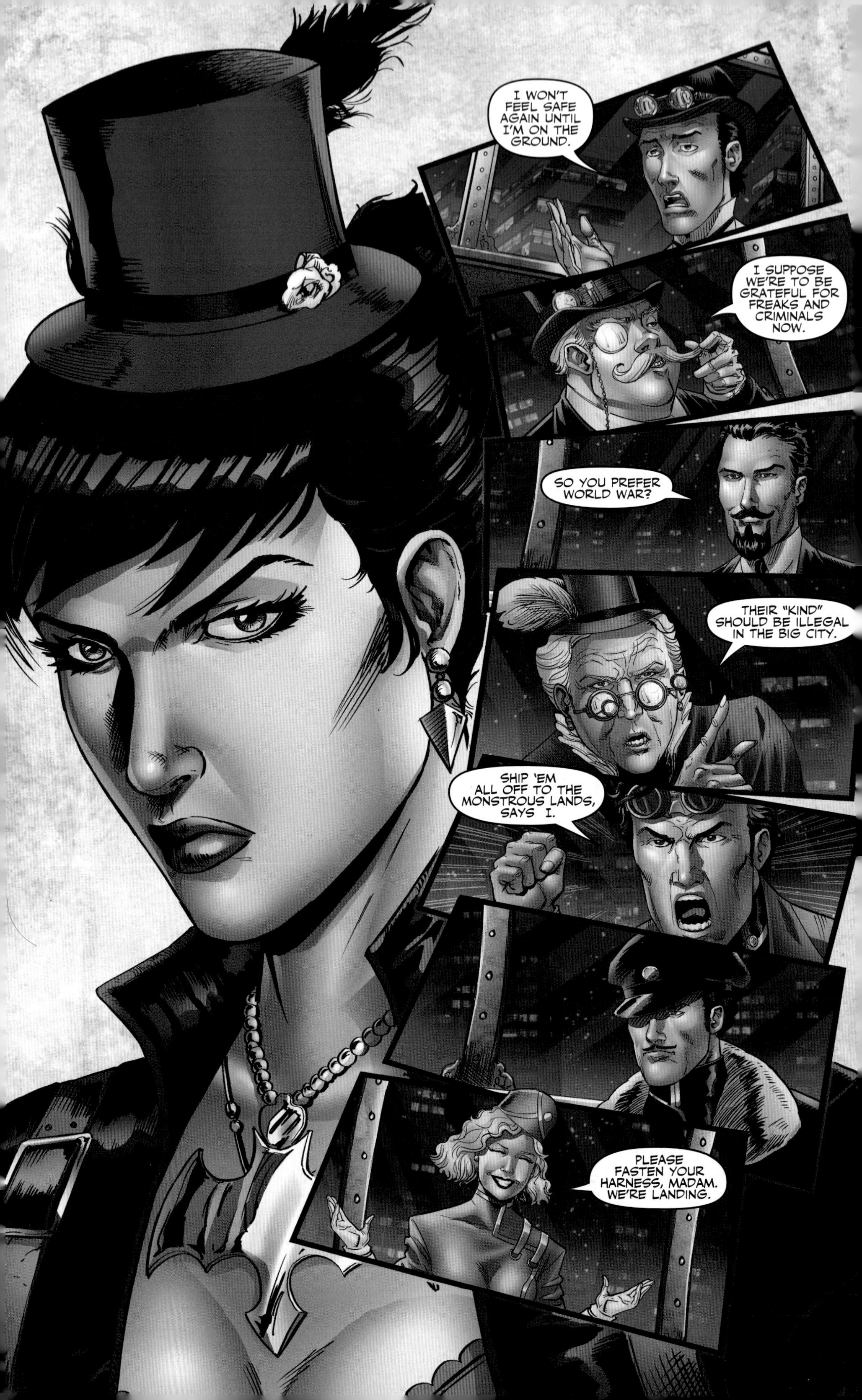
I WON'T FEEL SAFE AGAIN UNTIL I'M ON THE GROUND.
I SUPPOSE WE'RE TO BE GRATEFUL FOR FREAKS AND CRIMINALS NOW.
SO YOU PREFER WORLD WAR?
THEIR "KIND" SHOULD BE ILLEGAL IN THE BIG CITY.
SHIP 'EM ALL OFF TO THE MONSTROUS LANDS, SAYS I.
PLEASE FASTEN YOUR HARNESS, MADAM. WE'RE LANDING.

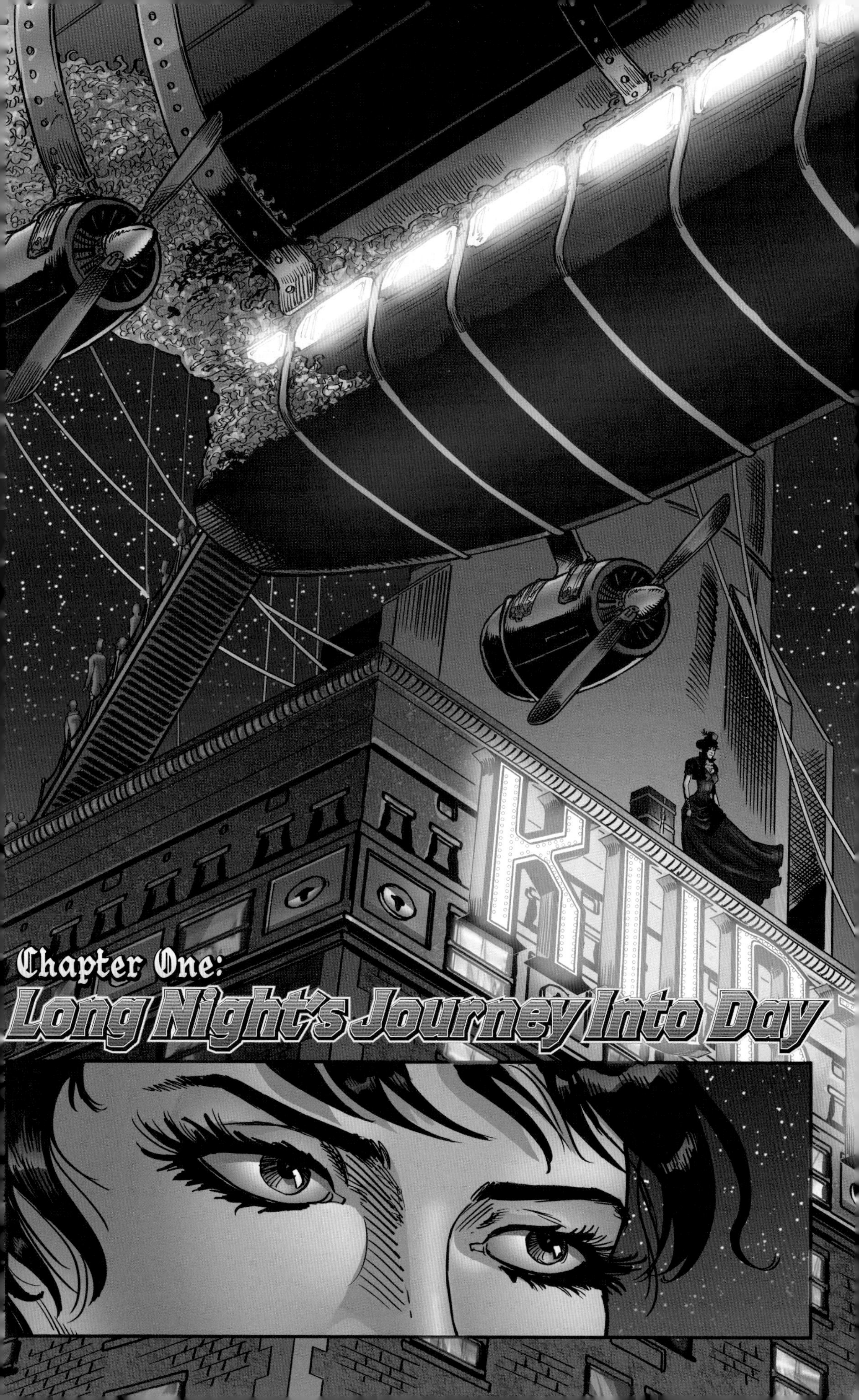
Chapter One:
Long Night's Journey Into Day

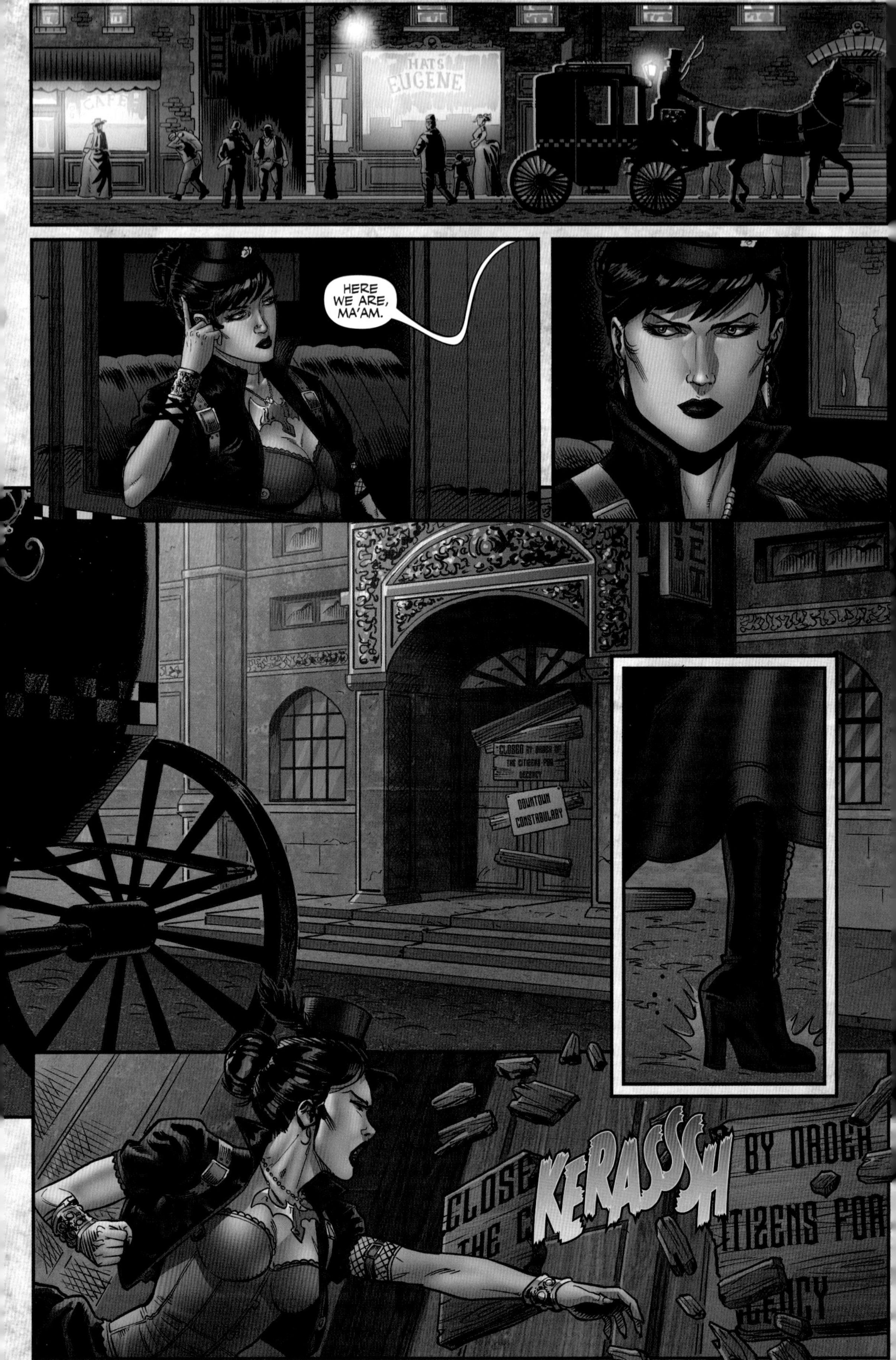
HATS
EUGENE
CAFE
HERE WE ARE, MA'AM.
DOWNTOWN CONSTABULARY
KERASSSH

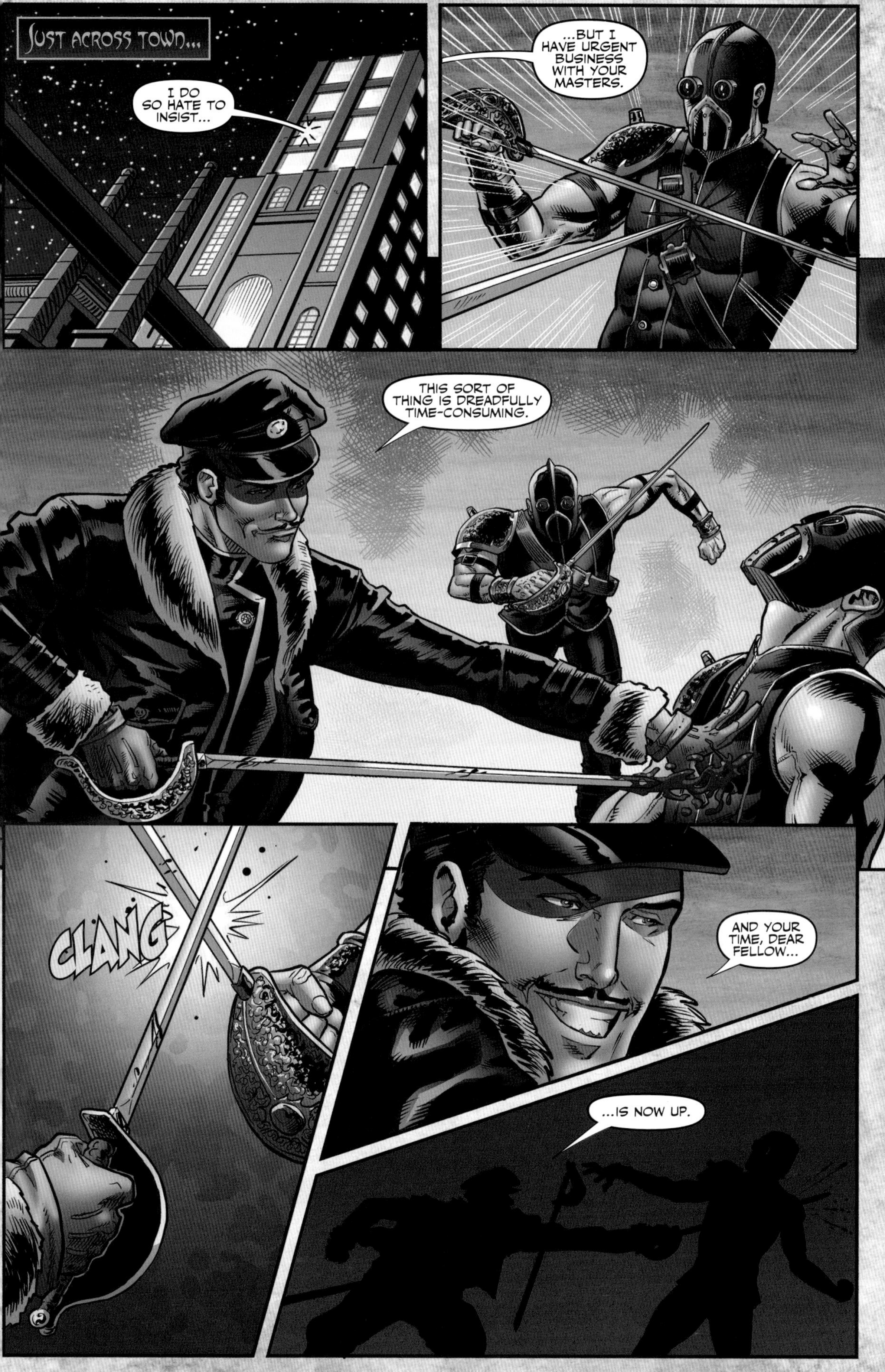
JUST ACROSS TOWN...
I DO SO HATE TO INSIST...
...BUT I HAVE URGENT BUSINESS WITH YOUR MASTERS.
THIS SORT OF THING IS DREADFULLY TIME-CONSUMING.
CLANG
AND YOUR TIME, DEAR FELLOW...
...IS NOW UP.

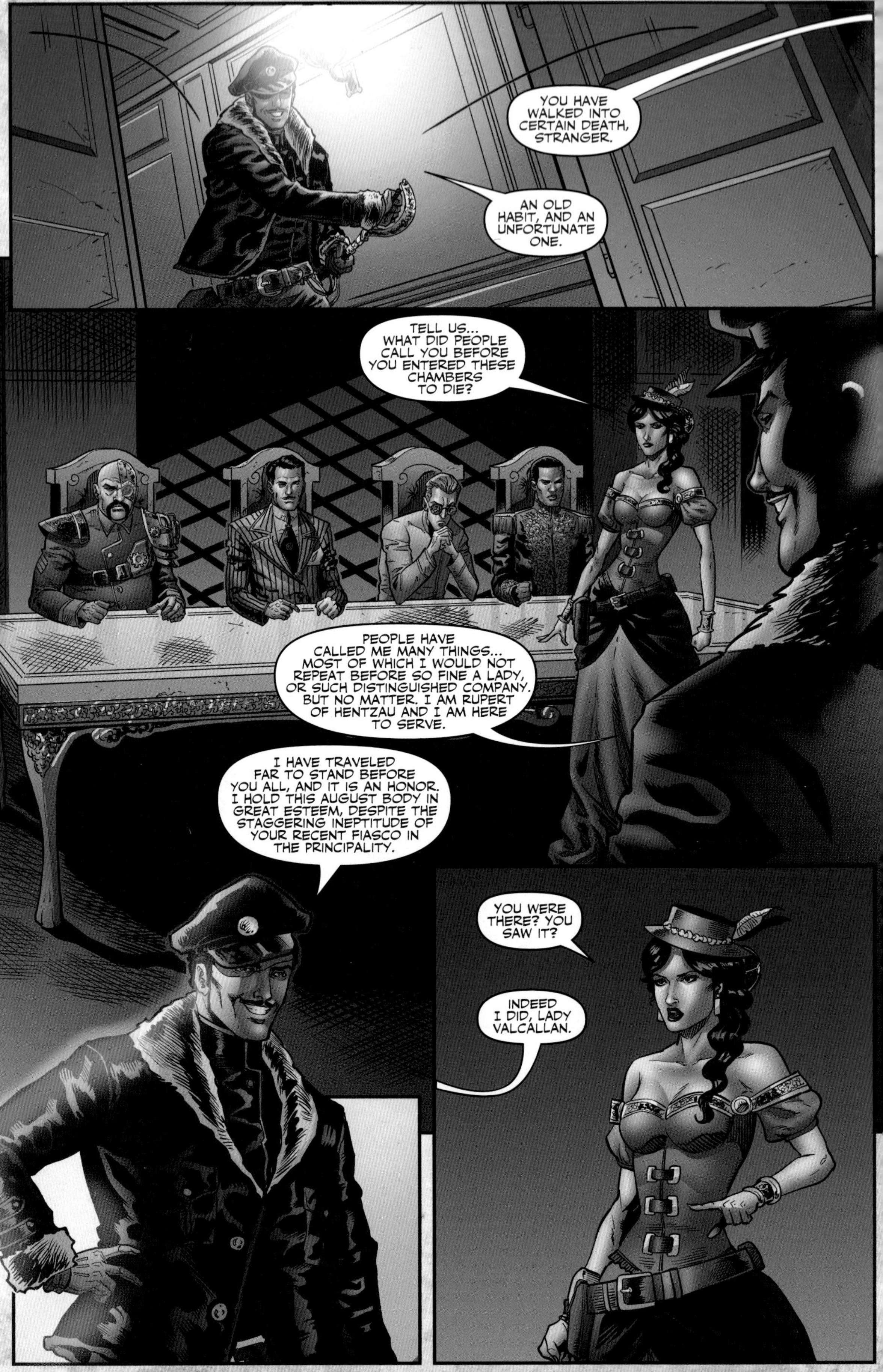
YOU HAVE WALKED INTO CERTAIN DEATH, STRANGER.
AN OLD HABIT, AND AN UNFORTUNATE ONE.
TELL US... WHAT DID PEOPLE CALL YOU BEFORE YOU ENTERED THESE CHAMBERS TO DIE?
PEOPLE HAVE CALLED ME MANY THINGS... MOST OF WHICH I WOULD NOT REPEAT BEFORE SO FINE A LADY, OR SUCH DISTINGUISHED COMPANY. BUT NO MATTER. I AM RUPERT OF HENTZAU AND I AM HERE TO SERVE.
I HAVE TRAVELED FAR TO STAND BEFORE YOU ALL, AND IT IS AN HONOR. I HOLD THIS AUGUST BODY IN GREAT ESTEEM, DESPITE THE STAGGERING INEPTITUDE OF YOUR RECENT FIASCO IN THE PRINCIPALITY.
YOU WERE THERE? YOU SAW IT?
INDEED I DID, LADY VALCALLAN.

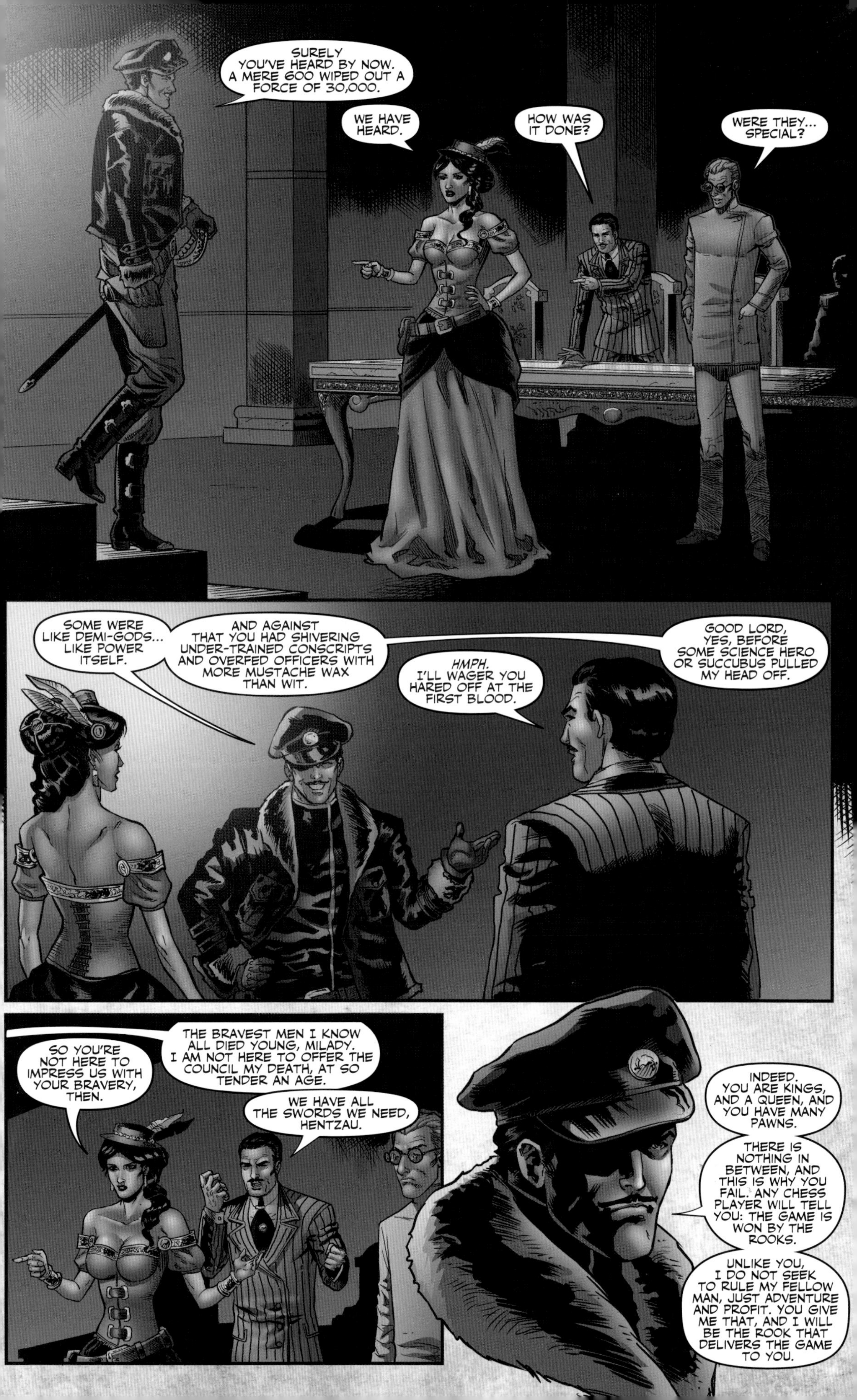
SURELY YOU'VE HEARD BY NOW. A MERE 600 WIPED OUT A FORCE OF 30,000.
WE HAVE HEARD.
HOW WAS IT DONE?
WERE THEY... SPECIAL?
SOME WERE LIKE DEMI-GODS... LIKE POWER ITSELF.
AND AGAINST THAT YOU HAD SHIVERING UNDER-TRAINED CONSCRIPTS AND OVERFED OFFICERS WITH MORE MUSTACHE WAX THAN WIT.
HMPH. I'LL WAGER YOU HARED OFF AT THE FIRST BLOOD.
GOOD LORD, YES, BEFORE SOME SCIENCE HERO OR SUCCUBUS PULLED MY HEAD OFF.
SO YOU'RE NOT HERE TO IMPRESS US WITH YOUR BRAVERY, THEN.
THE BRAVEST MEN I KNOW ALL DIED YOUNG, MILADY. I AM NOT HERE TO OFFER THE COUNCIL MY DEATH, AT SO TENDER AN AGE.
WE HAVE ALL THE SWORDS WE NEED, HENTZAU.
INDEED. YOU ARE KINGS, AND A QUEEN, AND YOU HAVE MANY PAWNS.
THERE IS NOTHING IN BETWEEN, AND THIS IS WHY YOU FAIL. ANY CHESS PLAYER WILL TELL YOU: THE GAME IS WON BY THE ROOKS.
UNLIKE YOU, I DO NOT SEEK TO RULE MY FELLOW MAN, JUST ADVENTURE AND PROFIT. YOU GIVE ME THAT, AND I WILL BE THE ROOK THAT DELIVERS THE GAME TO YOU.

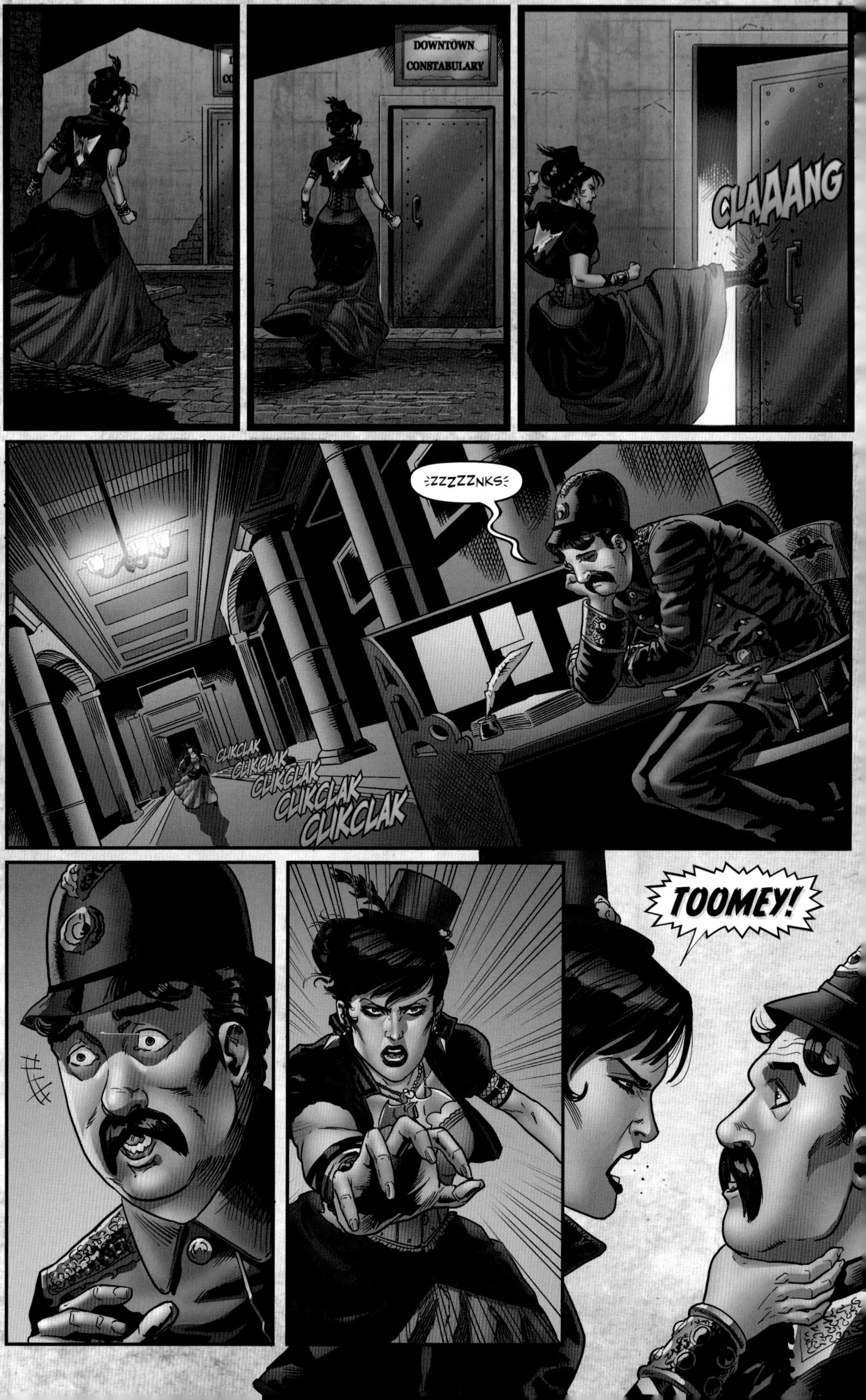
DOWNTOWN
CONSTABULARY
CLAAANG
ZZZZZNKS
CLIKCLAK
CLIKCLAK
CLIKCLAK
CLIKCLAK
CLIKCLAK
TOOMEY!

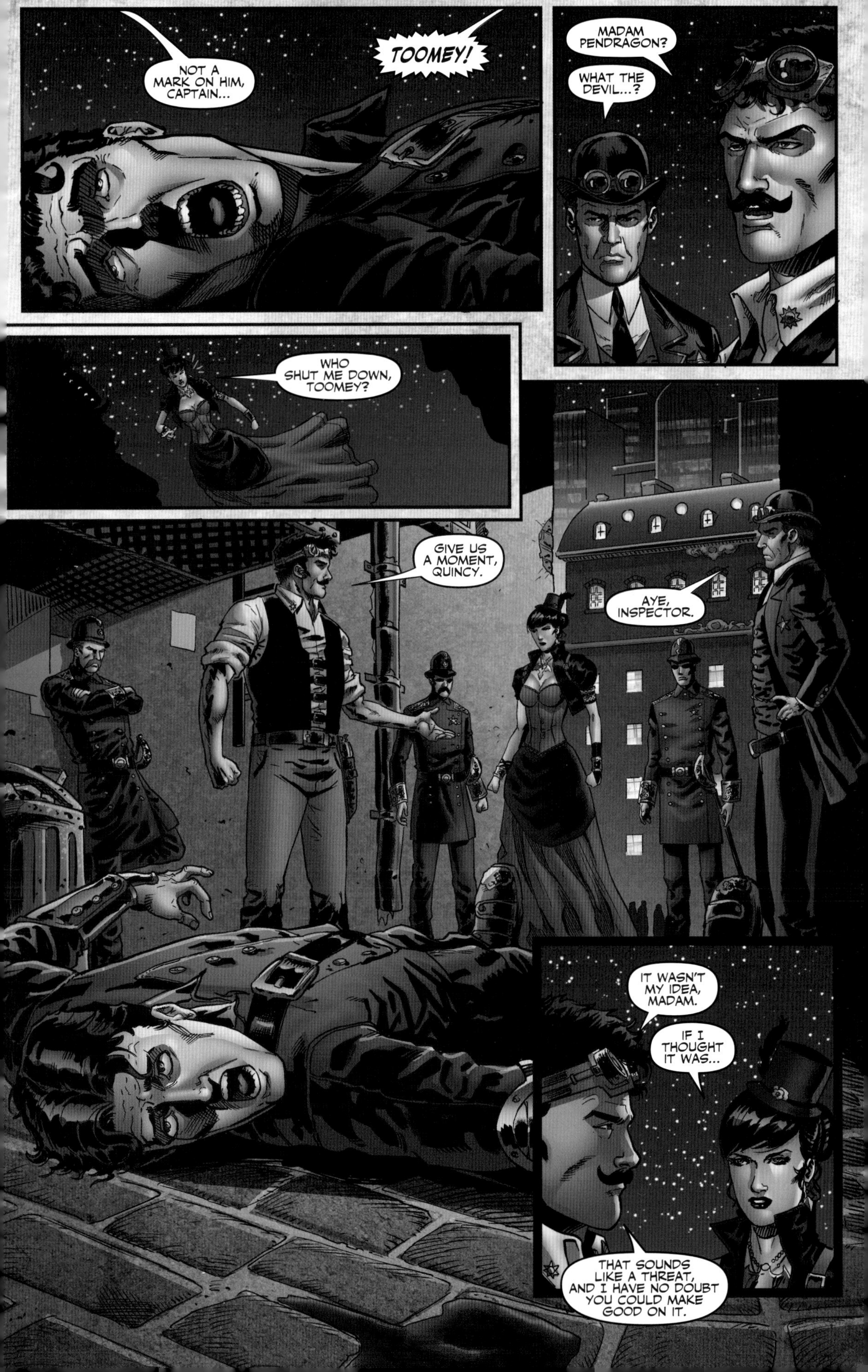
NOT A MARK ON HIM, CAPTAIN...
TOOMEY!
MADAM PENDRAGON?
WHAT THE DEVIL...?
WHO SHUT ME DOWN, TOOMEY?
GIVE US A MOMENT, QUINCY.
AYE, INSPECTOR.
IT WASN'T MY IDEA, MADAM.
IF I THOUGHT IT WAS...
THAT SOUNDS LIKE A THREAT, AND I HAVE NO DOUBT YOU COULD MAKE GOOD ON IT.

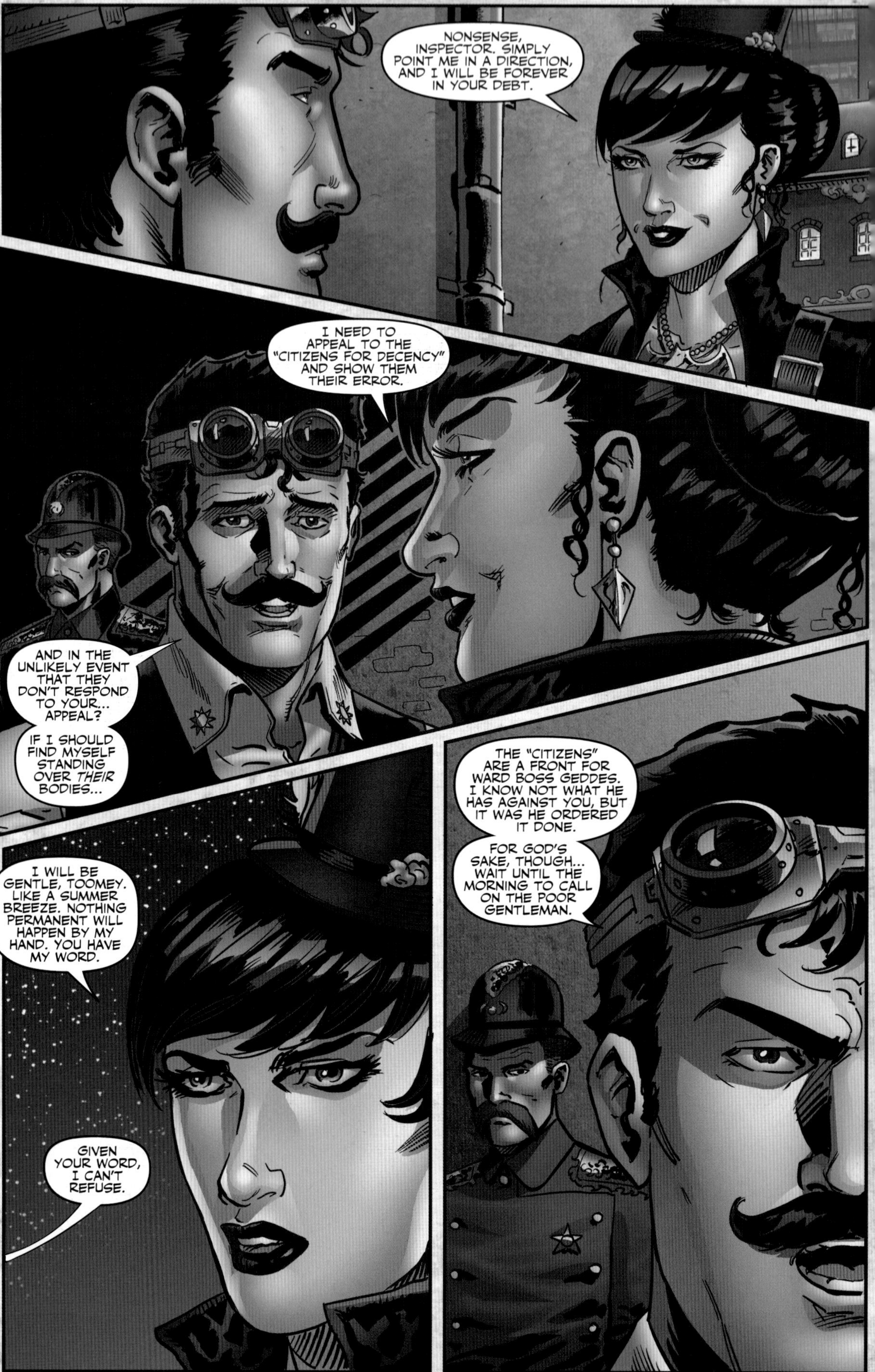
NONSENSE, INSPECTOR. SIMPLY POINT ME IN A DIRECTION, AND I WILL BE FOREVER IN YOUR DEBT.
I NEED TO APPEAL TO THE "CITIZENS FOR DECENCY" AND SHOW THEM THEIR ERROR.
AND IN THE UNLIKELY EVENT THAT THEY DON'T RESPOND TO YOUR... APPEAL?
IF I SHOULD FIND MYSELF STANDING OVER *THEIR* BODIES...
I WILL BE GENTLE, TOOMEY. LIKE A SUMMER BREEZE. NOTHING PERMANENT WILL HAPPEN BY MY HAND. YOU HAVE MY WORD.
GIVEN YOUR WORD, I CAN'T REFUSE.
THE "CITIZENS" ARE A FRONT FOR WARD BOSS GEDDES. I KNOW NOT WHAT HE HAS AGAINST YOU, BUT IT WAS HE ORDERED IT DONE.
FOR GOD'S SAKE, THOUGH... WAIT UNTIL THE MORNING TO CALL ON THE POOR GENTLEMAN.

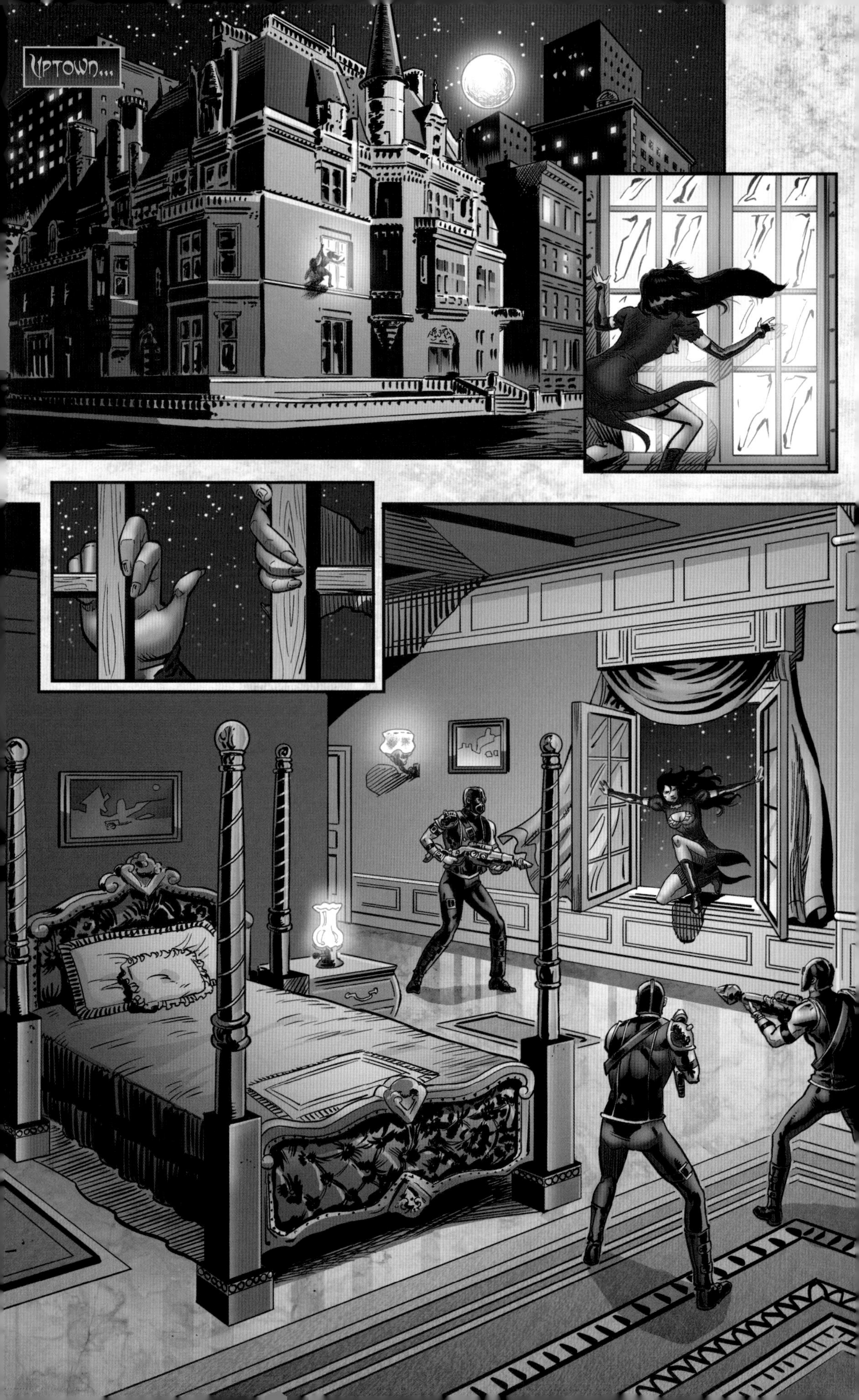
Uptown...

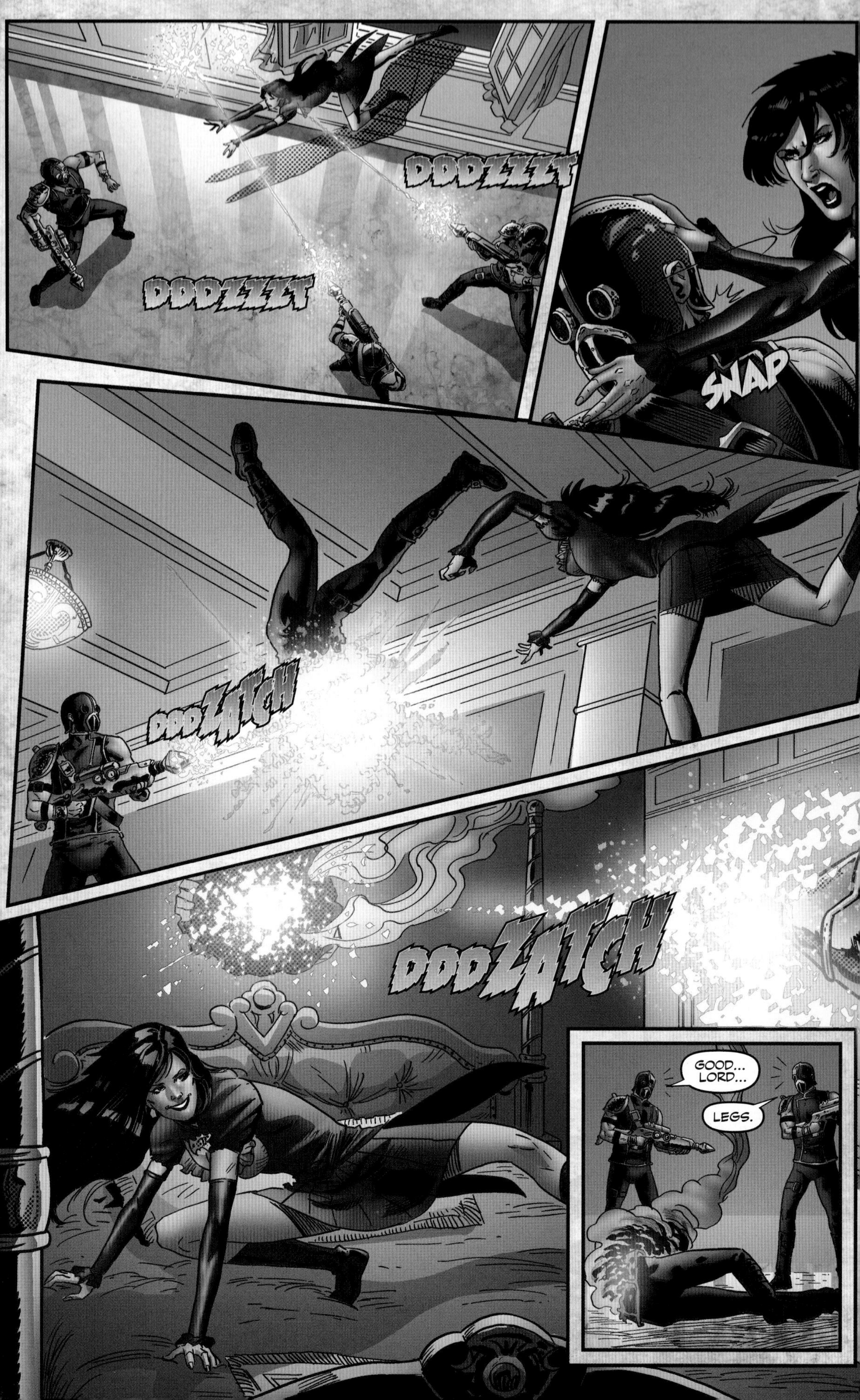

DDDZZZZT
DDDZZZZT
SNAP
DDDZATCH
DDDZATCH
GOOD... LORD...
LEGS.

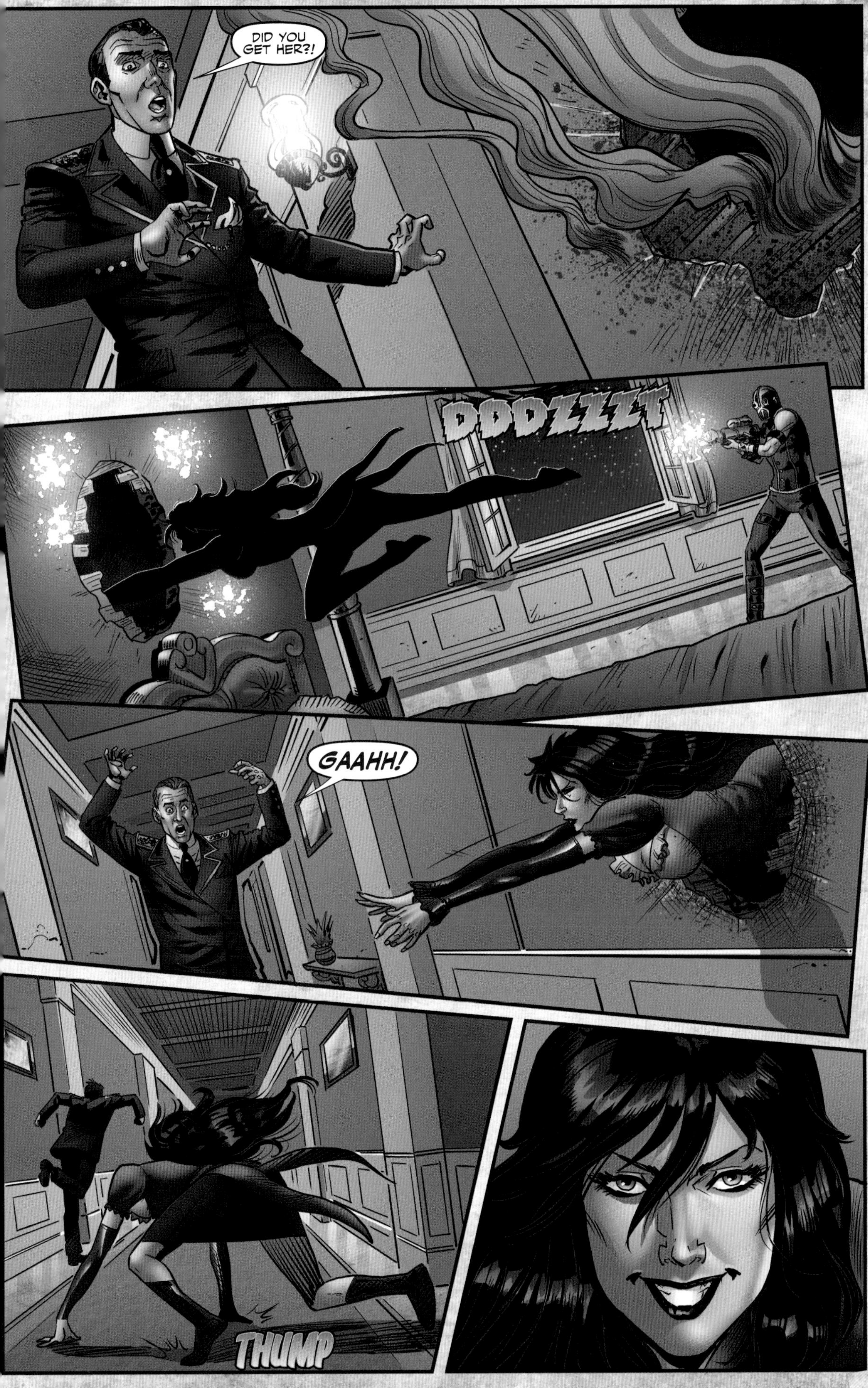
DID YOU GET HER?!
DDDZZZT
GAAHH!
THUMP

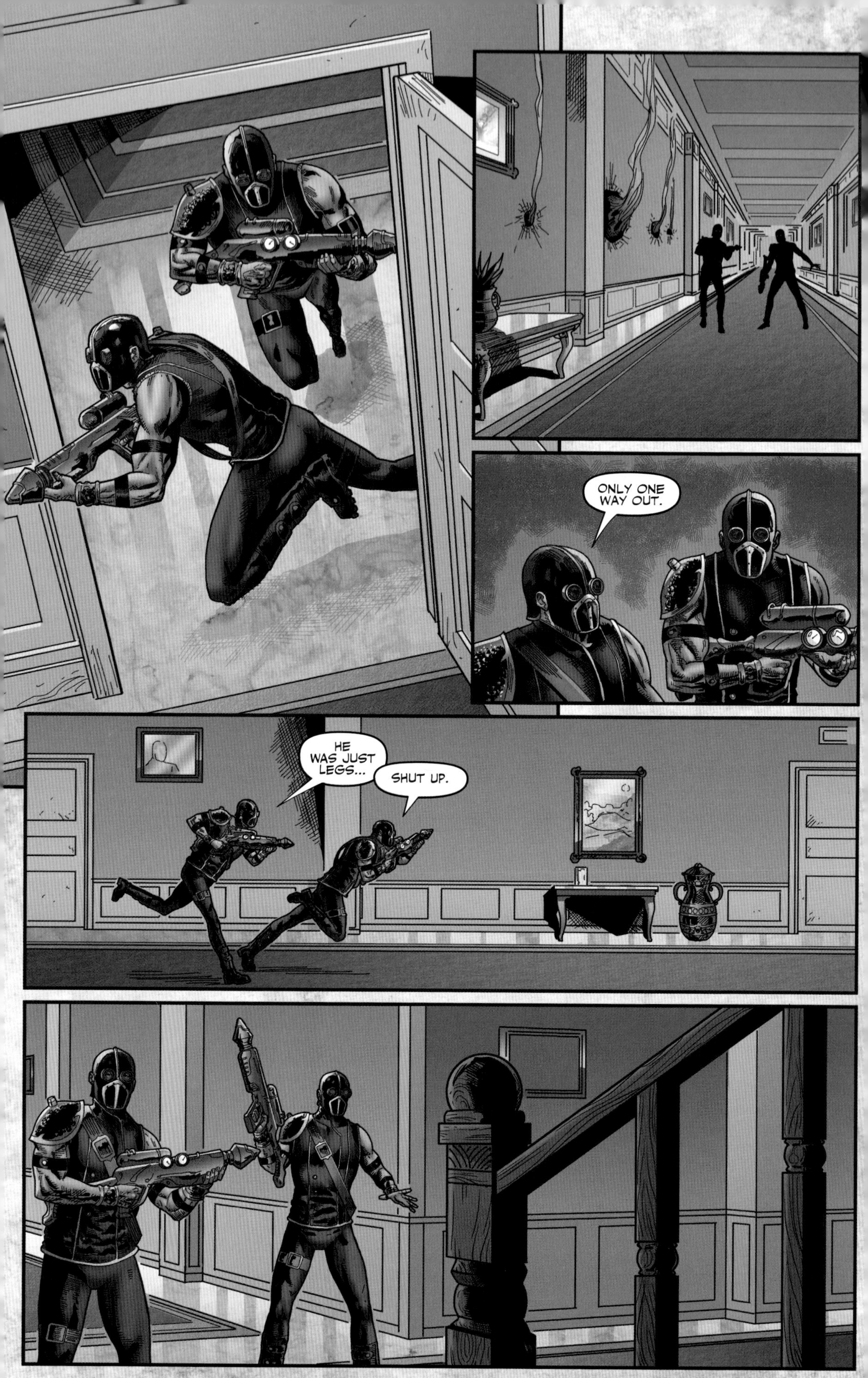
ONLY ONE WAY OUT.
HE WAS JUST LEGS...
SHUT UP.

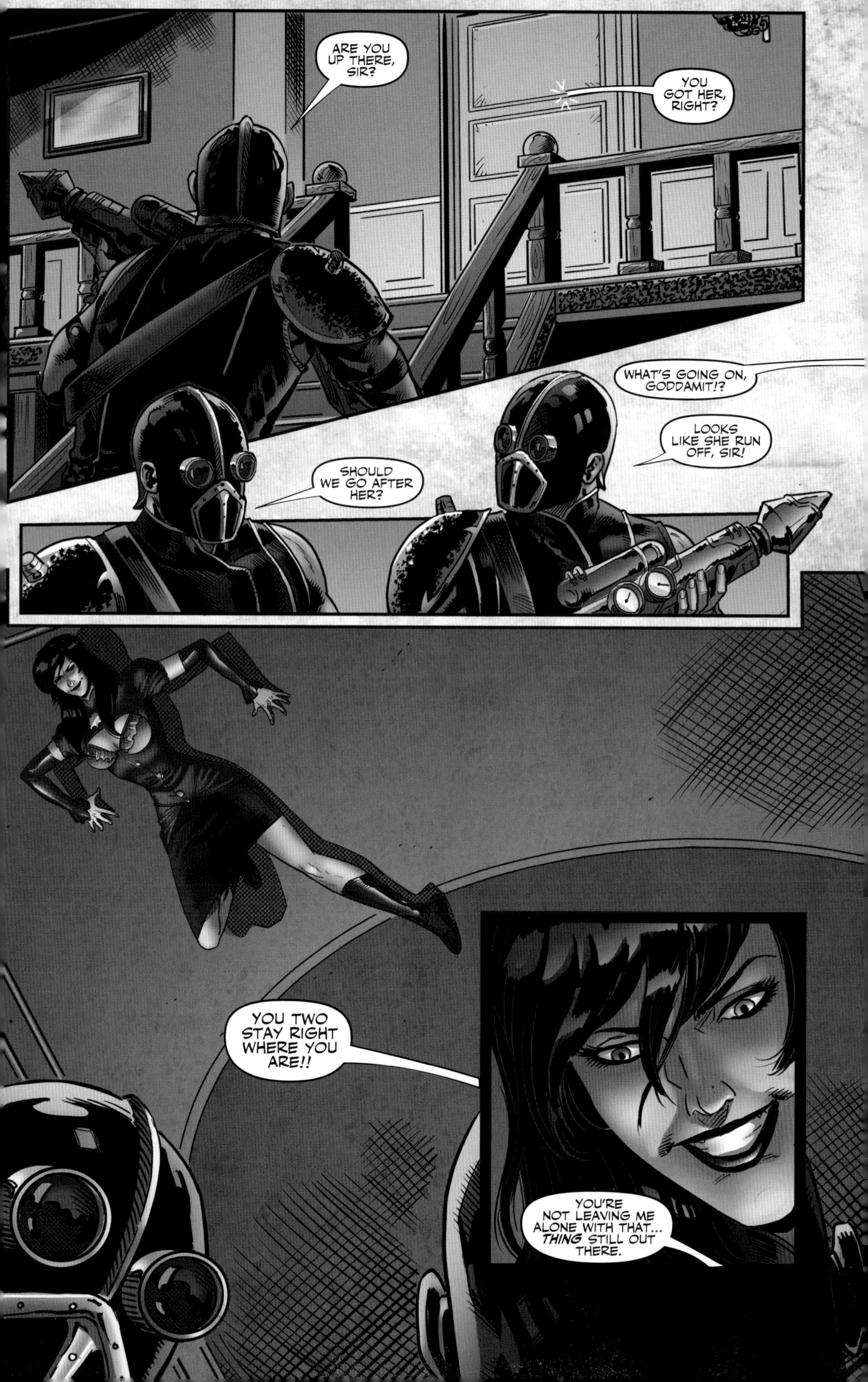
ARE YOU UP THERE, SIR?
YOU GOT HER, RIGHT?
WHAT'S GOING ON, GODDAMIT!?
LOOKS LIKE SHE RUN OFF, SIR!
SHOULD WE GO AFTER HER?
YOU TWO STAY RIGHT WHERE YOU ARE!!
YOU'RE NOT LEAVING ME ALONE WITH THAT... *THING* STILL OUT THERE.

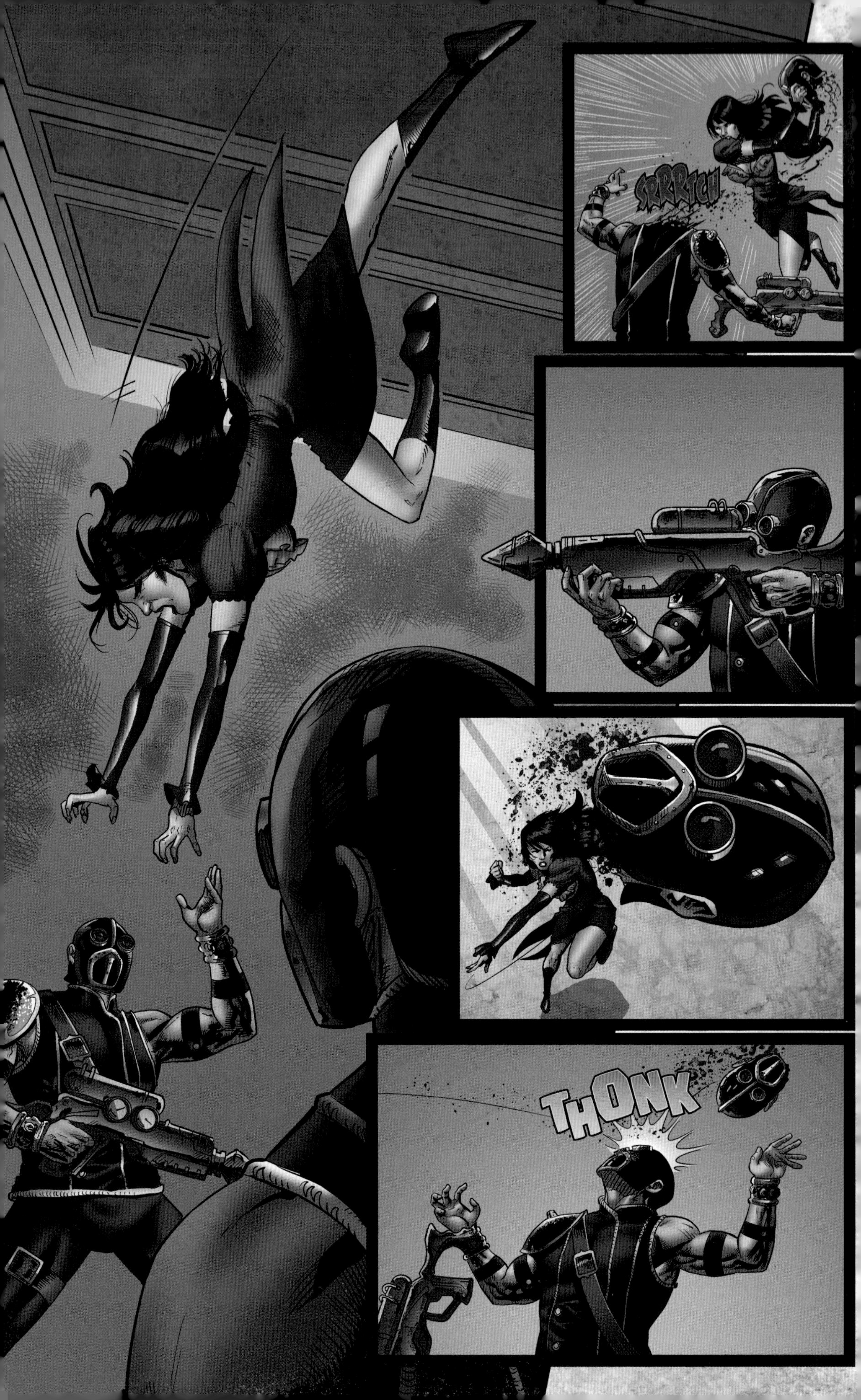
SRRRTCH
THONK

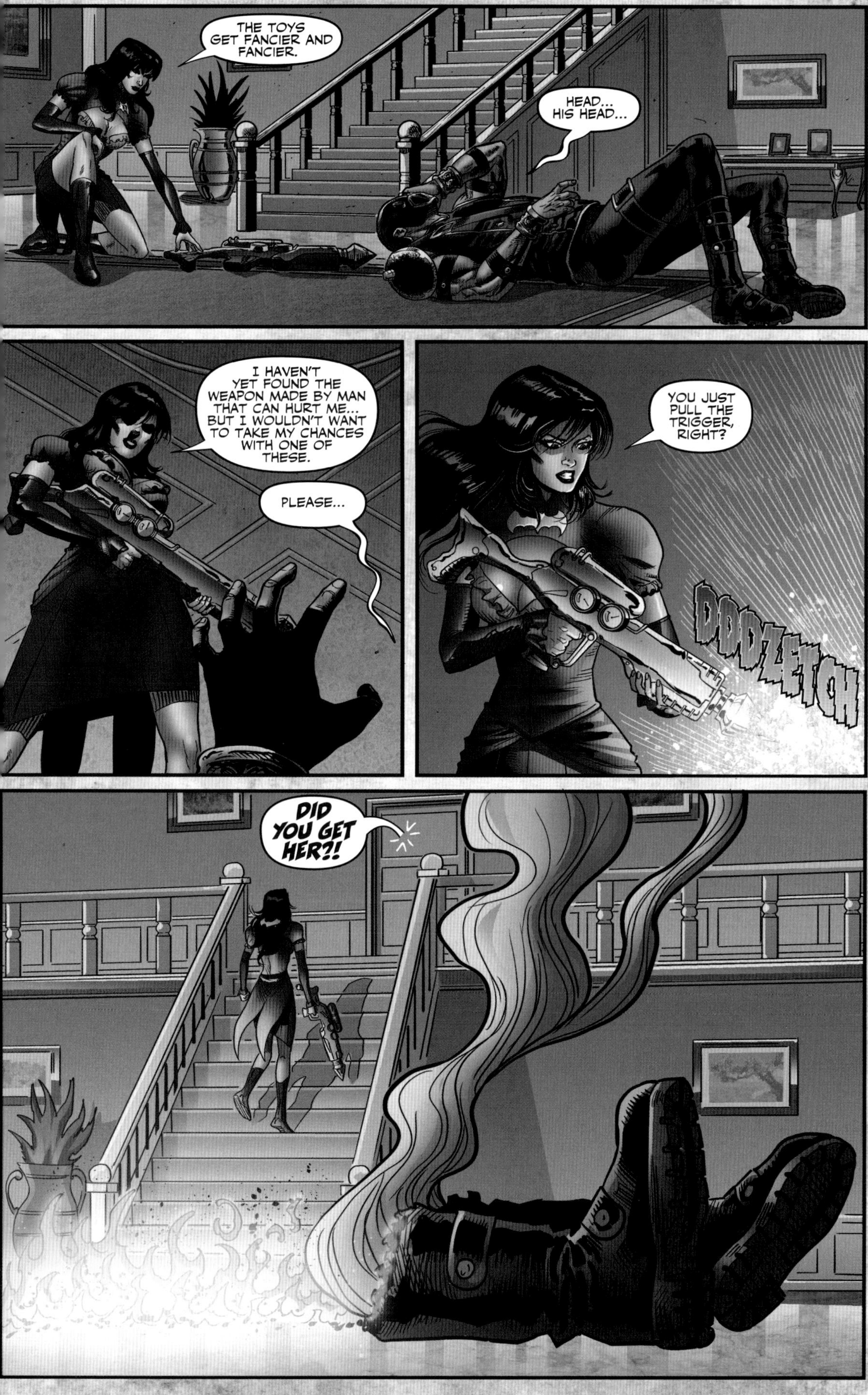
THE TOYS GET FANCIER AND FANCIER.
HEAD... HIS HEAD...
I HAVEN'T YET FOUND THE WEAPON MADE BY MAN THAT CAN HURT ME... BUT I WOULDN'T WANT TO TAKE MY CHANCES WITH ONE OF THESE.
PLEASE...
YOU JUST PULL THE TRIGGER, RIGHT?
DDDZETCH
DID YOU GET HER?!

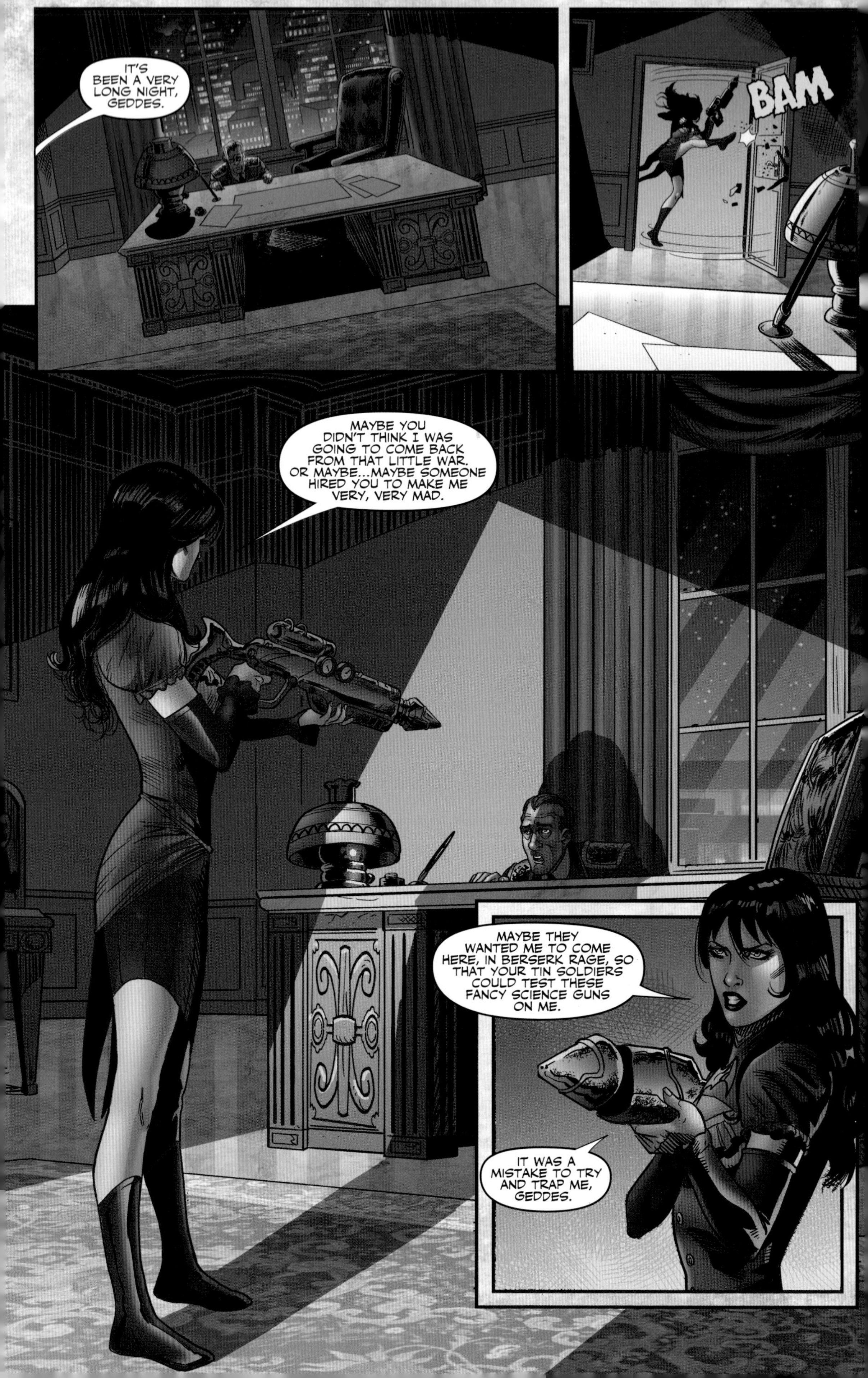
IT'S BEEN A VERY LONG NIGHT, GEDDES.
BAM
MAYBE YOU DIDN'T THINK I WAS GOING TO COME BACK FROM THAT LITTLE WAR. OR MAYBE...MAYBE SOMEONE HIRED YOU TO MAKE ME VERY, VERY MAD.
MAYBE THEY WANTED ME TO COME HERE, IN BERSERK RAGE, SO THAT YOUR TIN SOLDIERS COULD TEST THESE FANCY SCIENCE GUNS ON ME.
IT WAS A MISTAKE TO TRY AND TRAP ME, GEDDES.

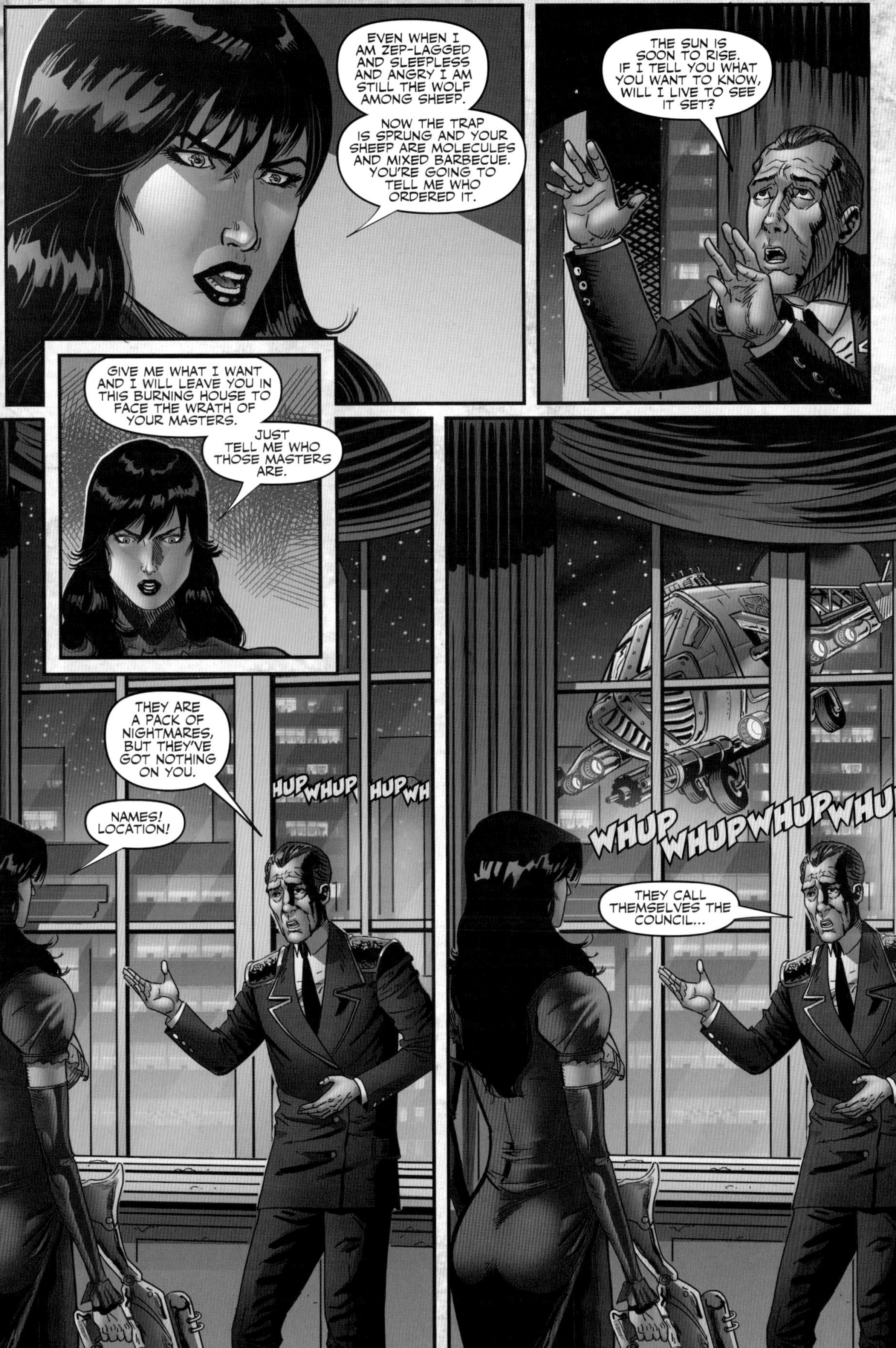
EVEN WHEN I AM ZEP-LAGGED AND SLEEPLESS AND ANGRY I AM STILL THE WOLF AMONG SHEEP.
NOW THE TRAP IS SPRUNG AND YOUR SHEEP ARE MOLECULES AND MIXED BARBECUE. YOU'RE GOING TO TELL ME WHO ORDERED IT.
THE SUN IS SOON TO RISE. IF I TELL YOU WHAT YOU WANT TO KNOW, WILL I LIVE TO SEE IT SET?
GIVE ME WHAT I WANT AND I WILL LEAVE YOU IN THIS BURNING HOUSE TO FACE THE WRATH OF YOUR MASTERS.
JUST TELL ME WHO THOSE MASTERS ARE.
THEY ARE A PACK OF NIGHTMARES, BUT THEY'VE GOT NOTHING ON YOU.
NAMES! LOCATION!
HUP WHUP HUP WH
WHUP WHUP WHUP WHU
THEY CALL THEMSELVES THE COUNCIL...

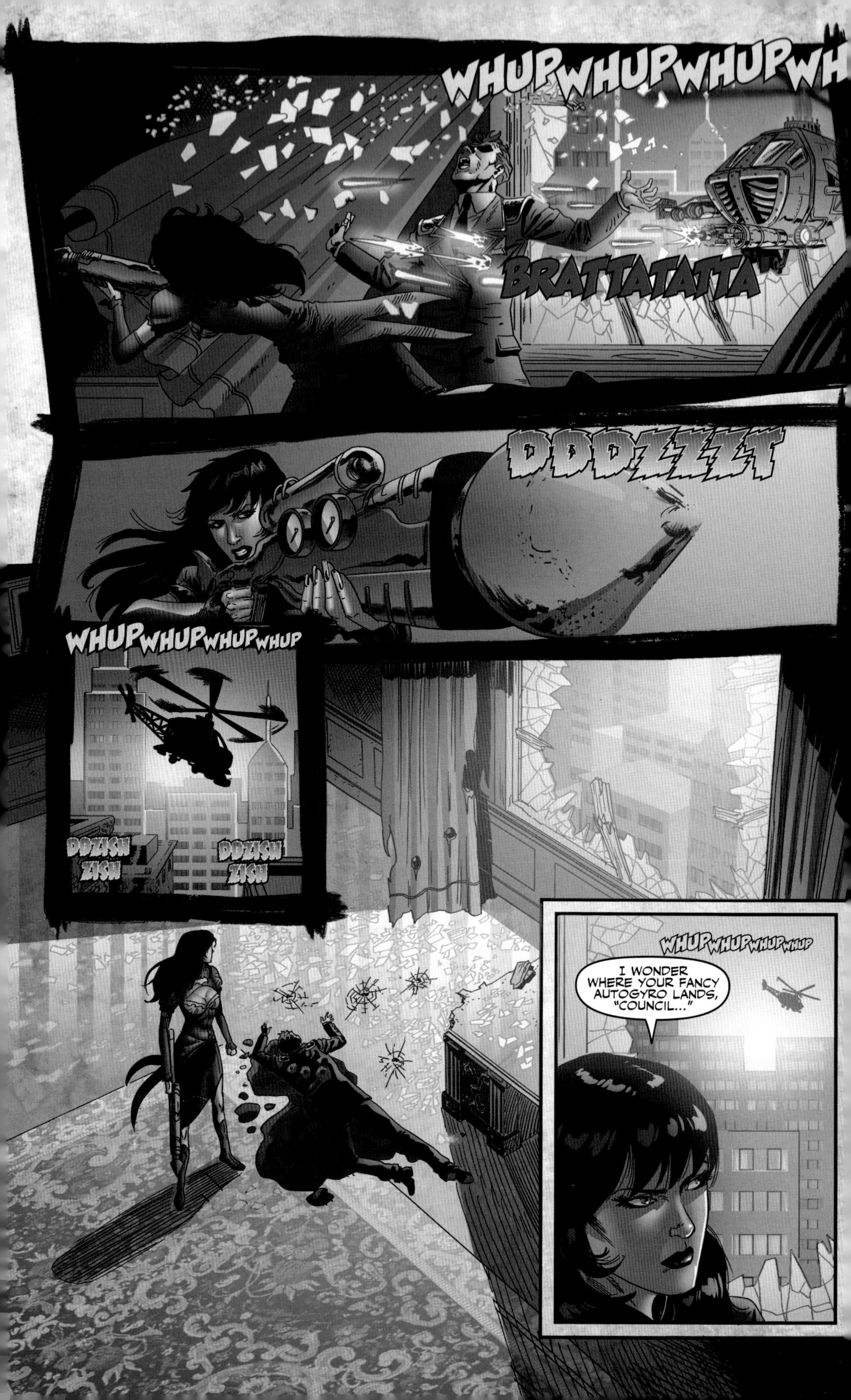
WHUPWHUPWHUPWH
BRATTATATTA
DDDZZZT
WHUPWHUPWHUPWHUP
DDZISH ZISH
DDZISH ZISH
WHUPWHUPWHUPWHUP
I WONDER WHERE YOUR FANCY AUTOGYRO LANDS, "COUNCIL..."

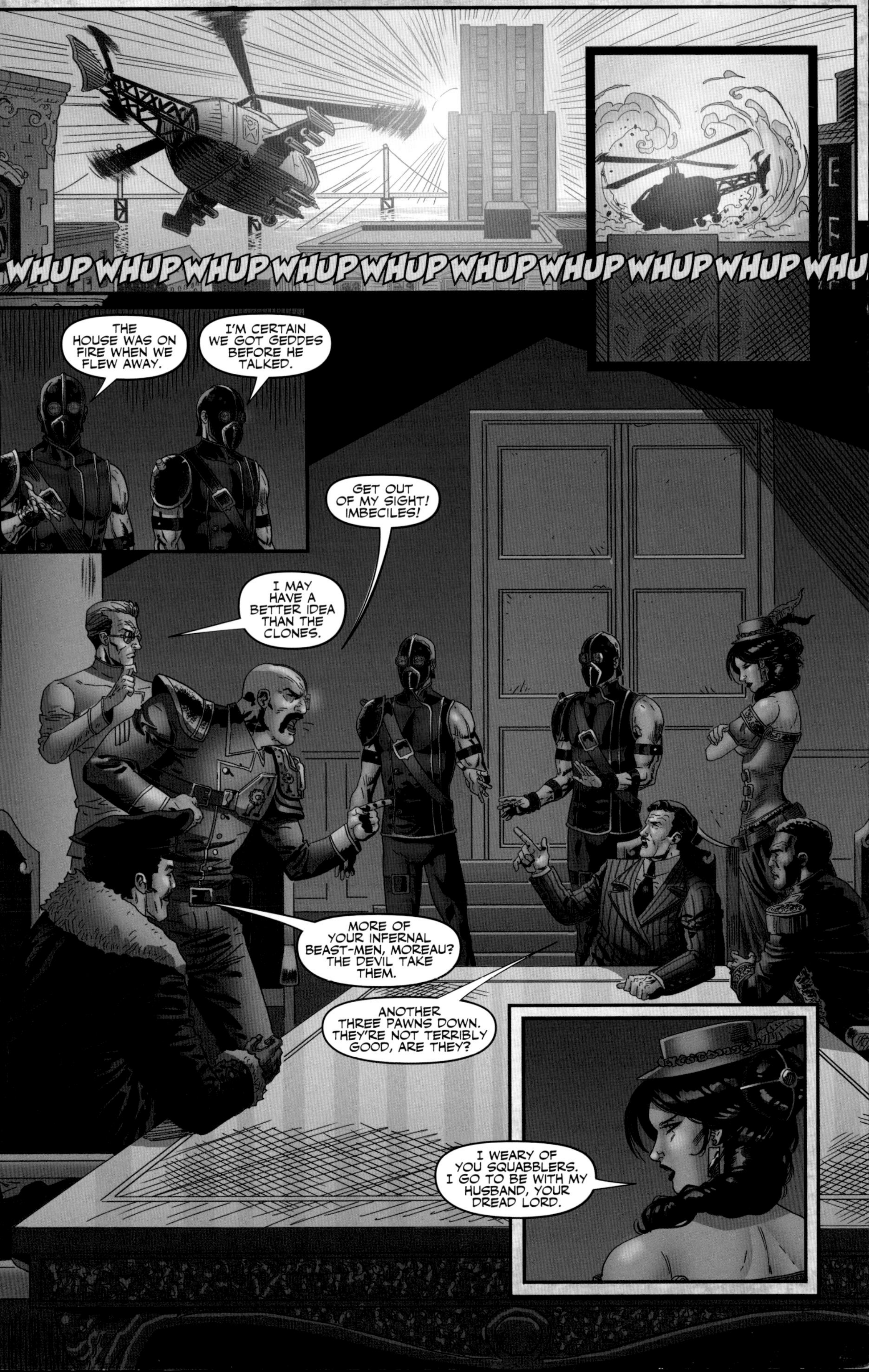
WHUP WHUP WHUP WHUP WHUP WHUP WHUP WHUP WHU
THE HOUSE WAS ON FIRE WHEN WE FLEW AWAY.
I'M CERTAIN WE GOT GEDDES BEFORE HE TALKED.
GET OUT OF MY SIGHT! IMBECILES!
I MAY HAVE A BETTER IDEA THAN THE CLONES.
MORE OF YOUR INFERNAL BEAST-MEN, MOREAU? THE DEVIL TAKE THEM.
ANOTHER THREE PAWNS DOWN. THEY'RE NOT TERRIBLY GOOD, ARE THEY?
I WEARY OF YOU SQUABBLERS. I GO TO BE WITH MY HUSBAND, YOUR DREAD LORD.

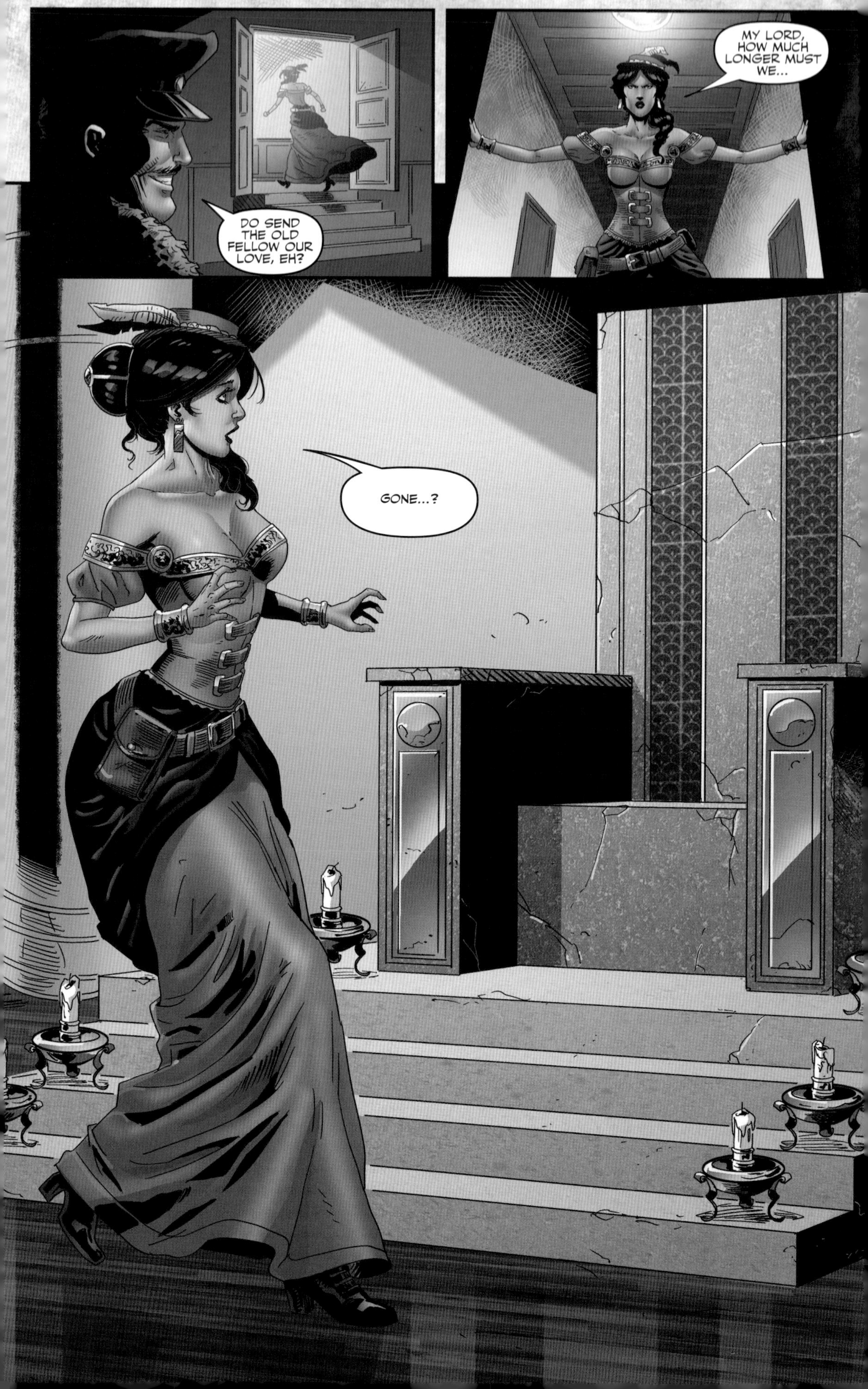
DO SEND THE OLD FELLOW OUR LOVE, EH?
MY LORD, HOW MUCH LONGER MUST WE...
GONE...?

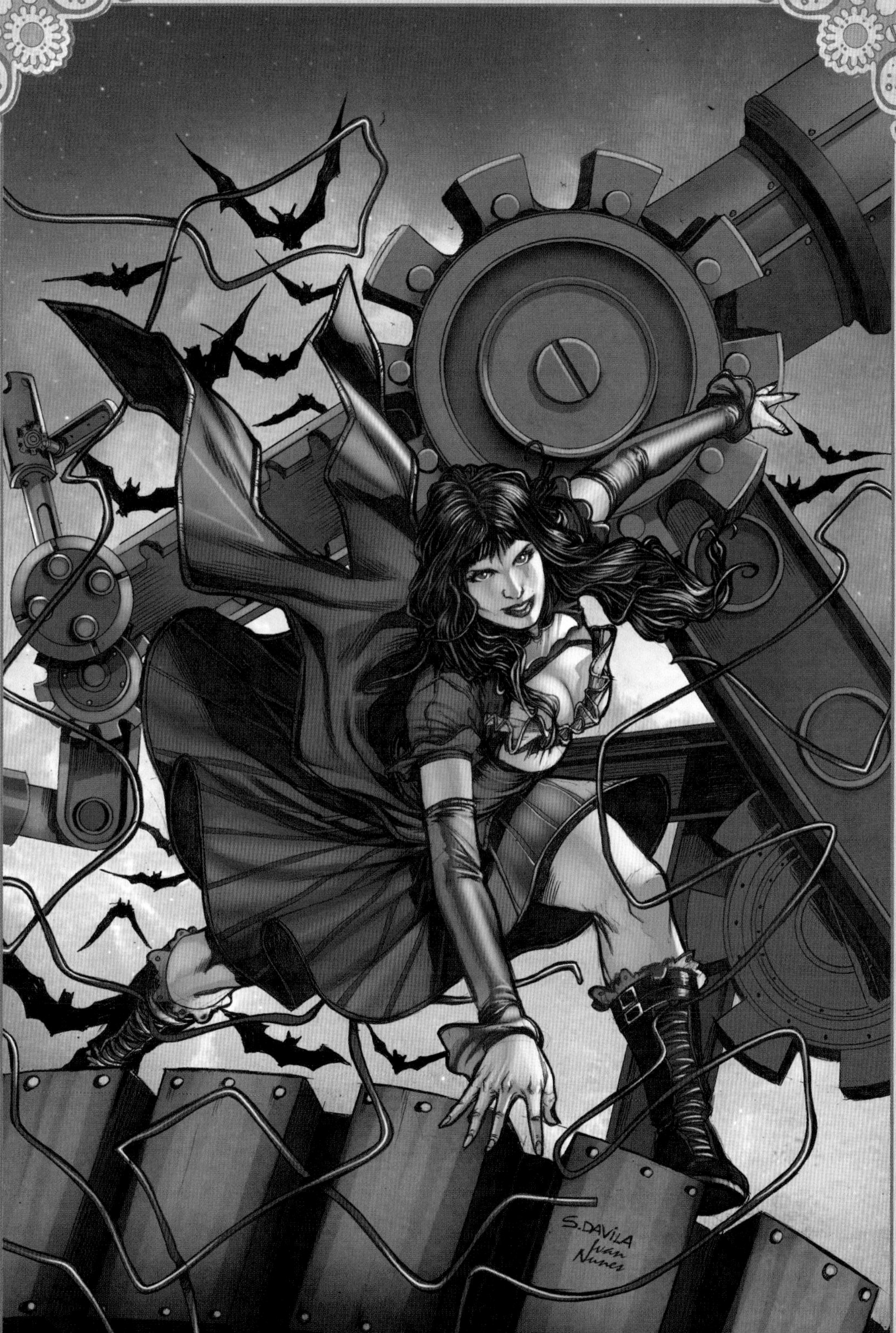
S.DAVILA
Ivan
Nunes

ISSUE TWO

cover by Sergio Dávila and Ivan Nunes

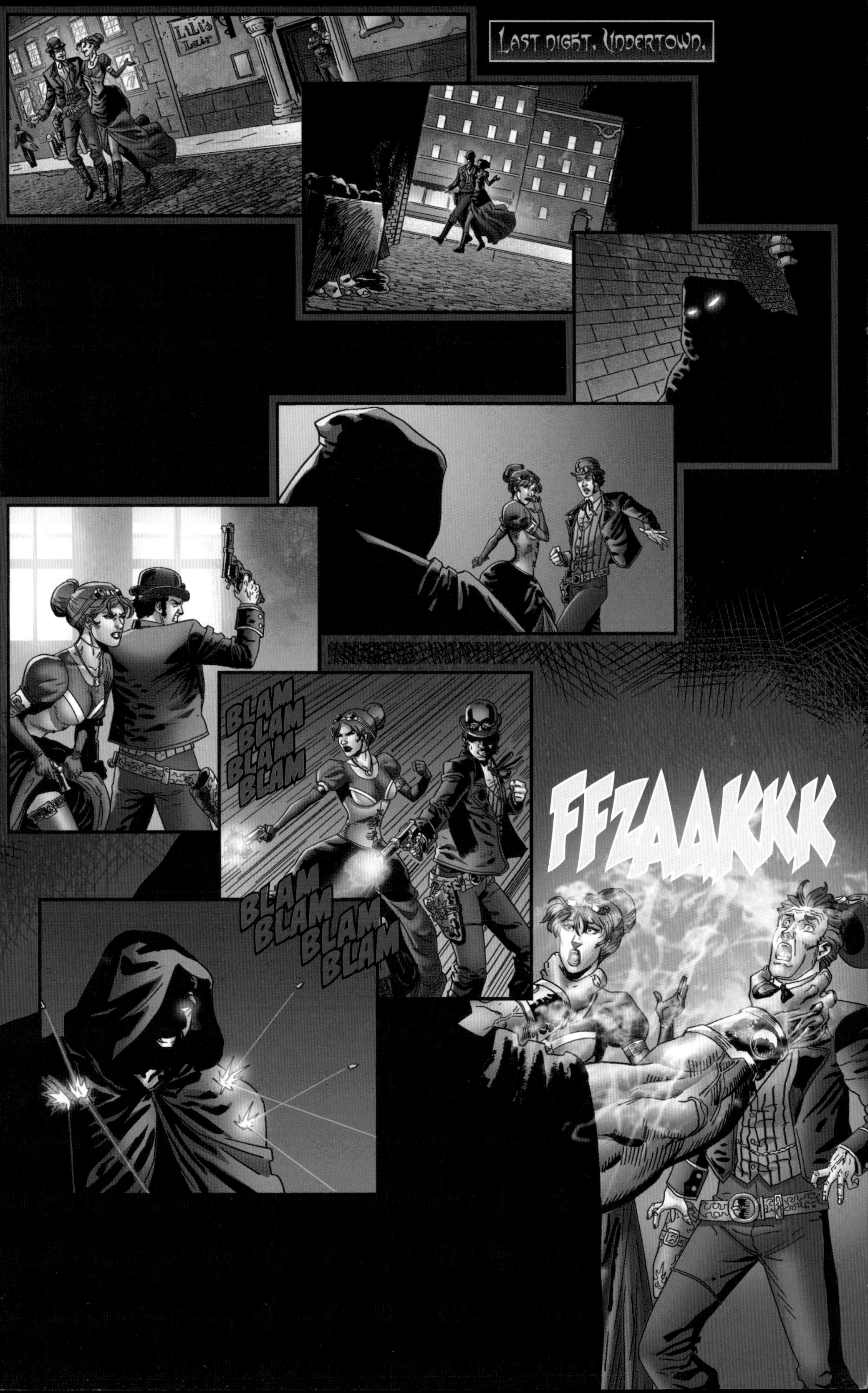
Lili's Lair
Last night, Undertown.
BLAM
BLAM
BLAM
BLAM
BLAM
BLAM
BLAM
BLAM
FFZAAKKK

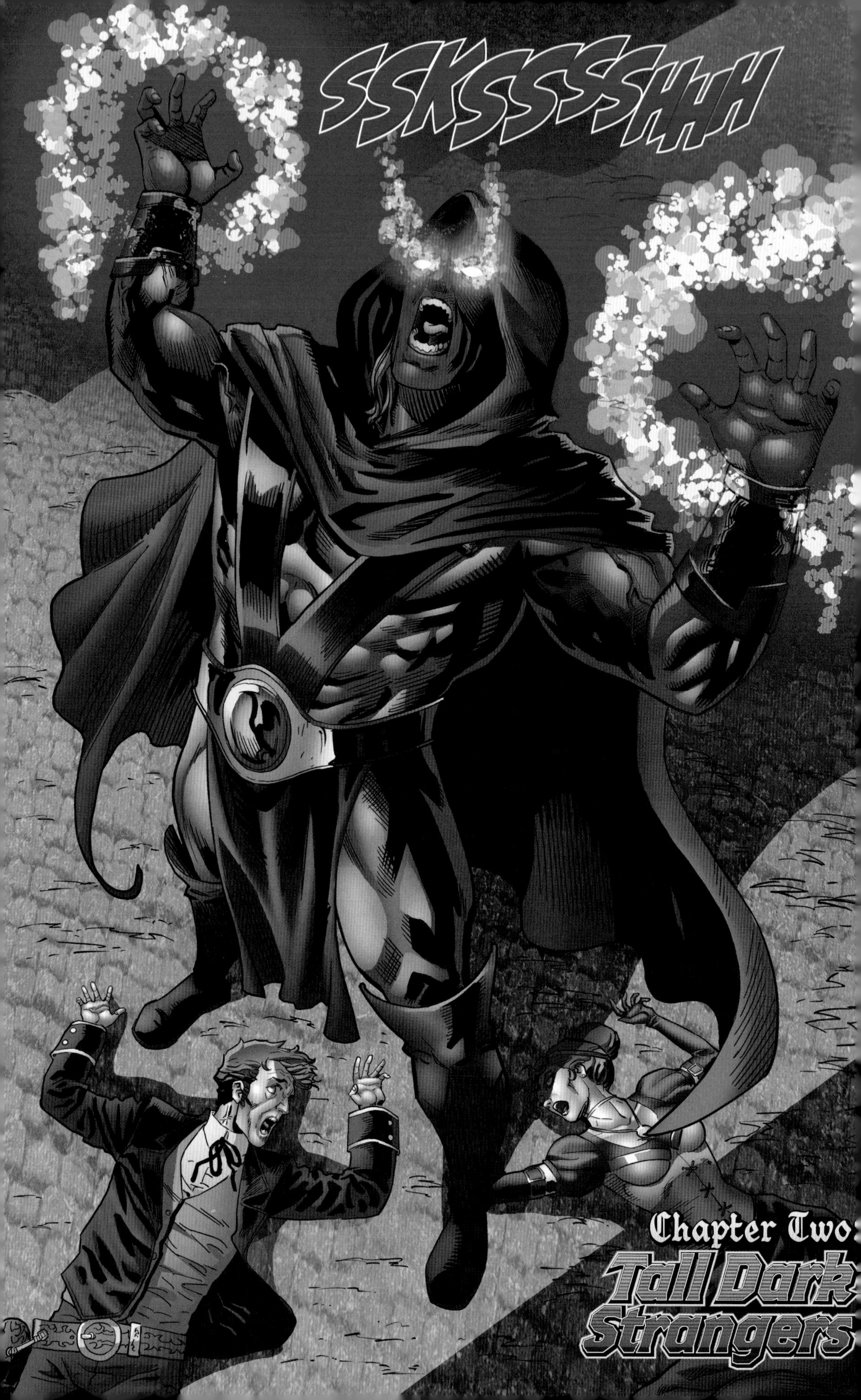
SSKSSSSHHH
Chapter Two:
Tall Dark Strangers

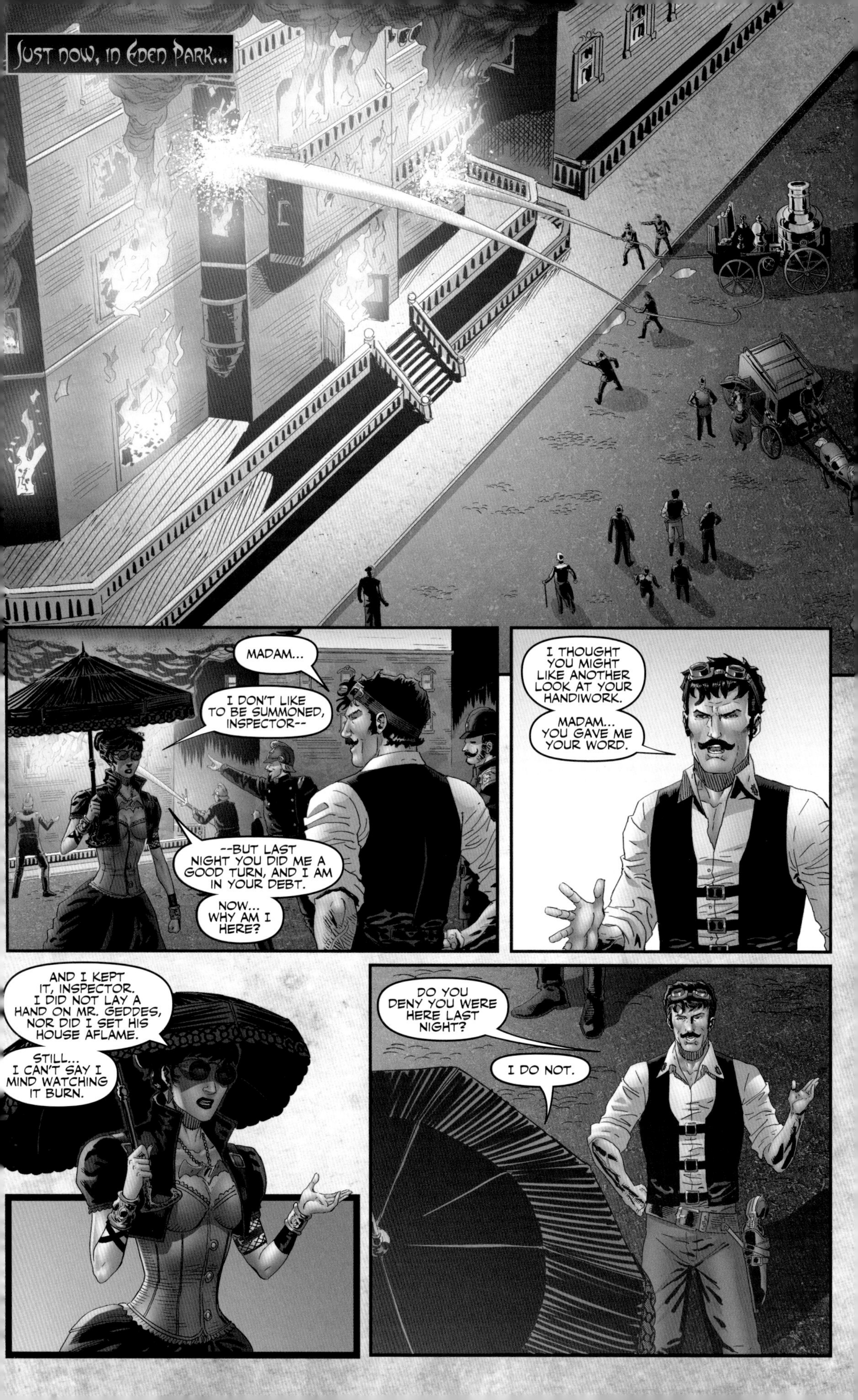
Just now, in Eden Park...
MADAM...
I DON'T LIKE TO BE SUMMONED, INSPECTOR--
--BUT LAST NIGHT YOU DID ME A GOOD TURN, AND I AM IN YOUR DEBT.
NOW... WHY AM I HERE?
I THOUGHT YOU MIGHT LIKE ANOTHER LOOK AT YOUR HANDIWORK.
MADAM... YOU GAVE ME YOUR WORD.
AND I KEPT IT, INSPECTOR. I DID NOT LAY A HAND ON MR. GEDDES, NOR DID I SET HIS HOUSE AFLAME.
STILL... I CAN'T SAY I MIND WATCHING IT BURN.
DO YOU DENY YOU WERE HERE LAST NIGHT?
I DO NOT.

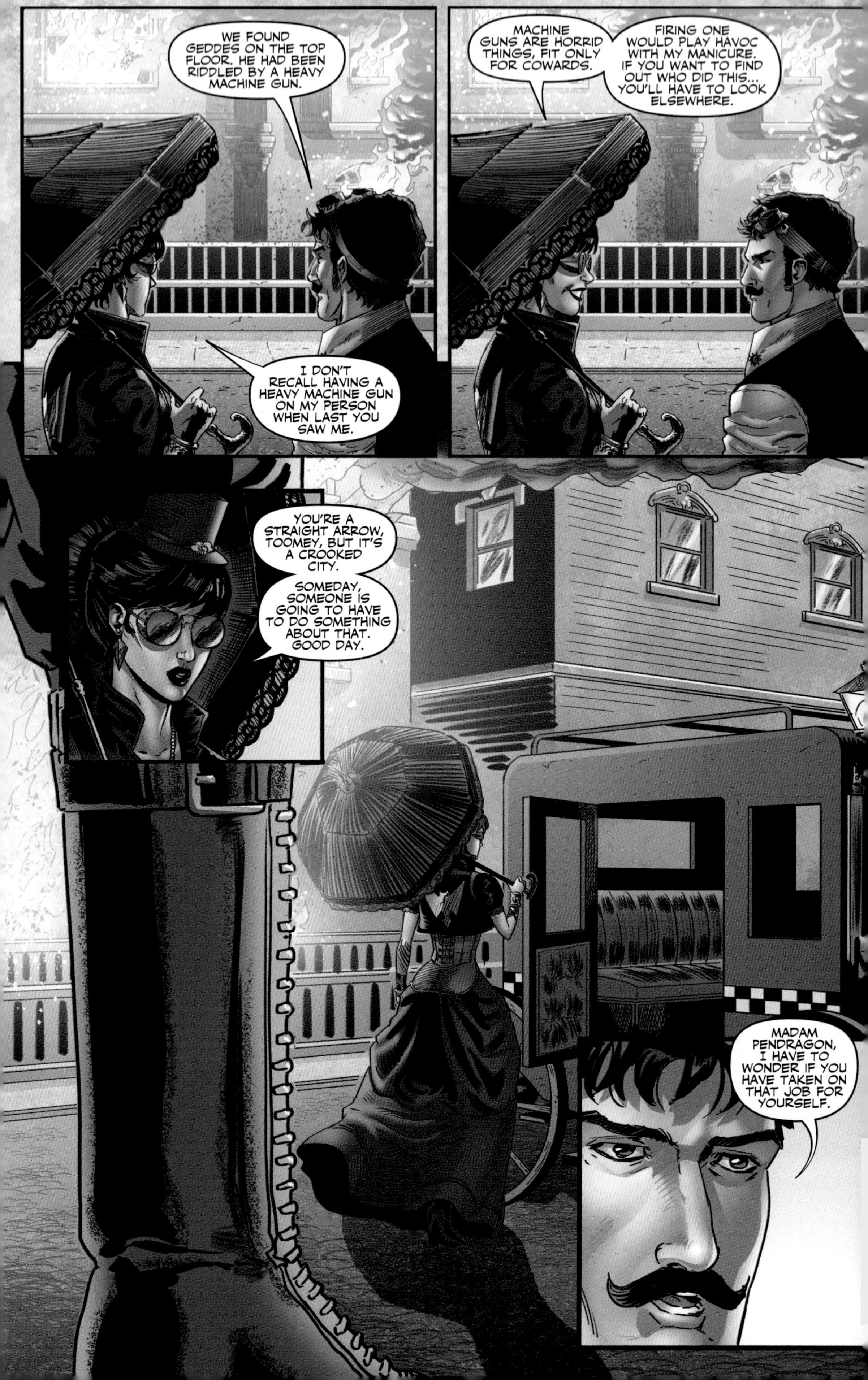
WE FOUND GEDDES ON THE TOP FLOOR. HE HAD BEEN RIDDLED BY A HEAVY MACHINE GUN.
I DON'T RECALL HAVING A HEAVY MACHINE GUN ON MY PERSON WHEN LAST YOU SAW ME.
MACHINE GUNS ARE HORRID THINGS, FIT ONLY FOR COWARDS.
FIRING ONE WOULD PLAY HAVOC WITH MY MANICURE. IF YOU WANT TO FIND OUT WHO DID THIS... YOU'LL HAVE TO LOOK ELSEWHERE.
YOU'RE A STRAIGHT ARROW, TOOMEY, BUT IT'S A CROOKED CITY.
SOMEDAY, SOMEONE IS GOING TO HAVE TO DO SOMETHING ABOUT THAT. GOOD DAY.
MADAM PENDRAGON, I HAVE TO WONDER IF YOU HAVE TAKEN ON THAT JOB FOR YOURSELF.

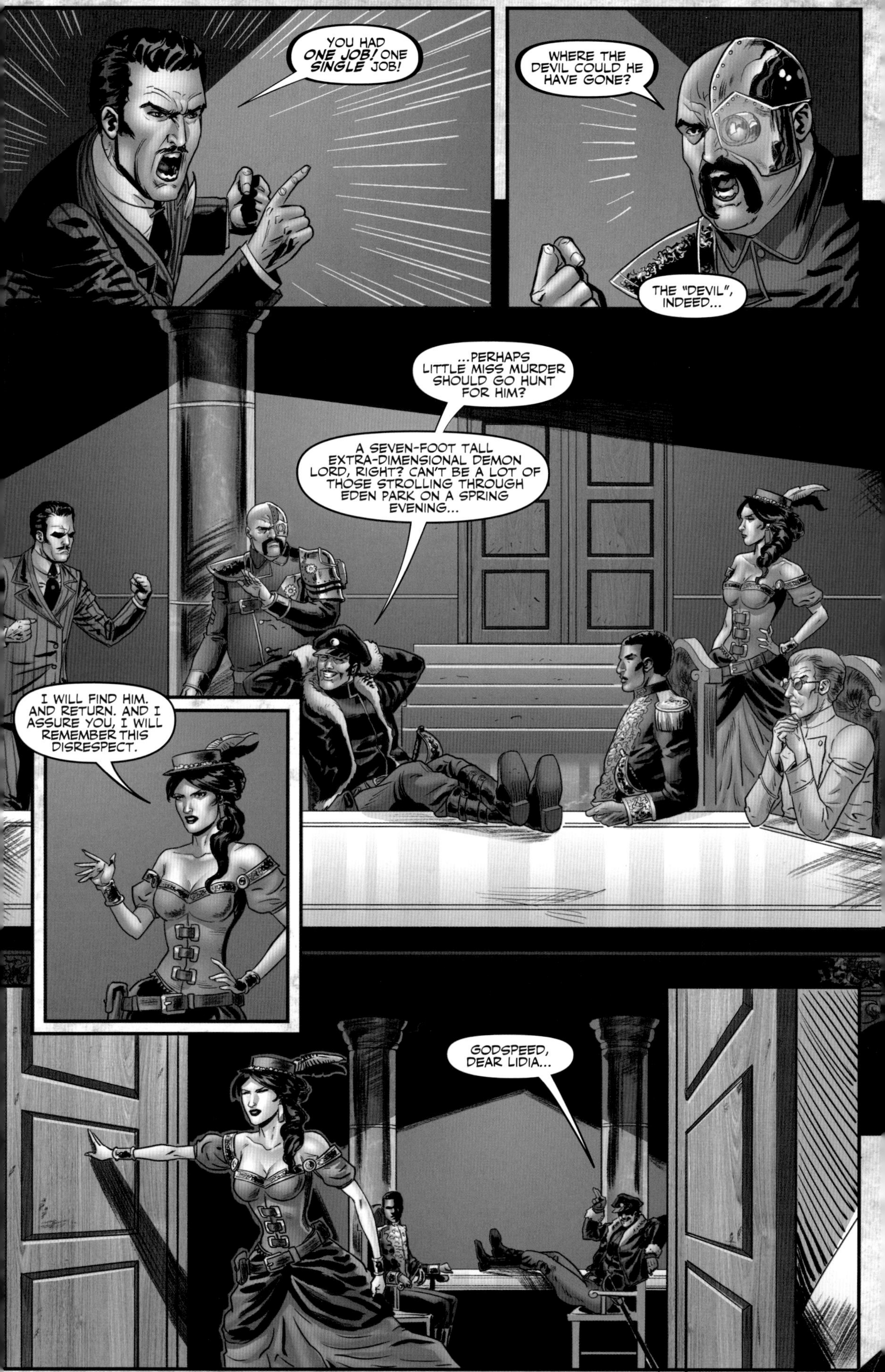
YOU HAD ONE JOB! ONE SINGLE JOB!
WHERE THE DEVIL COULD HE HAVE GONE?
THE "DEVIL", INDEED...
...PERHAPS LITTLE MISS MURDER SHOULD GO HUNT FOR HIM?
A SEVEN-FOOT TALL EXTRA-DIMENSIONAL DEMON LORD, RIGHT? CAN'T BE A LOT OF THOSE STROLLING THROUGH EDEN PARK ON A SPRING EVENING...
I WILL FIND HIM. AND RETURN. AND I ASSURE YOU, I WILL REMEMBER THIS DISRESPECT.
GODSPEED, DEAR LIDIA...

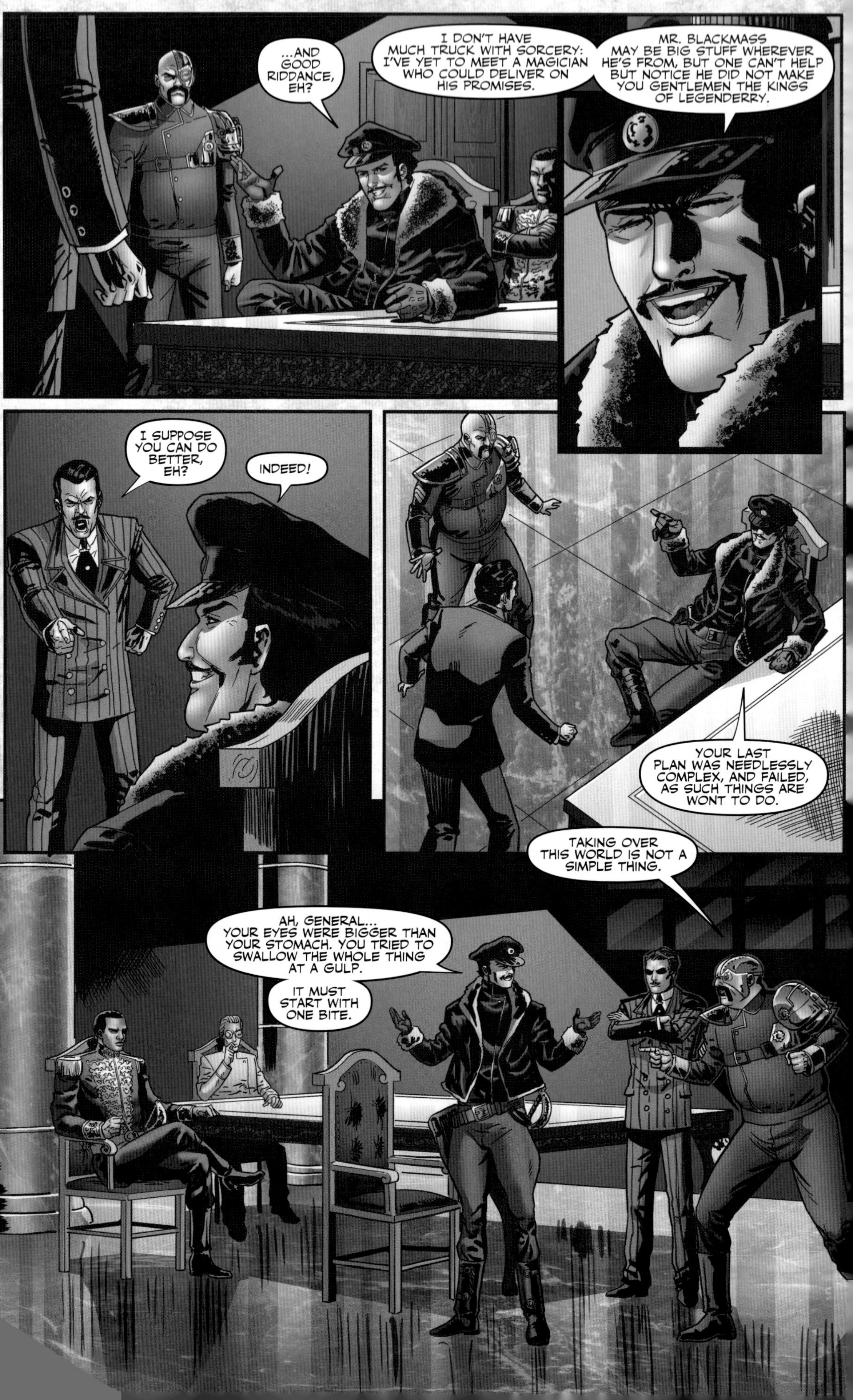
...AND GOOD RIDDANCE, EH?
I DON'T HAVE MUCH TRUCK WITH SORCERY: I'VE YET TO MEET A MAGICIAN WHO COULD DELIVER ON HIS PROMISES.
MR. BLACKMASS MAY BE BIG STUFF WHEREVER HE'S FROM, BUT ONE CAN'T HELP BUT NOTICE HE DID NOT MAKE YOU GENTLEMEN THE KINGS OF LEGENDERRY.
I SUPPOSE YOU CAN DO BETTER, EH?
INDEED!
YOUR LAST PLAN WAS NEEDLESSLY COMPLEX, AND FAILED, AS SUCH THINGS ARE WONT TO DO.
TAKING OVER THIS WORLD IS NOT A SIMPLE THING.
AH, GENERAL... YOUR EYES WERE BIGGER THAN YOUR STOMACH. YOU TRIED TO SWALLOW THE WHOLE THING AT A GULP.
IT MUST START WITH ONE BITE.

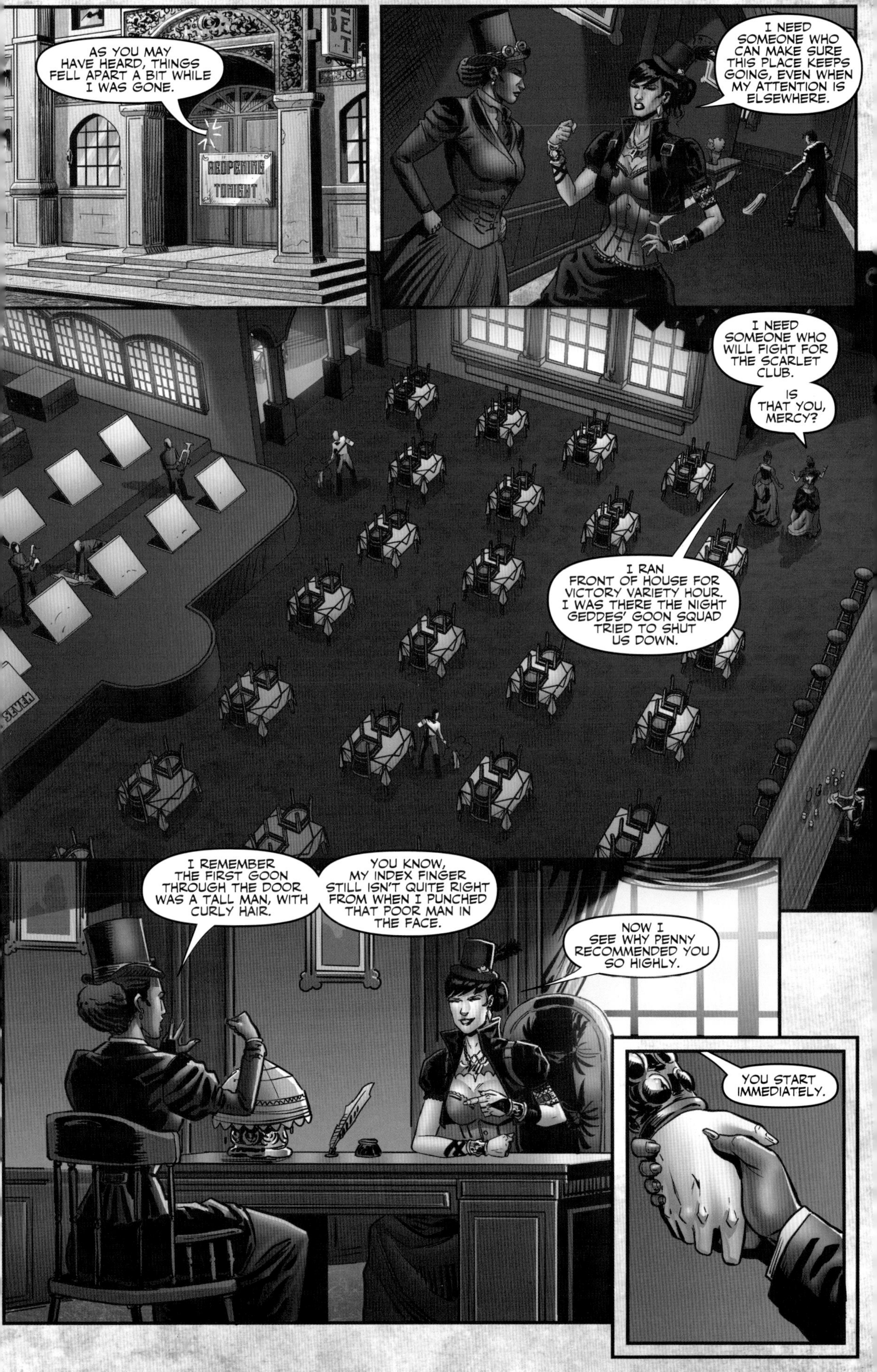
AS YOU MAY HAVE HEARD, THINGS FELL APART A BIT WHILE I WAS GONE.
REOPENING TONIGHT
I NEED SOMEONE WHO CAN MAKE SURE THIS PLACE KEEPS GOING, EVEN WHEN MY ATTENTION IS ELSEWHERE.
I NEED SOMEONE WHO WILL FIGHT FOR THE SCARLET CLUB.
IS THAT YOU, MERCY?
I RAN FRONT OF HOUSE FOR VICTORY VARIETY HOUR. I WAS THERE THE NIGHT GEDDES' GOON SQUAD TRIED TO SHUT US DOWN.
I REMEMBER THE FIRST GOON THROUGH THE DOOR WAS A TALL MAN, WITH CURLY HAIR.
YOU KNOW, MY INDEX FINGER STILL ISN'T QUITE RIGHT FROM WHEN I PUNCHED THAT POOR MAN IN THE FACE.
NOW I SEE WHY PENNY RECOMMENDED YOU SO HIGHLY.
YOU START IMMEDIATELY.

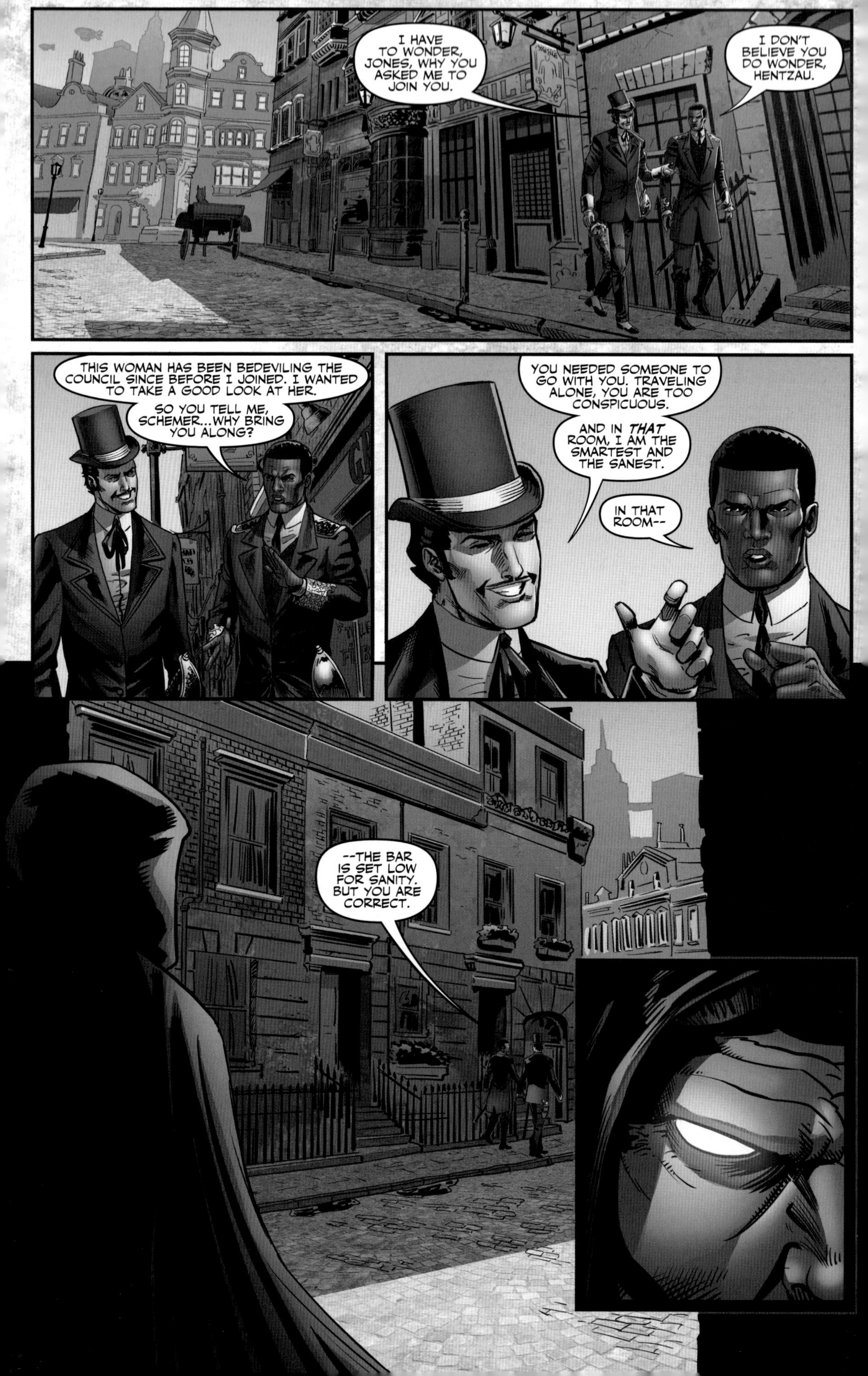
I HAVE TO WONDER, JONES, WHY YOU ASKED ME TO JOIN YOU.
I DON'T BELIEVE YOU DO WONDER, HENTZAU.
THIS WOMAN HAS BEEN BEDEVILING THE COUNCIL SINCE BEFORE I JOINED. I WANTED TO TAKE A GOOD LOOK AT HER.
SO YOU TELL ME, SCHEMER...WHY BRING YOU ALONG?
YOU NEEDED SOMEONE TO GO WITH YOU. TRAVELING ALONE, YOU ARE TOO CONSPICUOUS.
AND IN *THAT* ROOM, I AM THE SMARTEST AND THE SANEST.
IN THAT ROOM--
--THE BAR IS SET LOW FOR SANITY. BUT YOU ARE CORRECT.

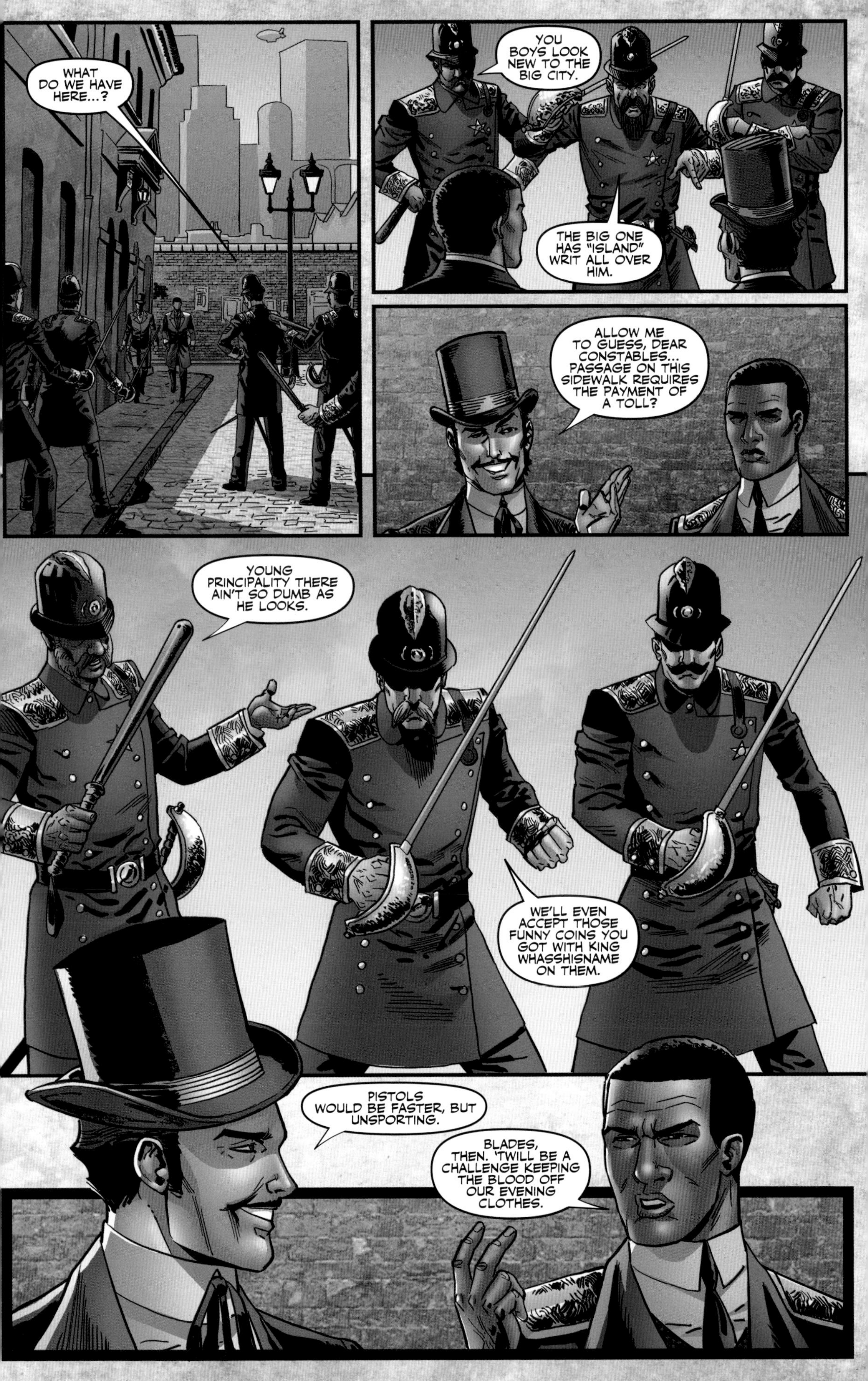
WHAT DO WE HAVE HERE...?
YOU BOYS LOOK NEW TO THE BIG CITY.
THE BIG ONE HAS "ISLAND" WRIT ALL OVER HIM.
ALLOW ME TO GUESS, DEAR CONSTABLES... PASSAGE ON THIS SIDEWALK REQUIRES THE PAYMENT OF A TOLL?
YOUNG PRINCIPALITY THERE AIN'T SO DUMB AS HE LOOKS.
WE'LL EVEN ACCEPT THOSE FUNNY COINS YOU GOT WITH KING WHASSHISNAME ON THEM.
PISTOLS WOULD BE FASTER, BUT UNSPORTING.
BLADES, THEN. 'TWILL BE A CHALLENGE KEEPING THE BLOOD OFF OUR EVENING CLOTHES.

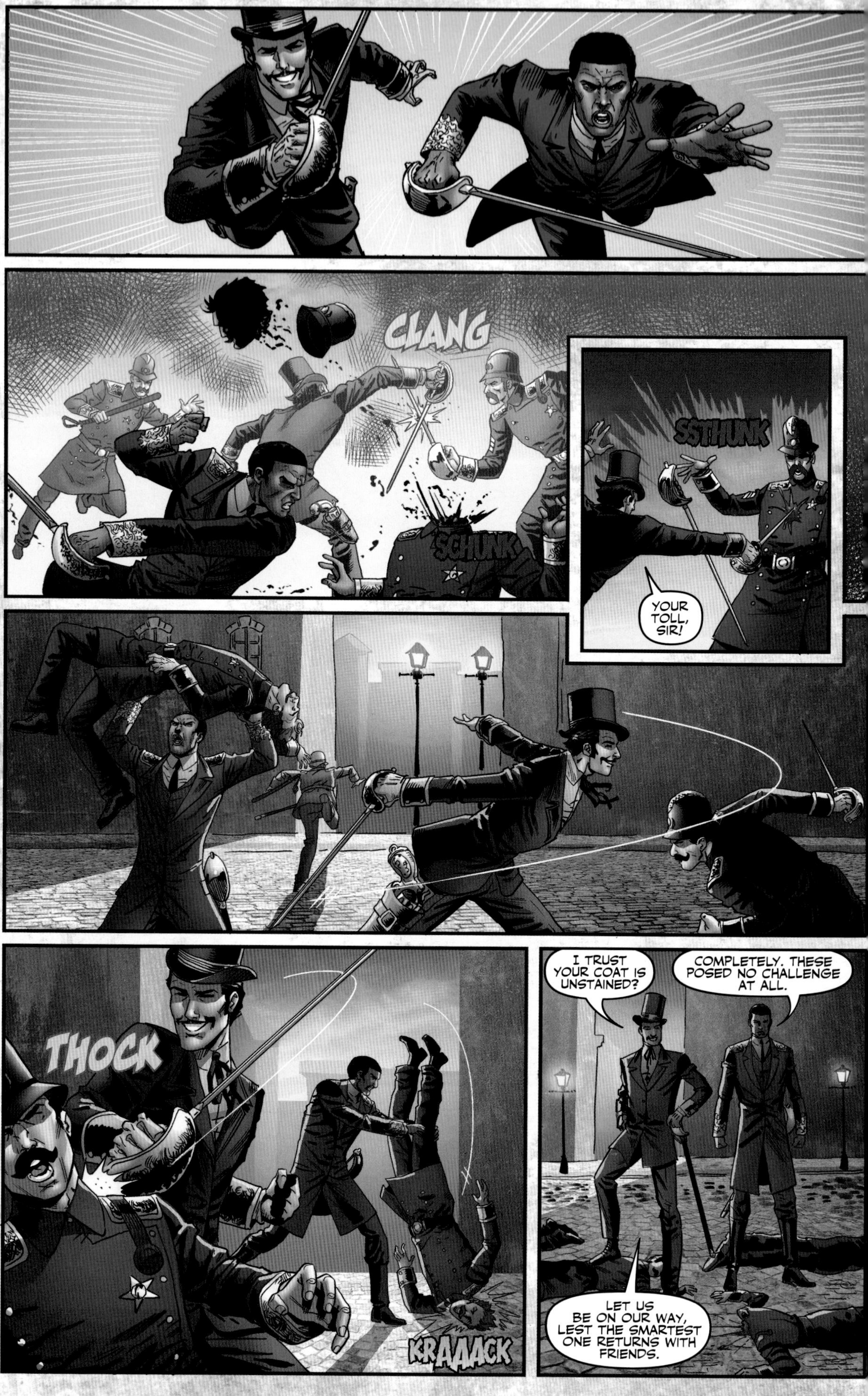
CLANG
SCHUNK
SSTHUNK
YOUR TOLL, SIR!
THOCK
KRAAACK
I TRUST YOUR COAT IS UNSTAINED?
COMPLETELY. THESE POSED NO CHALLENGE AT ALL.
LET US BE ON OUR WAY, LEST THE SMARTEST ONE RETURNS WITH FRIENDS.

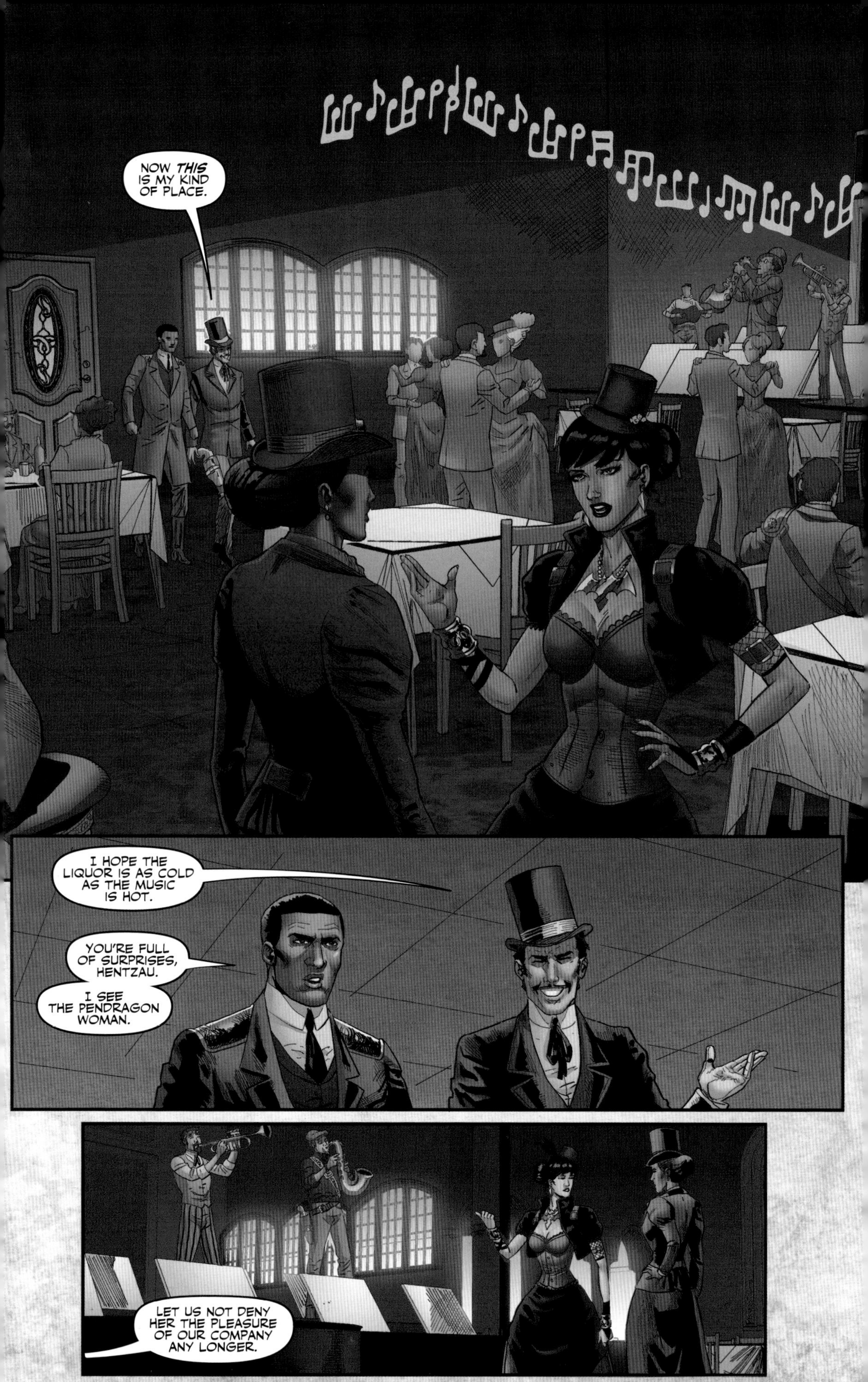
NOW THIS IS MY KIND OF PLACE.
I HOPE THE LIQUOR IS AS COLD AS THE MUSIC IS HOT.
YOU'RE FULL OF SURPRISES, HENTZAU.
I SEE THE PENDRAGON WOMAN.
LET US NOT DENY HER THE PLEASURE OF OUR COMPANY ANY LONGER.

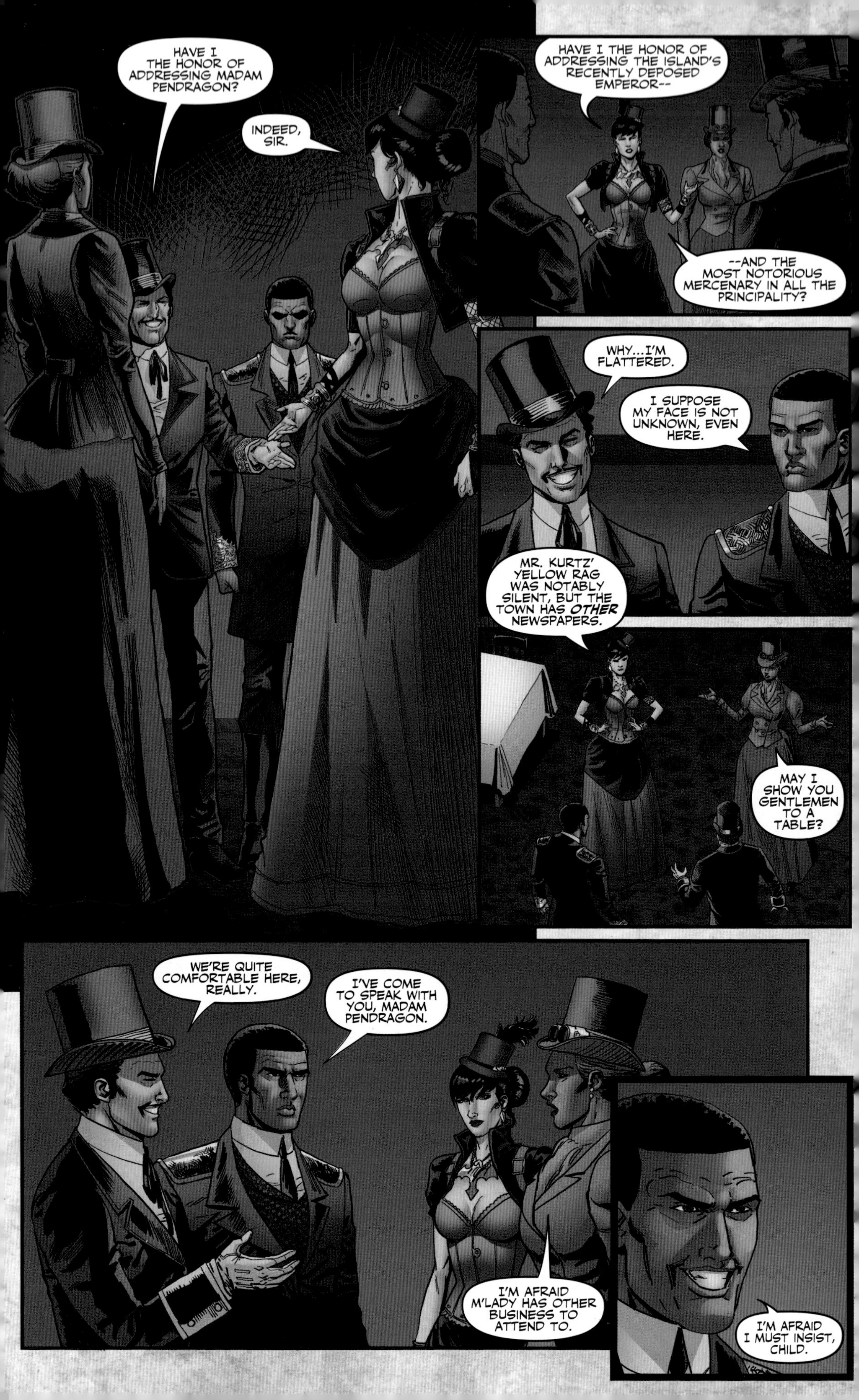
HAVE I THE HONOR OF ADDRESSING MADAM PENDRAGON?
INDEED, SIR.
HAVE I THE HONOR OF ADDRESSING THE ISLAND'S RECENTLY DEPOSED EMPEROR--
--AND THE MOST NOTORIOUS MERCENARY IN ALL THE PRINCIPALITY?
WHY...I'M FLATTERED.
I SUPPOSE MY FACE IS NOT UNKNOWN, EVEN HERE.
MR. KURTZ' YELLOW RAG WAS NOTABLY SILENT, BUT THE TOWN HAS *OTHER* NEWSPAPERS.
MAY I SHOW YOU GENTLEMEN TO A TABLE?
WE'RE QUITE COMFORTABLE HERE, REALLY.
I'VE COME TO SPEAK WITH YOU, MADAM PENDRAGON.
I'M AFRAID M'LADY HAS OTHER BUSINESS TO ATTEND TO.
I'M AFRAID I MUST INSIST, CHILD.

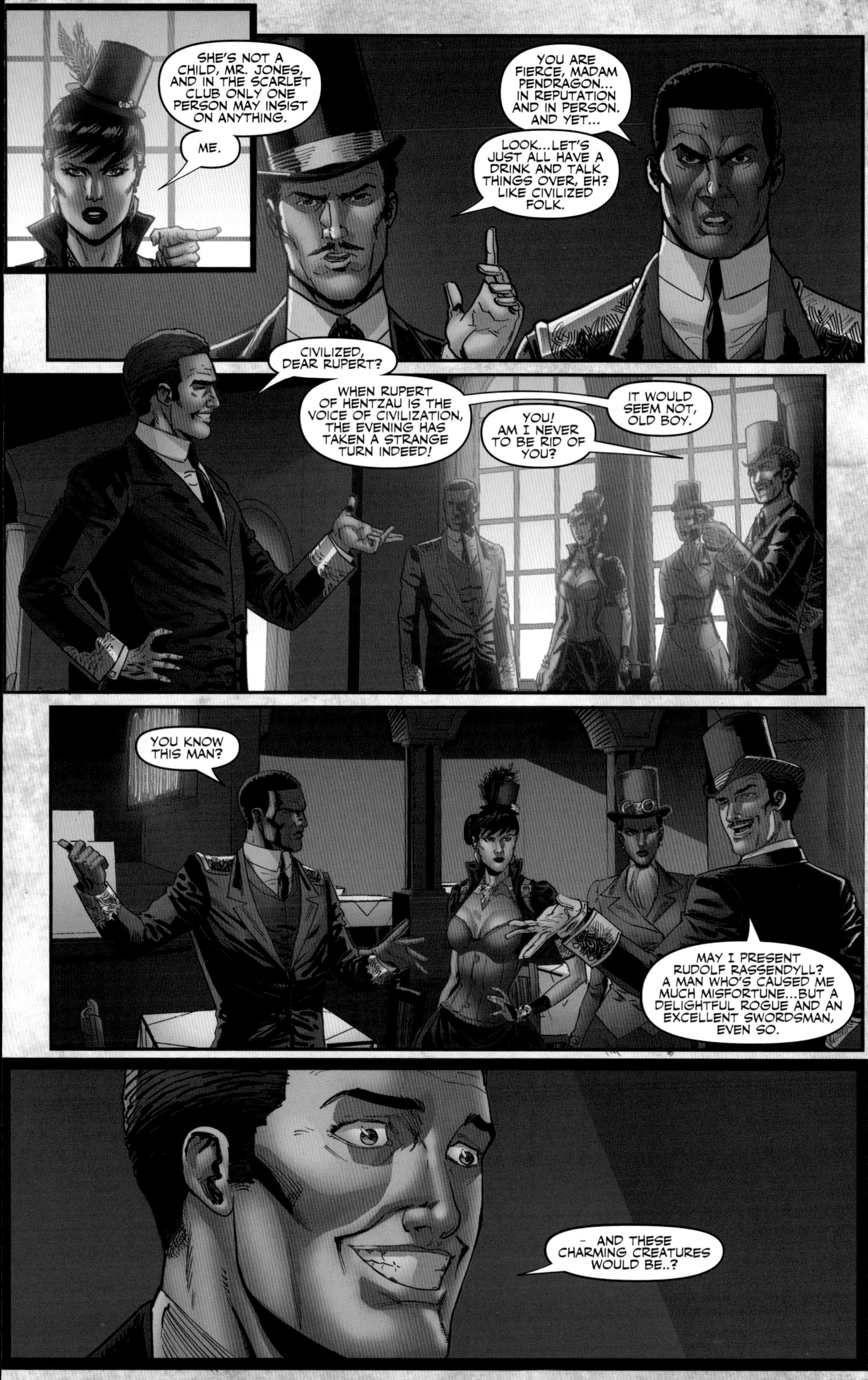
SHE'S NOT A CHILD, MR. JONES, AND IN THE SCARLET CLUB ONLY ONE PERSON MAY INSIST ON ANYTHING.
ME.
YOU ARE FIERCE, MADAM PENDRAGON... IN REPUTATION AND IN PERSON. AND YET...
LOOK...LET'S JUST ALL HAVE A DRINK AND TALK THINGS OVER, EH? LIKE CIVILIZED FOLK.
CIVILIZED, DEAR RUPERT?
WHEN RUPERT OF HENTZAU IS THE VOICE OF CIVILIZATION, THE EVENING HAS TAKEN A STRANGE TURN INDEED!
YOU! AM I NEVER TO BE RID OF YOU?
IT WOULD SEEM NOT, OLD BOY.
YOU KNOW THIS MAN?
MAY I PRESENT RUDOLF RASSENDYLL? A MAN WHO'S CAUSED ME MUCH MISFORTUNE...BUT A DELIGHTFUL ROGUE AND AN EXCELLENT SWORDSMAN, EVEN SO.
- AND THESE CHARMING CREATURES WOULD BE..?

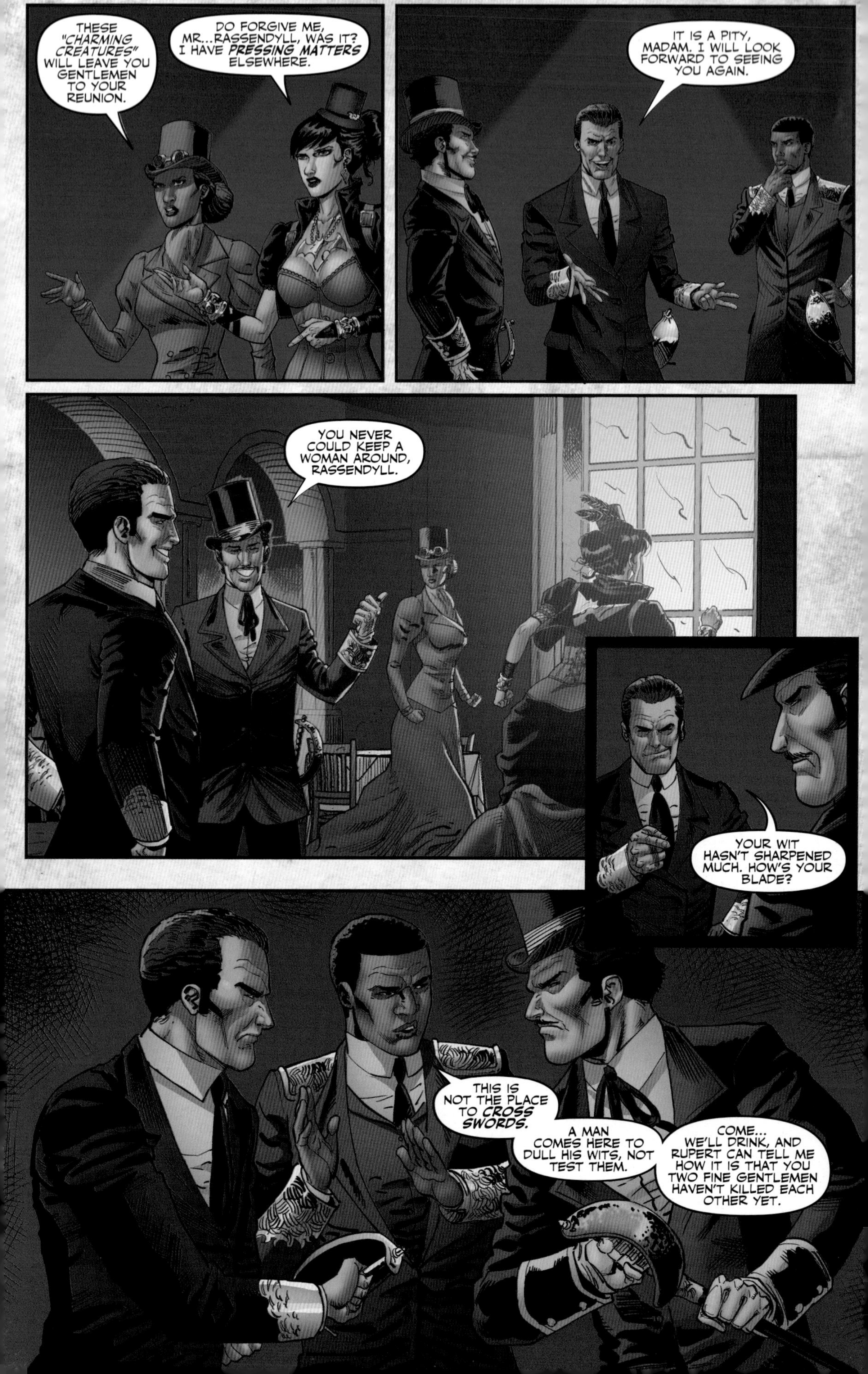

THESE "CHARMING CREATURES" WILL LEAVE YOU GENTLEMEN TO YOUR REUNION.
DO FORGIVE ME, MR...RASSENDYLL, WAS IT? I HAVE PRESSING MATTERS ELSEWHERE.
IT IS A PITY, MADAM. I WILL LOOK FORWARD TO SEEING YOU AGAIN.
YOU NEVER COULD KEEP A WOMAN AROUND, RASSENDYLL.
YOUR WIT HASN'T SHARPENED MUCH. HOW'S YOUR BLADE?
THIS IS NOT THE PLACE TO CROSS SWORDS.
A MAN COMES HERE TO DULL HIS WITS, NOT TEST THEM.
COME... WE'LL DRINK, AND RUPERT CAN TELL ME HOW IT IS THAT YOU TWO FINE GENTLEMEN HAVEN'T KILLED EACH OTHER YET.

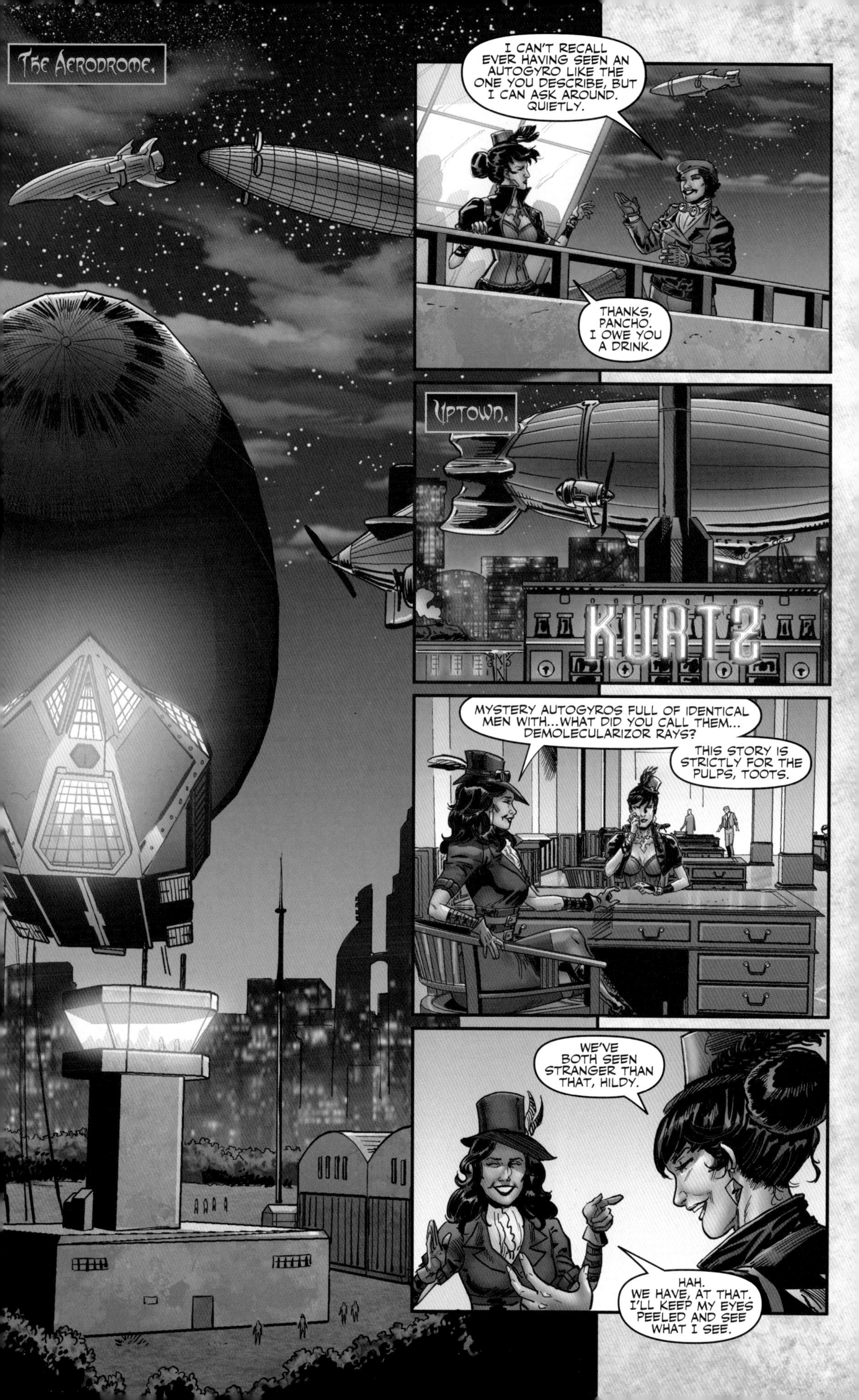
THE AERODROME.
I CAN'T RECALL EVER HAVING SEEN AN AUTOGYRO LIKE THE ONE YOU DESCRIBE, BUT I CAN ASK AROUND. QUIETLY.
THANKS, PANCHO. I OWE YOU A DRINK.
UPTOWN.
KURTZ
MYSTERY AUTOGYROS FULL OF IDENTICAL MEN WITH...WHAT DID YOU CALL THEM... DEMOLECULARIZOR RAYS?
THIS STORY IS STRICTLY FOR THE PULPS, TOOTS.
WE'VE BOTH SEEN STRANGER THAN THAT, HILDY.
HAH. WE HAVE, AT THAT. I'LL KEEP MY EYES PEELED AND SEE WHAT I SEE.

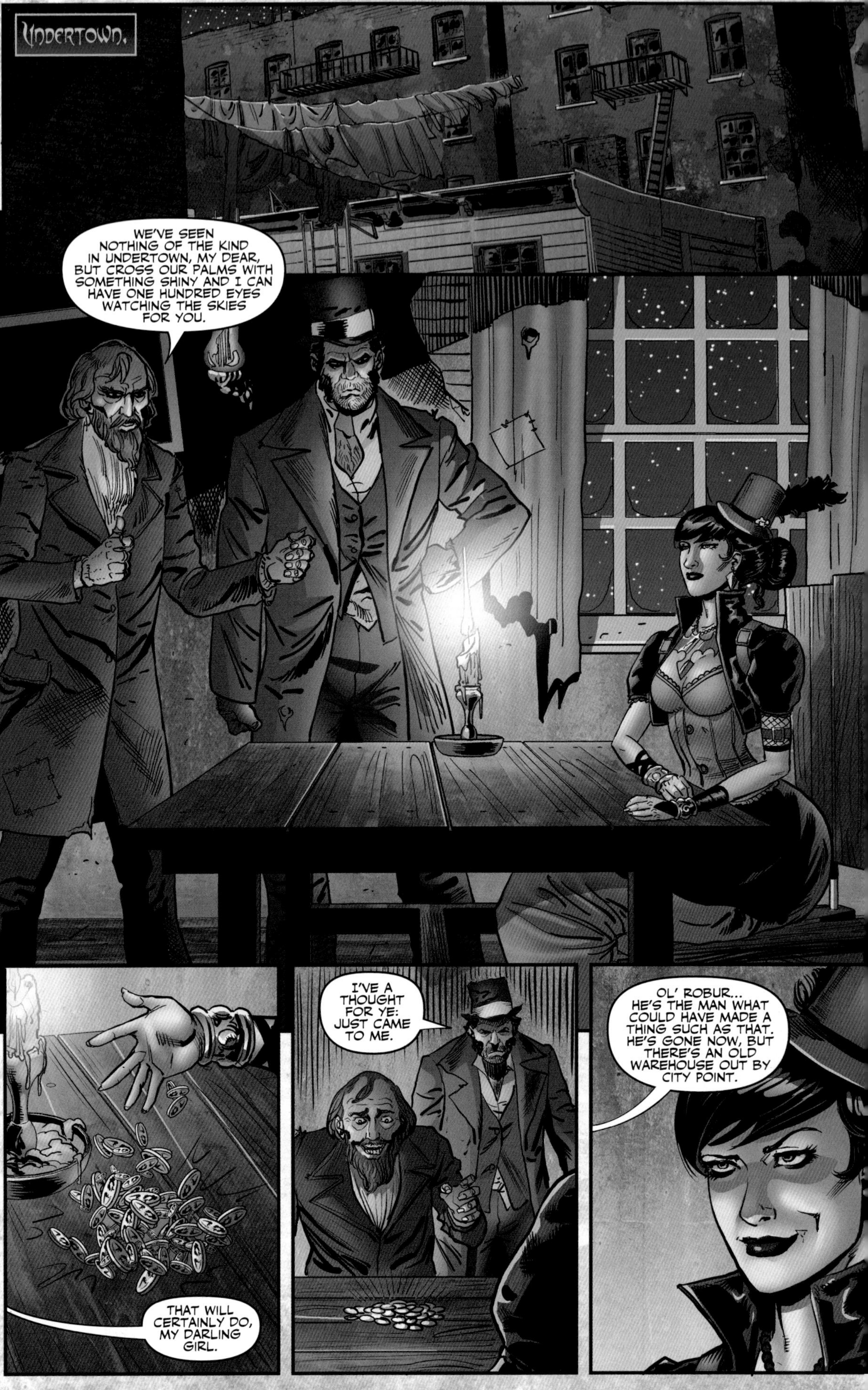
Undertown.
WE'VE SEEN NOTHING OF THE KIND IN UNDERTOWN, MY DEAR, BUT CROSS OUR PALMS WITH SOMETHING SHINY AND I CAN HAVE ONE HUNDRED EYES WATCHING THE SKIES FOR YOU.
THAT WILL CERTAINLY DO, MY DARLING GIRL.
I'VE A THOUGHT FOR YE: JUST CAME TO ME.
OL' ROBUR... HE'S THE MAN WHAT COULD HAVE MADE A THING SUCH AS THAT. HE'S GONE NOW, BUT THERE'S AN OLD WAREHOUSE OUT BY CITY POINT.

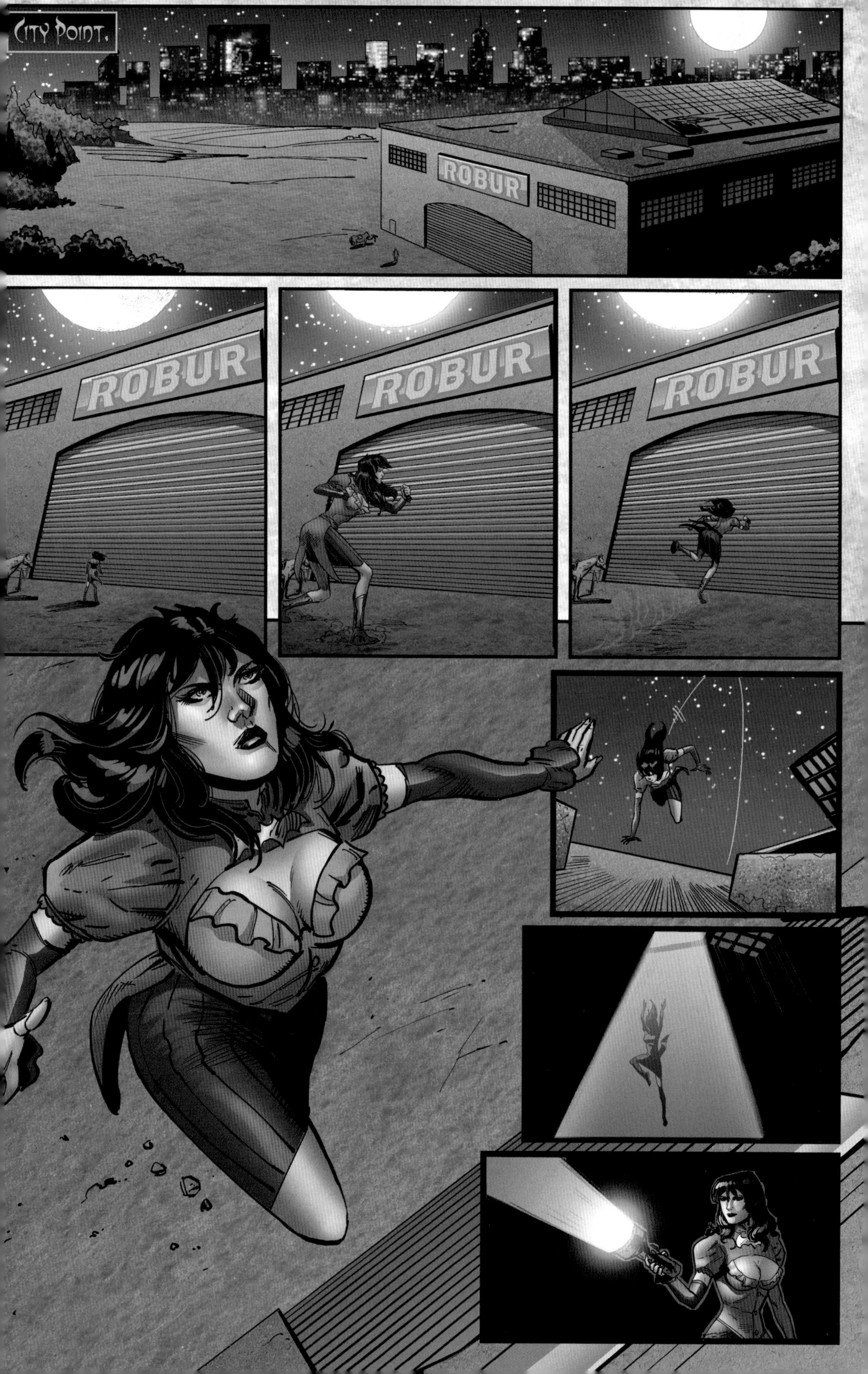
City Point.
ROBUR
ROBUR
ROBUR
ROBUR

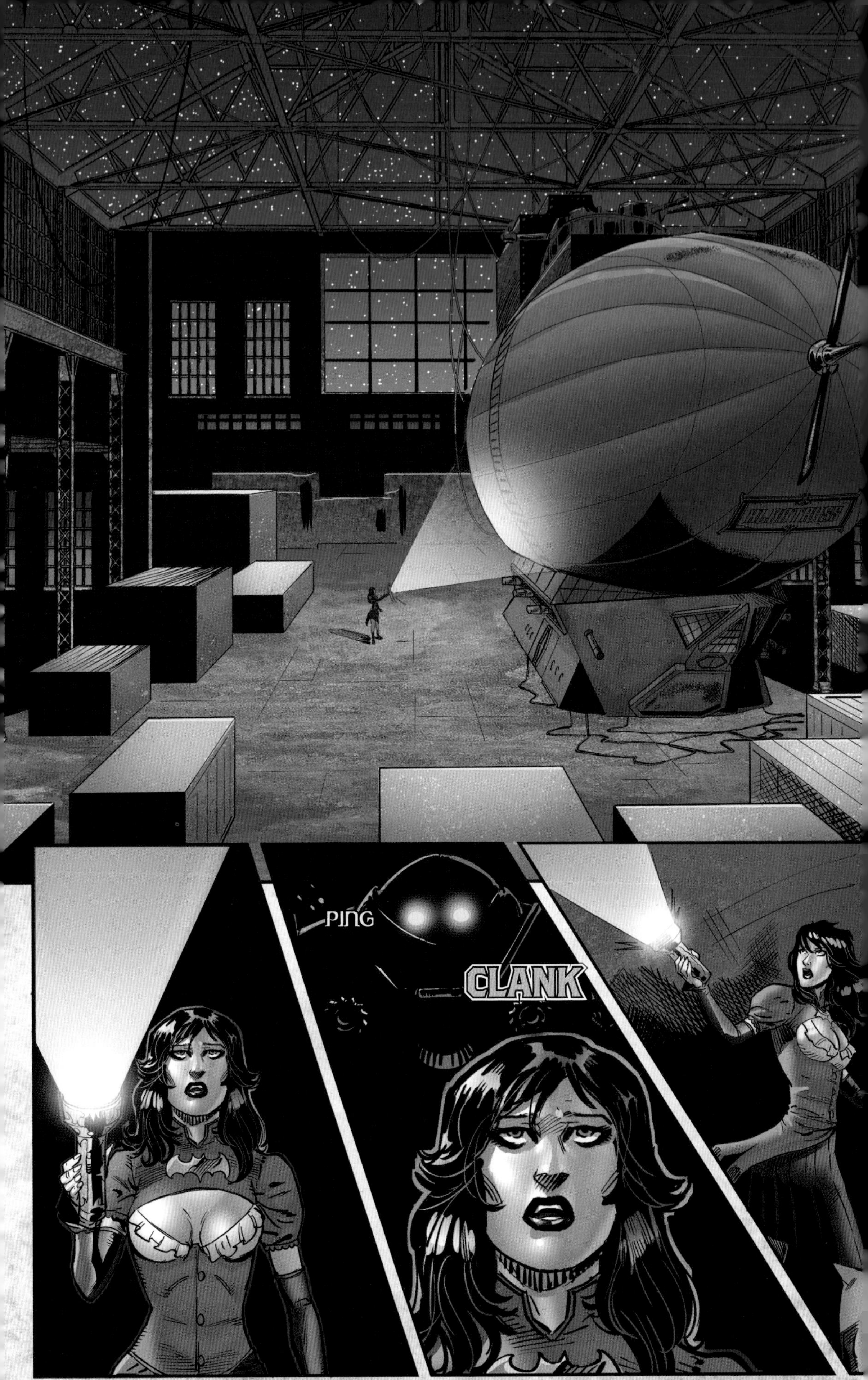
PING
CLANK

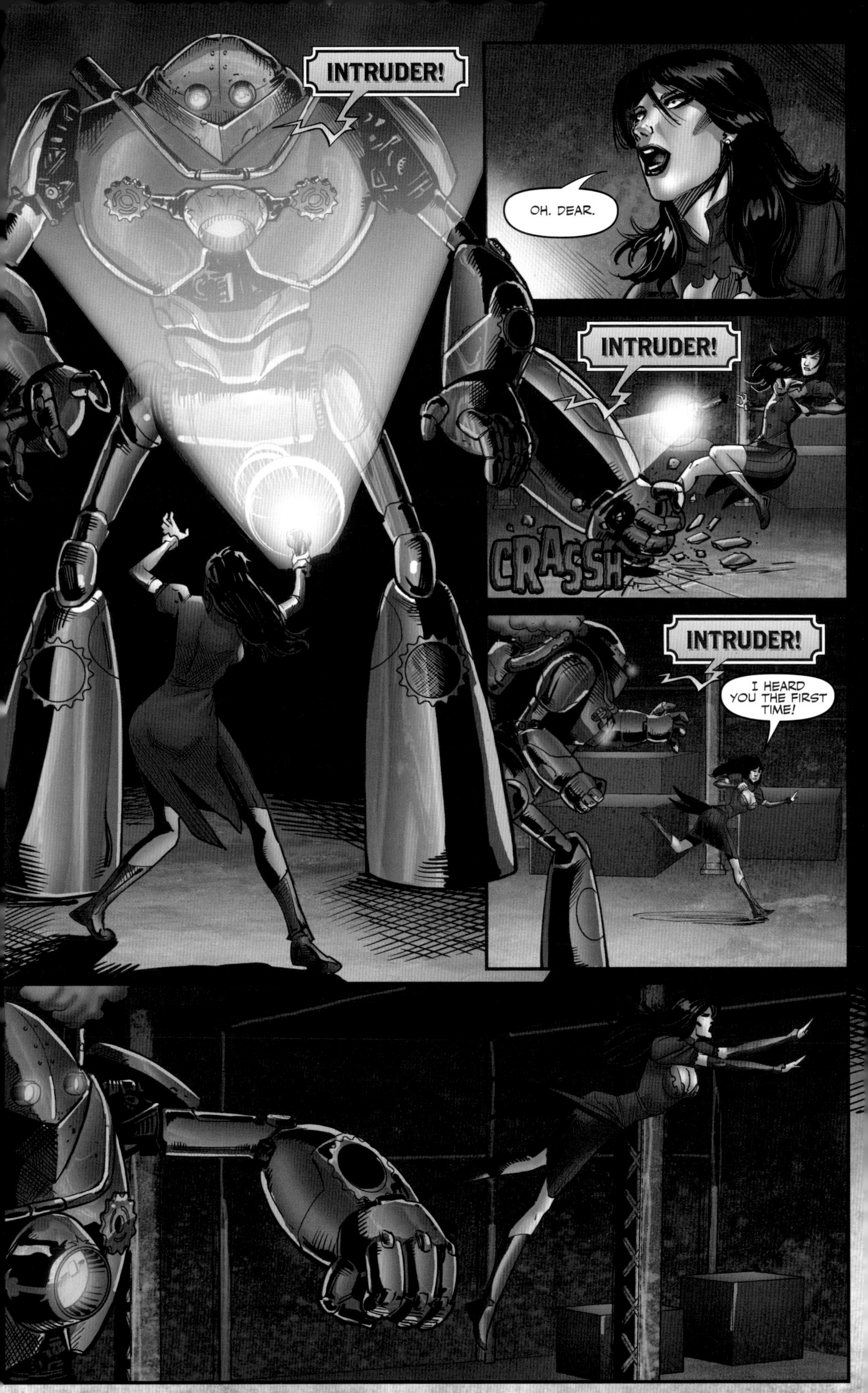
INTRUDER!
OH. DEAR.
INTRUDER!
CRASSH
INTRUDER!
I HEARD YOU THE FIRST TIME!

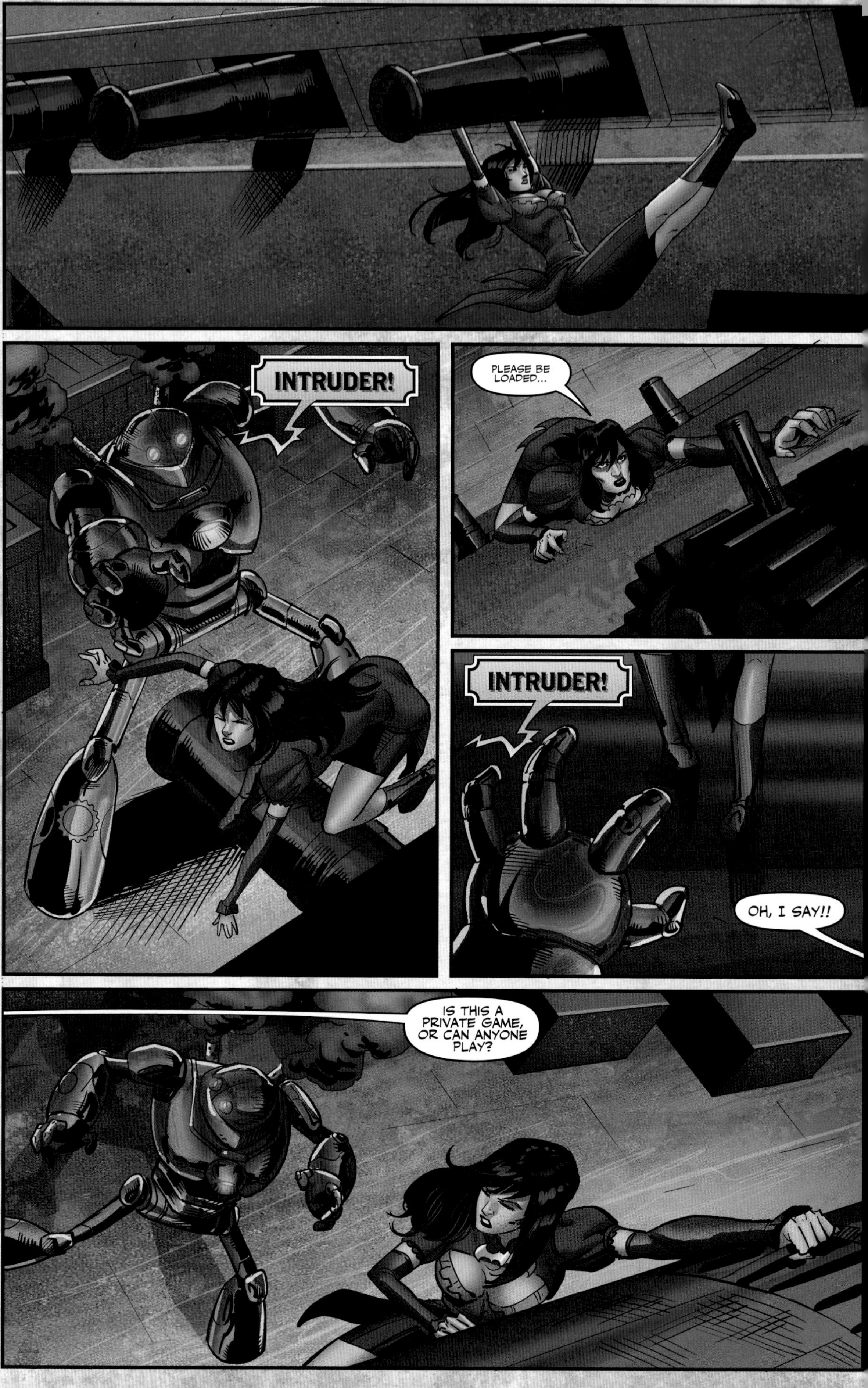
INTRUDER!
PLEASE BE LOADED...
INTRUDER!
OH, I SAY!!
IS THIS A PRIVATE GAME, OR CAN ANYONE PLAY?

INTRUDER!

RATHER RUDE OF YOU TO KEEP REMINDING ONE, BUT I CAN'T ARGUE THE PREMISE.

I DON'T IMAGINE THIS POP-GUN WILL DO MUCH GOOD... ARE YOU SURE THAT THING IS STILL LOADED!?

INTRUDER!

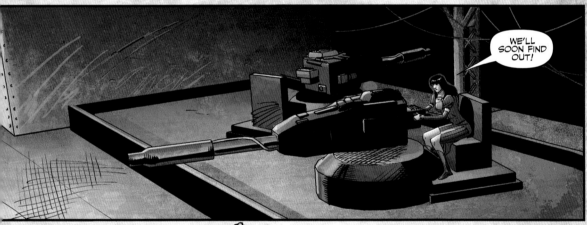

WE'LL SOON FIND OUT!

BLAM

INTRUDER!

SPANG
SPANG
SPANG
SPANG
SPANG

BLAM BLAM BLAM

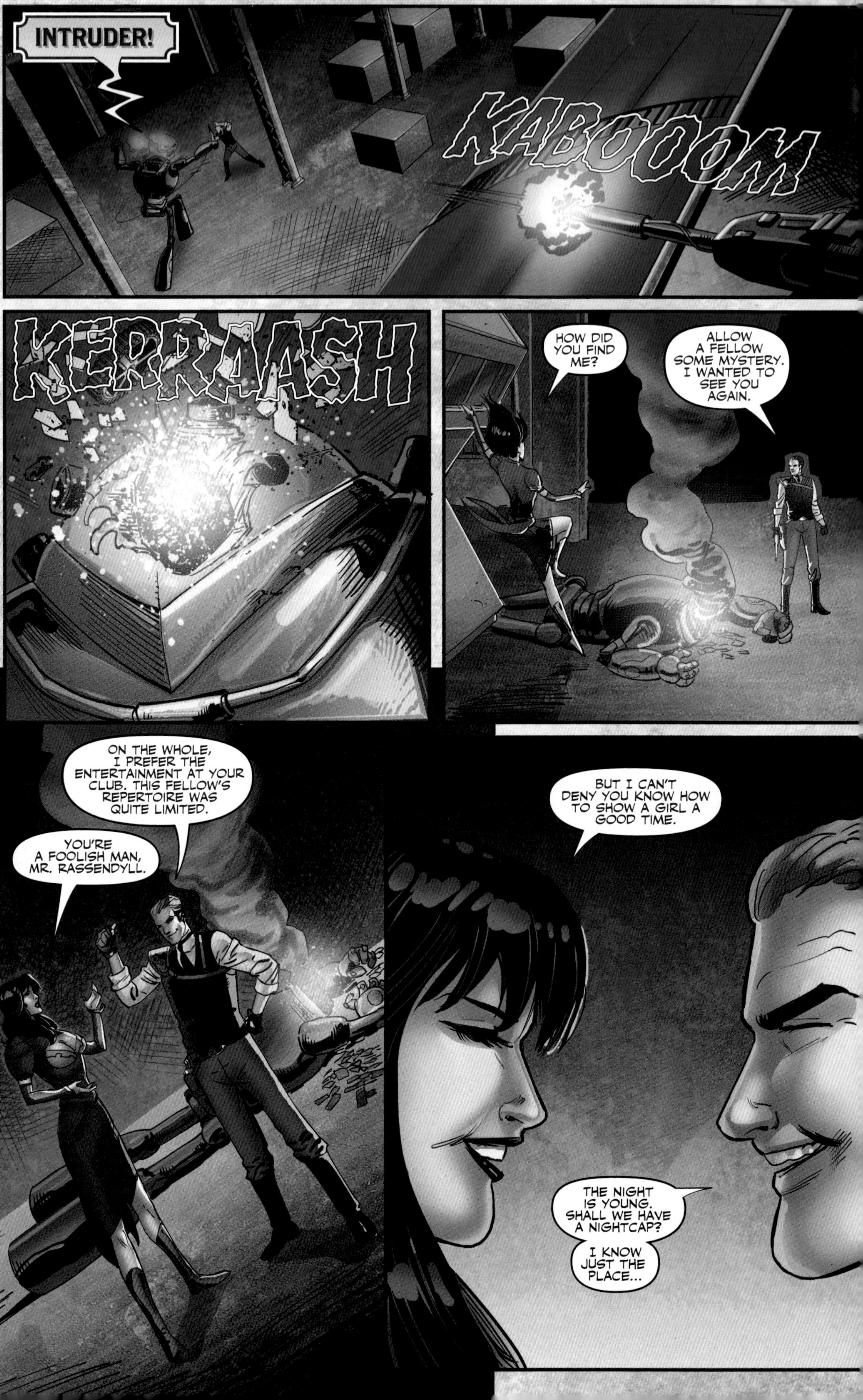
INTRUDER!
KABOOOM
KERRAASH
HOW DID YOU FIND ME?
ALLOW A FELLOW SOME MYSTERY. I WANTED TO SEE YOU AGAIN.
ON THE WHOLE, I PREFER THE ENTERTAINMENT AT YOUR CLUB. THIS FELLOW'S REPERTOIRE WAS QUITE LIMITED.
YOU'RE A FOOLISH MAN, MR. RASSENDYLL.
BUT I CAN'T DENY YOU KNOW HOW TO SHOW A GIRL A GOOD TIME.
THE NIGHT IS YOUNG. SHALL WE HAVE A NIGHTCAP?
I KNOW JUST THE PLACE...

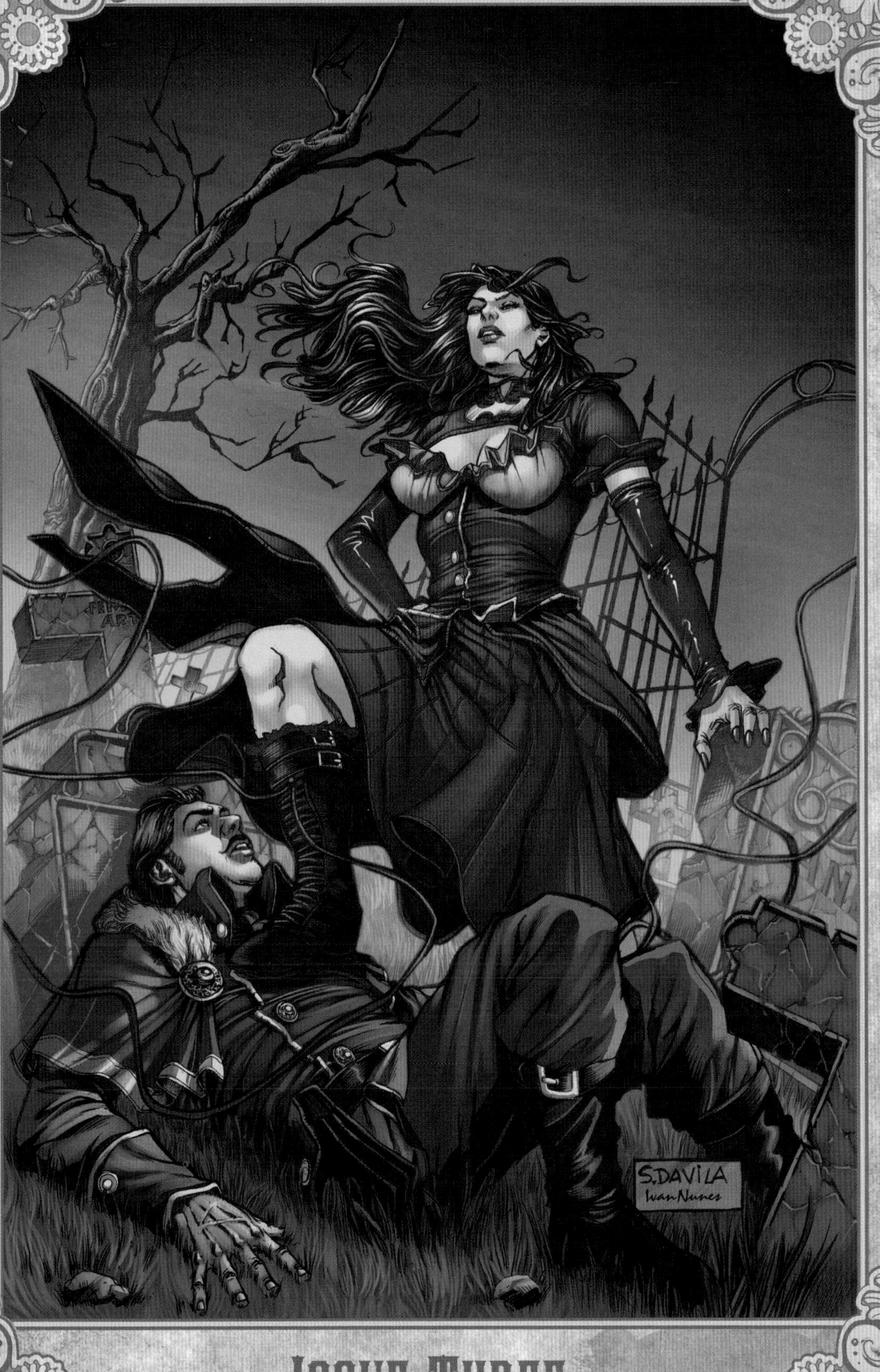
S.DAVILA
Ivan Nunes

ISSUE THREE

cover by Sergio Dávila and Ivan Nunes

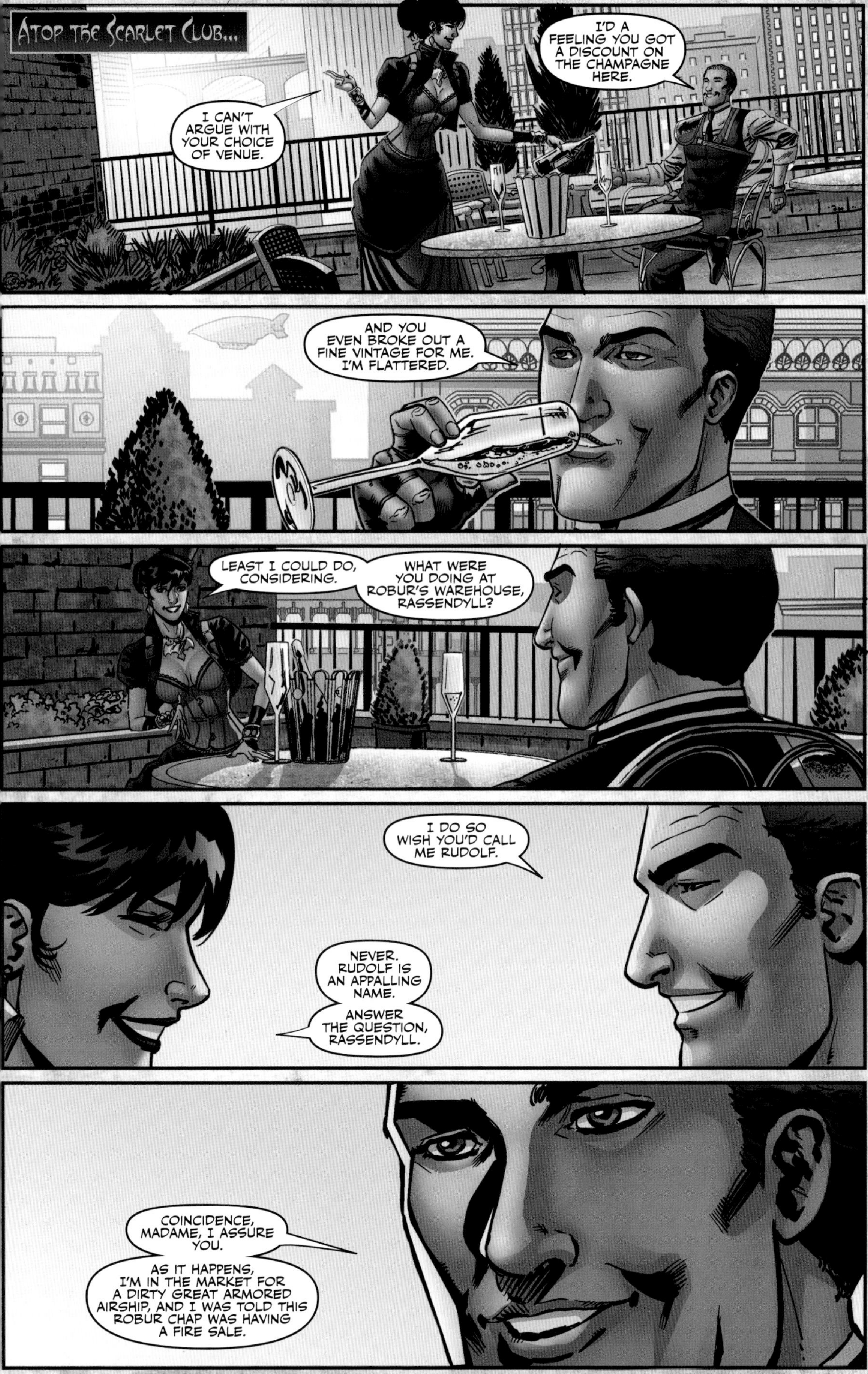
Atop the Scarlet Club...
I CAN'T ARGUE WITH YOUR CHOICE OF VENUE.
I'D A FEELING YOU GOT A DISCOUNT ON THE CHAMPAGNE HERE.
AND YOU EVEN BROKE OUT A FINE VINTAGE FOR ME. I'M FLATTERED.
LEAST I COULD DO, CONSIDERING.
WHAT WERE YOU DOING AT ROBUR'S WAREHOUSE, RASSENDYLL?
I DO SO WISH YOU'D CALL ME RUDOLF.
NEVER. RUDOLF IS AN APPALLING NAME.
ANSWER THE QUESTION, RASSENDYLL.
COINCIDENCE, MADAME, I ASSURE YOU.
AS IT HAPPENS, I'M IN THE MARKET FOR A DIRTY GREAT ARMORED AIRSHIP, AND I WAS TOLD THIS ROBUR CHAP WAS HAVING A FIRE SALE.

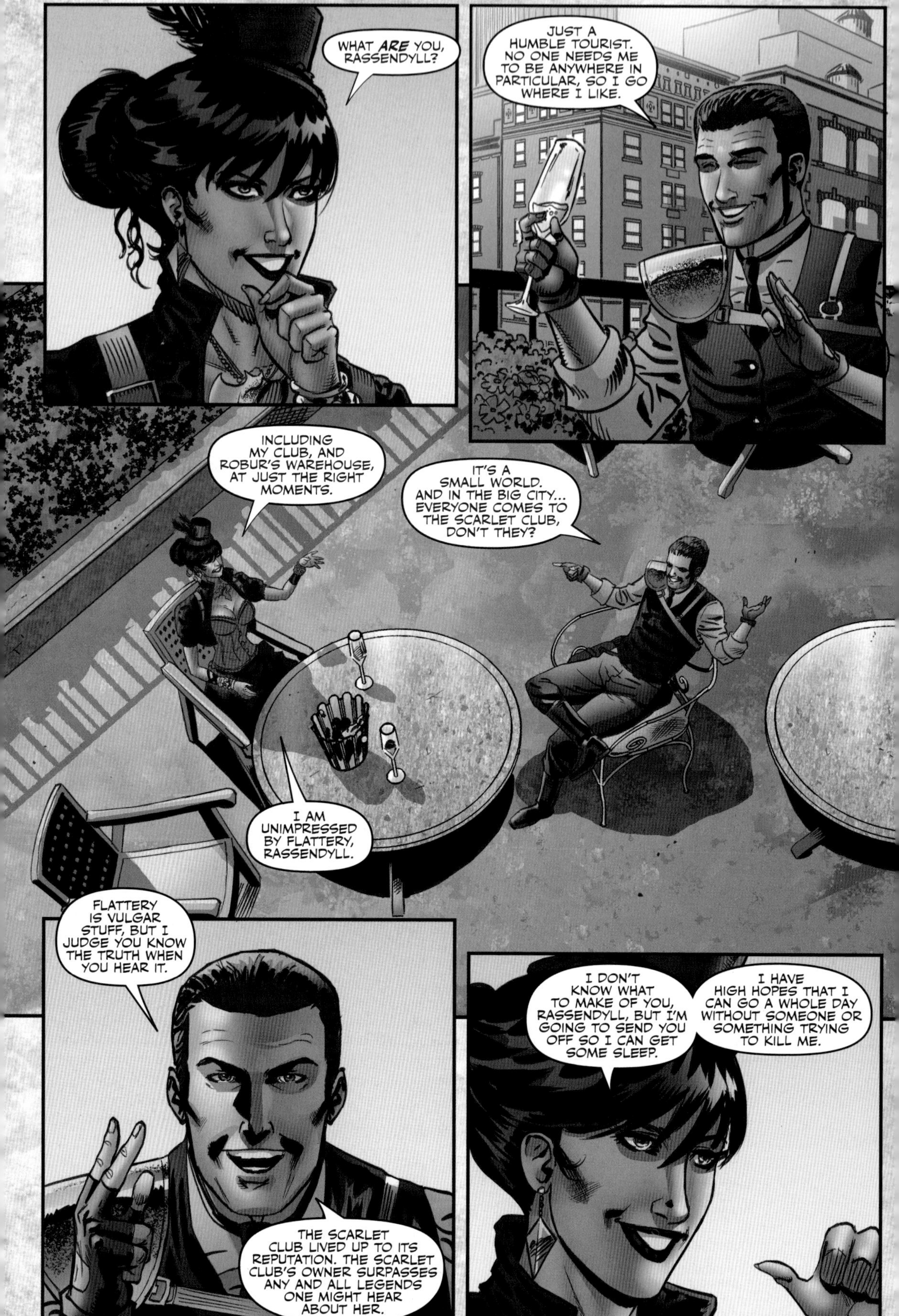

WHAT *ARE* YOU, RASSENDYLL?
JUST A HUMBLE TOURIST. NO ONE NEEDS ME TO BE ANYWHERE IN PARTICULAR, SO I GO WHERE I LIKE.
INCLUDING MY CLUB, AND ROBUR'S WAREHOUSE, AT JUST THE RIGHT MOMENTS.
IT'S A SMALL WORLD. AND IN THE BIG CITY... EVERYONE COMES TO THE SCARLET CLUB, DON'T THEY?
I AM UNIMPRESSED BY FLATTERY, RASSENDYLL.
FLATTERY IS VULGAR STUFF, BUT I JUDGE YOU KNOW THE TRUTH WHEN YOU HEAR IT.
THE SCARLET CLUB LIVED UP TO ITS REPUTATION. THE SCARLET CLUB'S OWNER SURPASSES ANY AND ALL LEGENDS ONE MIGHT HEAR ABOUT HER.
I DON'T KNOW WHAT TO MAKE OF YOU, RASSENDYLL, BUT I'M GOING TO SEND YOU OFF SO I CAN GET SOME SLEEP.
I HAVE HIGH HOPES THAT I CAN GO A WHOLE DAY WITHOUT SOMEONE OR SOMETHING TRYING TO KILL ME.

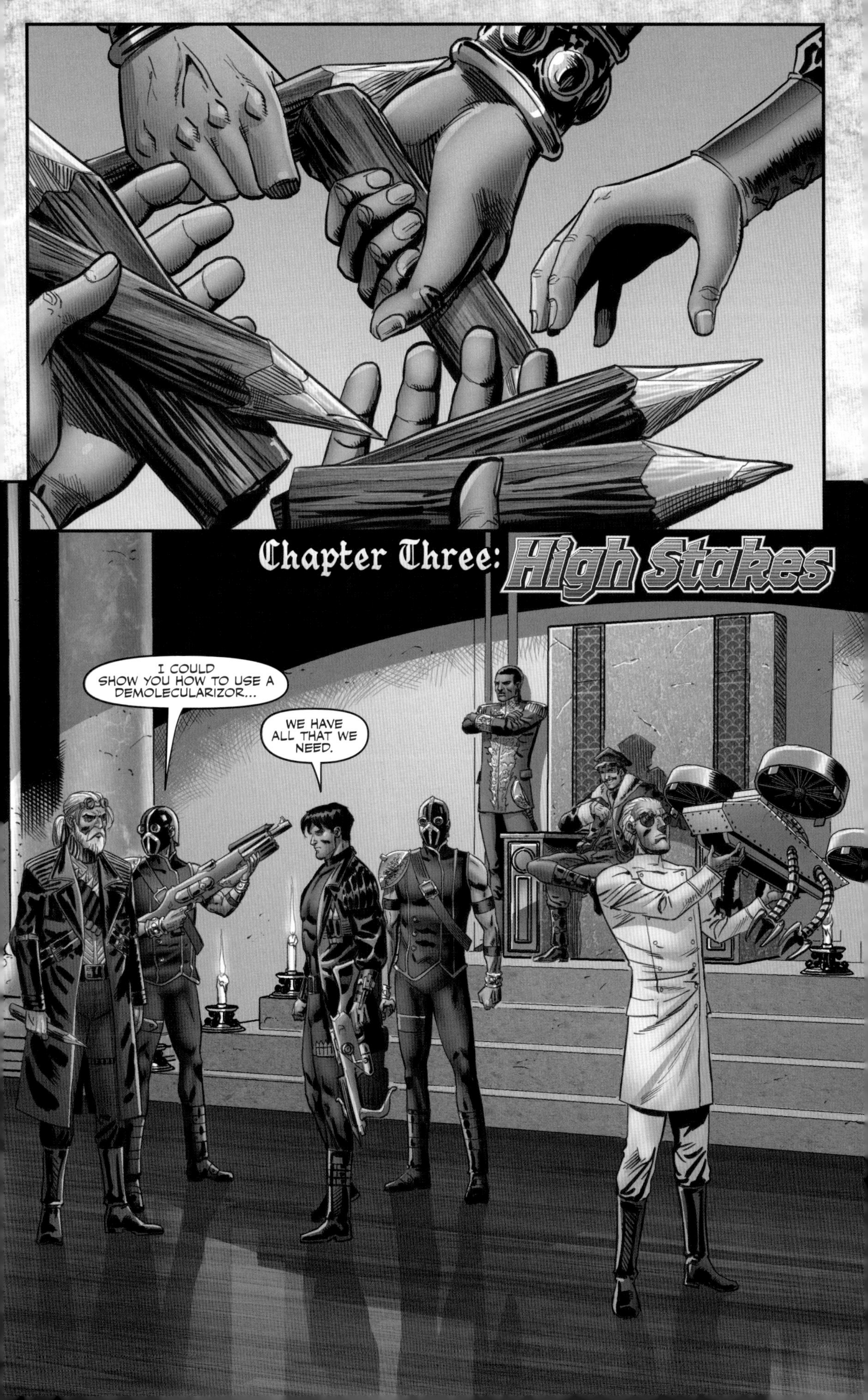
Chapter Three: High Stakes
I COULD SHOW YOU HOW TO USE A DEMOLECULARIZOR...
WE HAVE ALL THAT WE NEED.

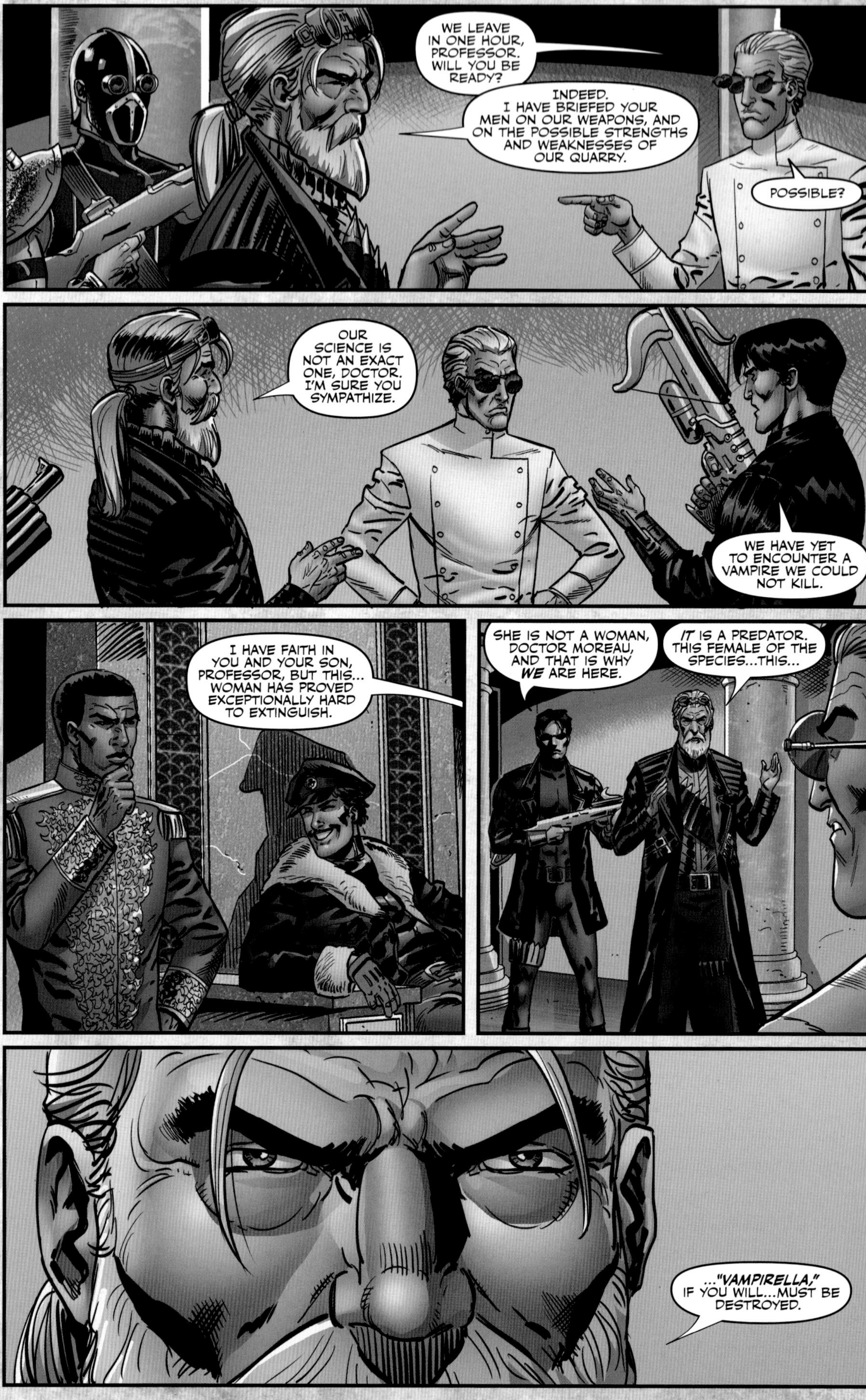
WE LEAVE IN ONE HOUR, PROFESSOR. WILL YOU BE READY?
INDEED. I HAVE BRIEFED YOUR MEN ON OUR WEAPONS, AND ON THE POSSIBLE STRENGTHS AND WEAKNESSES OF OUR QUARRY.
POSSIBLE?
OUR SCIENCE IS NOT AN EXACT ONE, DOCTOR. I'M SURE YOU SYMPATHIZE.
WE HAVE YET TO ENCOUNTER A VAMPIRE WE COULD NOT KILL.
I HAVE FAITH IN YOU AND YOUR SON, PROFESSOR, BUT THIS... WOMAN HAS PROVED EXCEPTIONALLY HARD TO EXTINGUISH.
SHE IS NOT A WOMAN, DOCTOR MOREAU, AND THAT IS WHY *WE* ARE HERE.
IT IS A PREDATOR. THIS FEMALE OF THE SPECIES...THIS...
...*"VAMPIRELLA,"* IF YOU WILL...MUST BE DESTROYED.

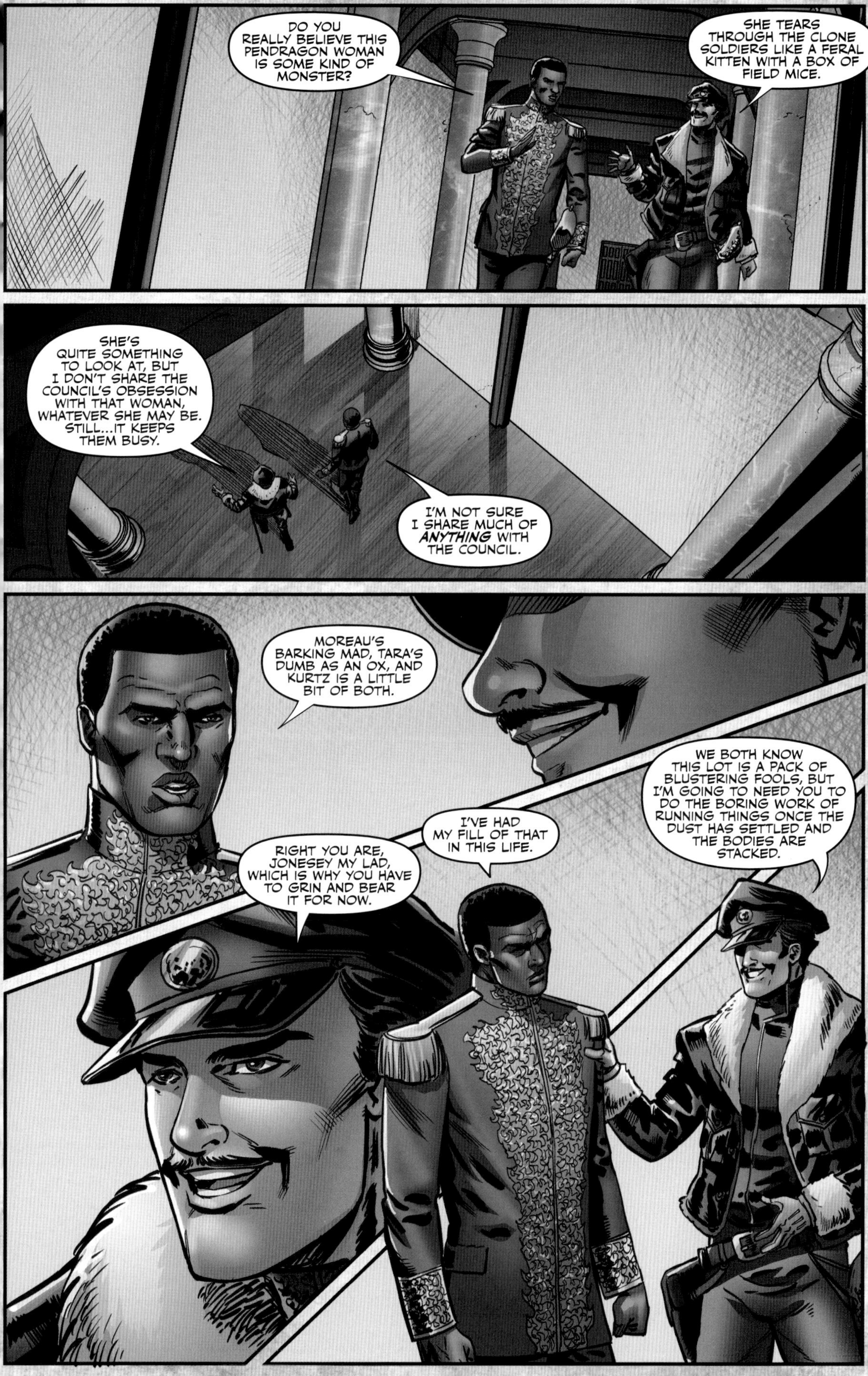
DO YOU REALLY BELIEVE THIS PENDRAGON WOMAN IS SOME KIND OF MONSTER?
SHE TEARS THROUGH THE CLONE SOLDIERS LIKE A FERAL KITTEN WITH A BOX OF FIELD MICE.
SHE'S QUITE SOMETHING TO LOOK AT, BUT I DON'T SHARE THE COUNCIL'S OBSESSION WITH THAT WOMAN, WHATEVER SHE MAY BE. STILL...IT KEEPS THEM BUSY.
I'M NOT SURE I SHARE MUCH OF *ANYTHING* WITH THE COUNCIL.
MOREAU'S BARKING MAD, TARA'S DUMB AS AN OX, AND KURTZ IS A LITTLE BIT OF BOTH.
WE BOTH KNOW THIS LOT IS A PACK OF BLUSTERING FOOLS, BUT I'M GOING TO NEED YOU TO DO THE BORING WORK OF RUNNING THINGS ONCE THE DUST HAS SETTLED AND THE BODIES ARE STACKED.
I'VE HAD MY FILL OF THAT IN THIS LIFE.
RIGHT YOU ARE, JONESEY MY LAD, WHICH IS WHY YOU HAVE TO GRIN AND BEAR IT FOR NOW.

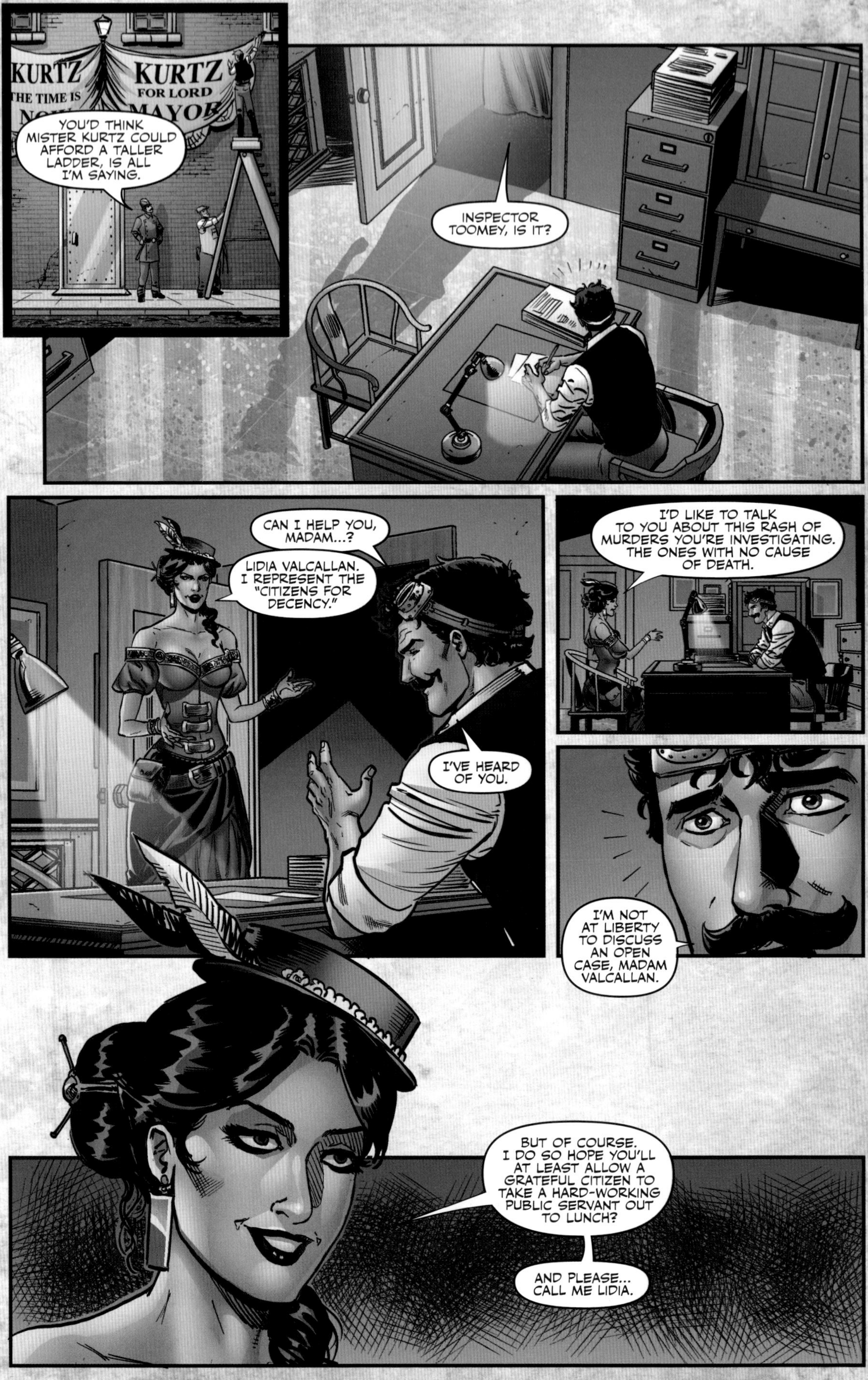
KURTZ
THE TIME IS
KURTZ
FOR LORD
MAYOR
YOU'D THINK MISTER KURTZ COULD AFFORD A TALLER LADDER, IS ALL I'M SAYING.
INSPECTOR TOOMEY, IS IT?
CAN I HELP YOU, MADAM...?
LIDIA VALCALLAN. I REPRESENT THE "CITIZENS FOR DECENCY."
I'VE HEARD OF YOU.
I'D LIKE TO TALK TO YOU ABOUT THIS RASH OF MURDERS YOU'RE INVESTIGATING. THE ONES WITH NO CAUSE OF DEATH.
I'M NOT AT LIBERTY TO DISCUSS AN OPEN CASE, MADAM VALCALLAN.
BUT OF COURSE. I DO SO HOPE YOU'LL AT LEAST ALLOW A GRATEFUL CITIZEN TO TAKE A HARD-WORKING PUBLIC SERVANT OUT TO LUNCH?
AND PLEASE... CALL ME LIDIA.

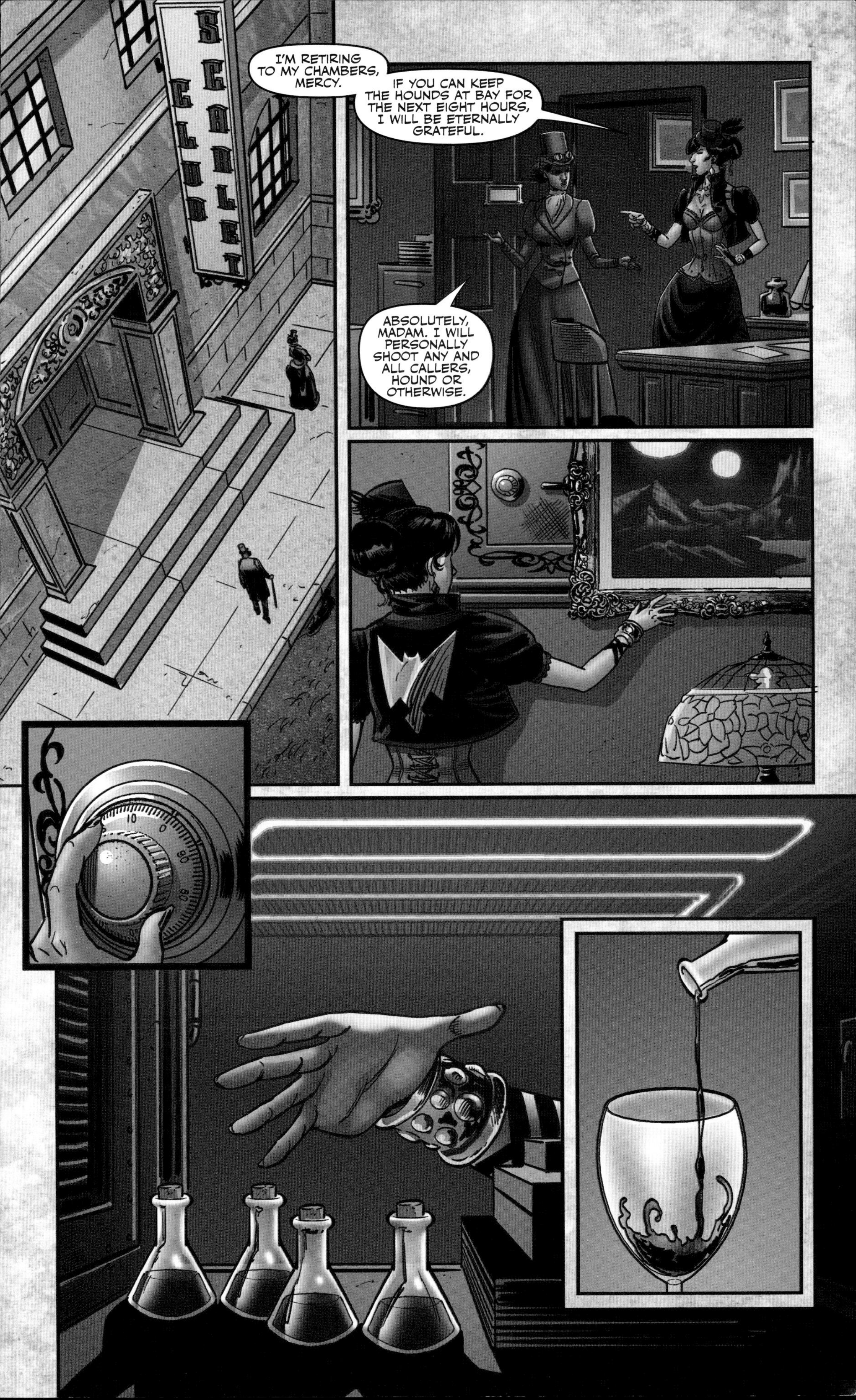
SCARLET CLUB
I'M RETIRING TO MY CHAMBERS, MERCY.
IF YOU CAN KEEP THE HOUNDS AT BAY FOR THE NEXT EIGHT HOURS, I WILL BE ETERNALLY GRATEFUL.
ABSOLUTELY, MADAM. I WILL PERSONALLY SHOOT ANY AND ALL CALLERS, HOUND OR OTHERWISE.

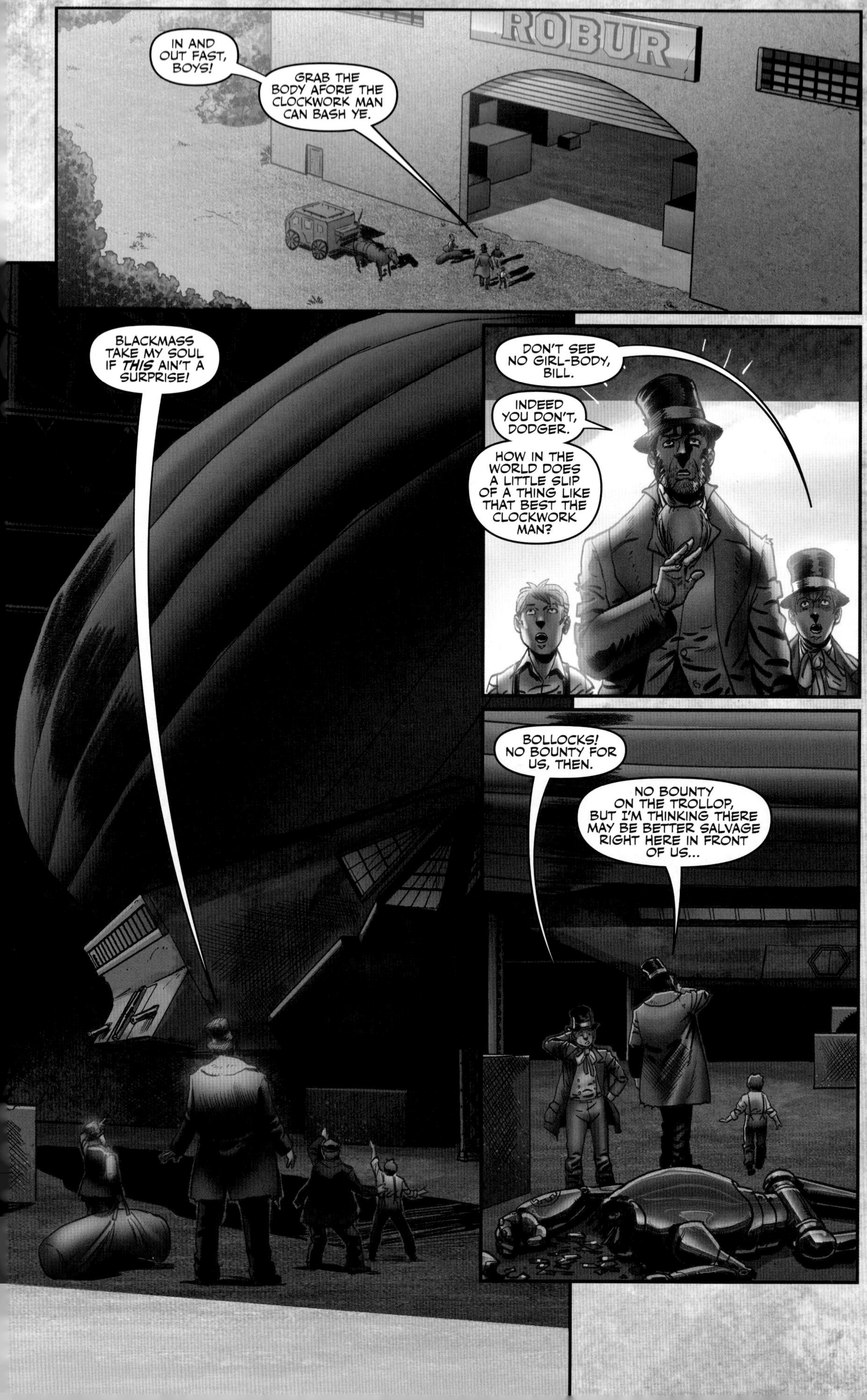
ROBUR
IN AND OUT FAST, BOYS!
GRAB THE BODY AFORE THE CLOCKWORK MAN CAN BASH YE.
BLACKMASS TAKE MY SOUL IF *THIS* AIN'T A SURPRISE!
DON'T SEE NO GIRL-BODY, BILL.
INDEED YOU DON'T, DODGER.
HOW IN THE WORLD DOES A LITTLE SLIP OF A THING LIKE THAT BEST THE CLOCKWORK MAN?
BOLLOCKS! NO BOUNTY FOR US, THEN.
NO BOUNTY ON THE TROLLOP, BUT I'M THINKING THERE MAY BE BETTER SALVAGE RIGHT HERE IN FRONT OF US...

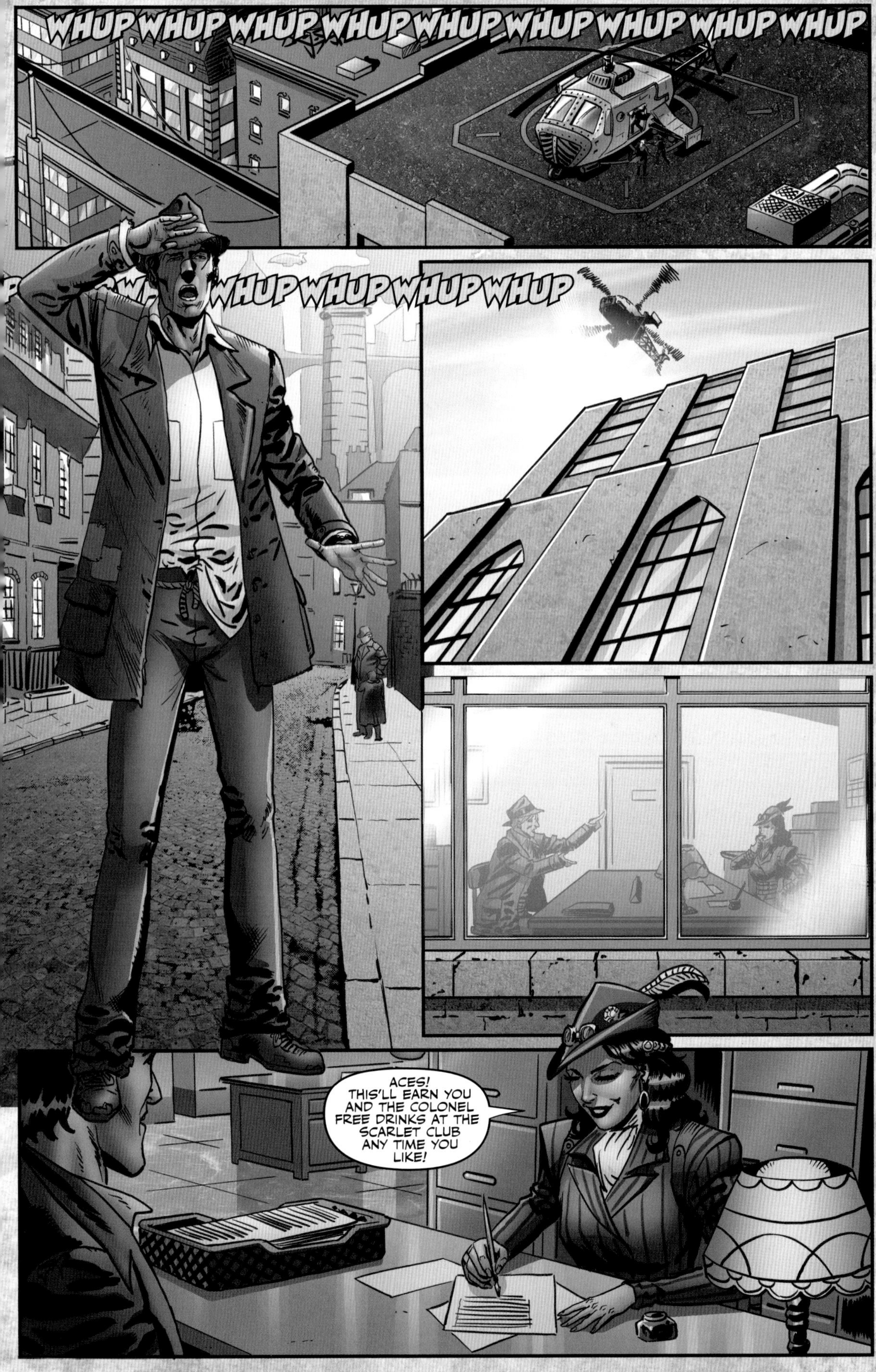
WHUP WHUP WHUP WHUP WHUP WHUP WHUP WHUP WHUP
WHUP WHUP WHUP WHUP
ACES! THIS'LL EARN YOU AND THE COLONEL FREE DRINKS AT THE SCARLET CLUB ANY TIME YOU LIKE!

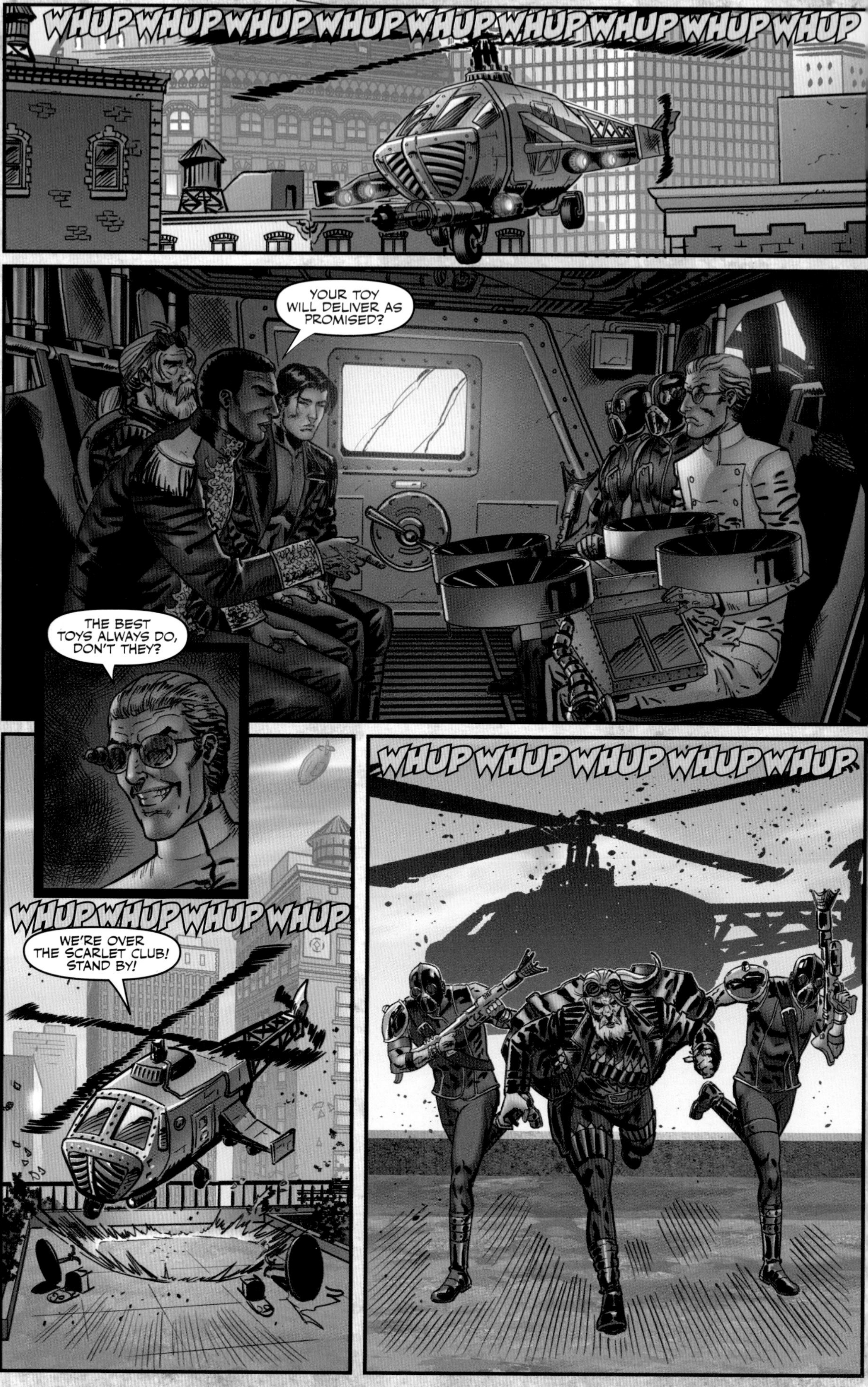
WHUP WHUP WHUP WHUP WHUP WHUP WHUP WHUP
YOUR TOY WILL DELIVER AS PROMISED?
THE BEST TOYS ALWAYS DO, DON'T THEY?
WHUP WHUP WHUP WHUP
WE'RE OVER THE SCARLET CLUB! STAND BY!
WHUP WHUP WHUP WHUP WHUP

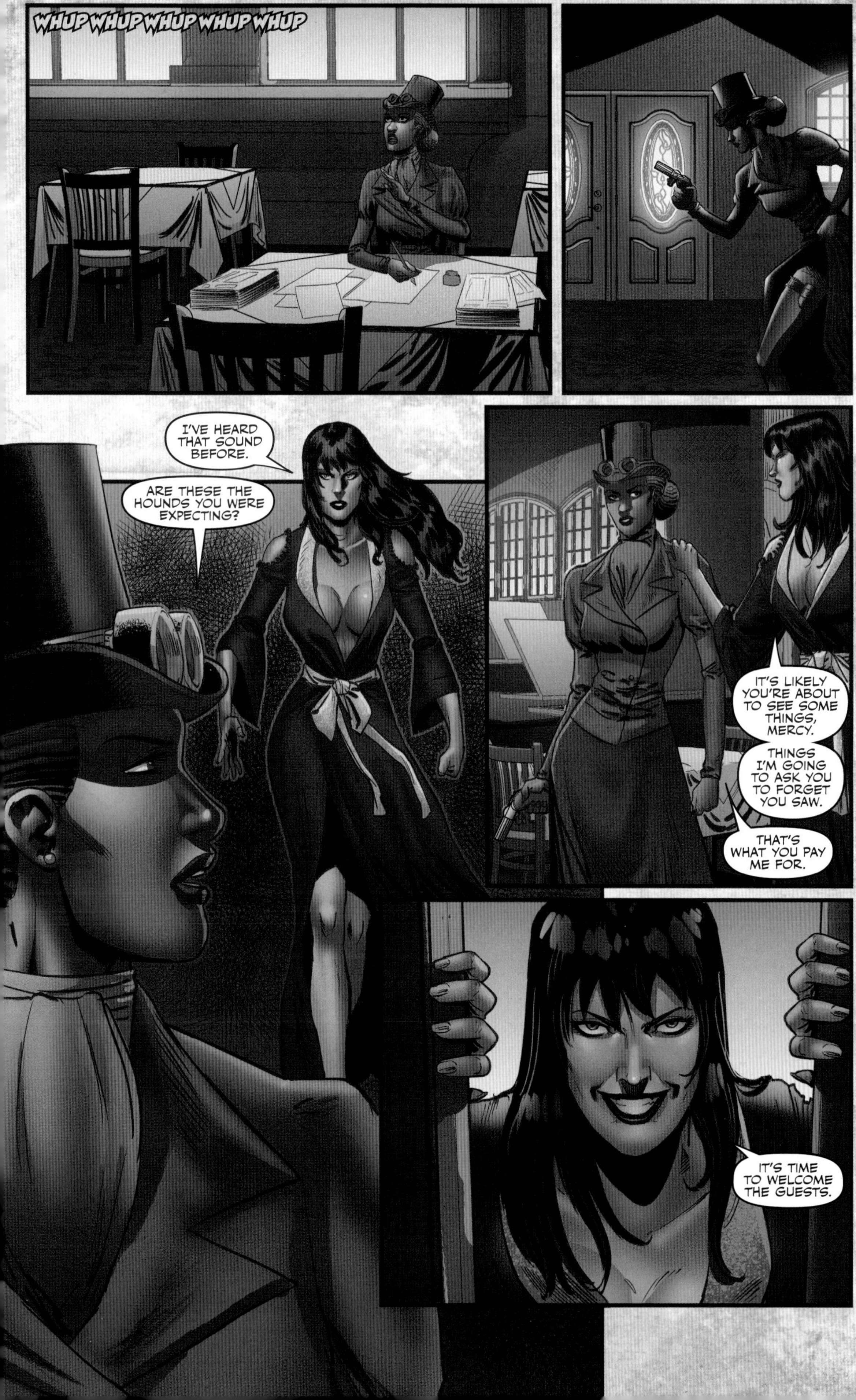
WHUP WHUP WHUP WHUP WHUP
I'VE HEARD THAT SOUND BEFORE.
ARE THESE THE HOUNDS YOU WERE EXPECTING?
IT'S LIKELY YOU'RE ABOUT TO SEE SOME THINGS, MERCY.
THINGS I'M GOING TO ASK YOU TO FORGET YOU SAW.
THAT'S WHAT YOU PAY ME FOR.
IT'S TIME TO WELCOME THE GUESTS.

YOU'RE EARLY, GENTLEMEN. DOORS ARE AT SIX.

DON'T MOCK US, MONSTER. YOU FACE YOUR DOOM!

"YOU FACE YOUR DOOM?" SERIOUSLY?

MONSTER-HUNTERS ARE BENT TOWARDS THE DRAMATIC.

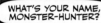

WHAT'S YOUR NAME, MONSTER-HUNTER?

I AM PROFESSOR CONRAD VAN HELSING.

I'VE HEARD OF YOU, PROFESSOR.

WHAT QUARREL HAVE YOU WITH ME?

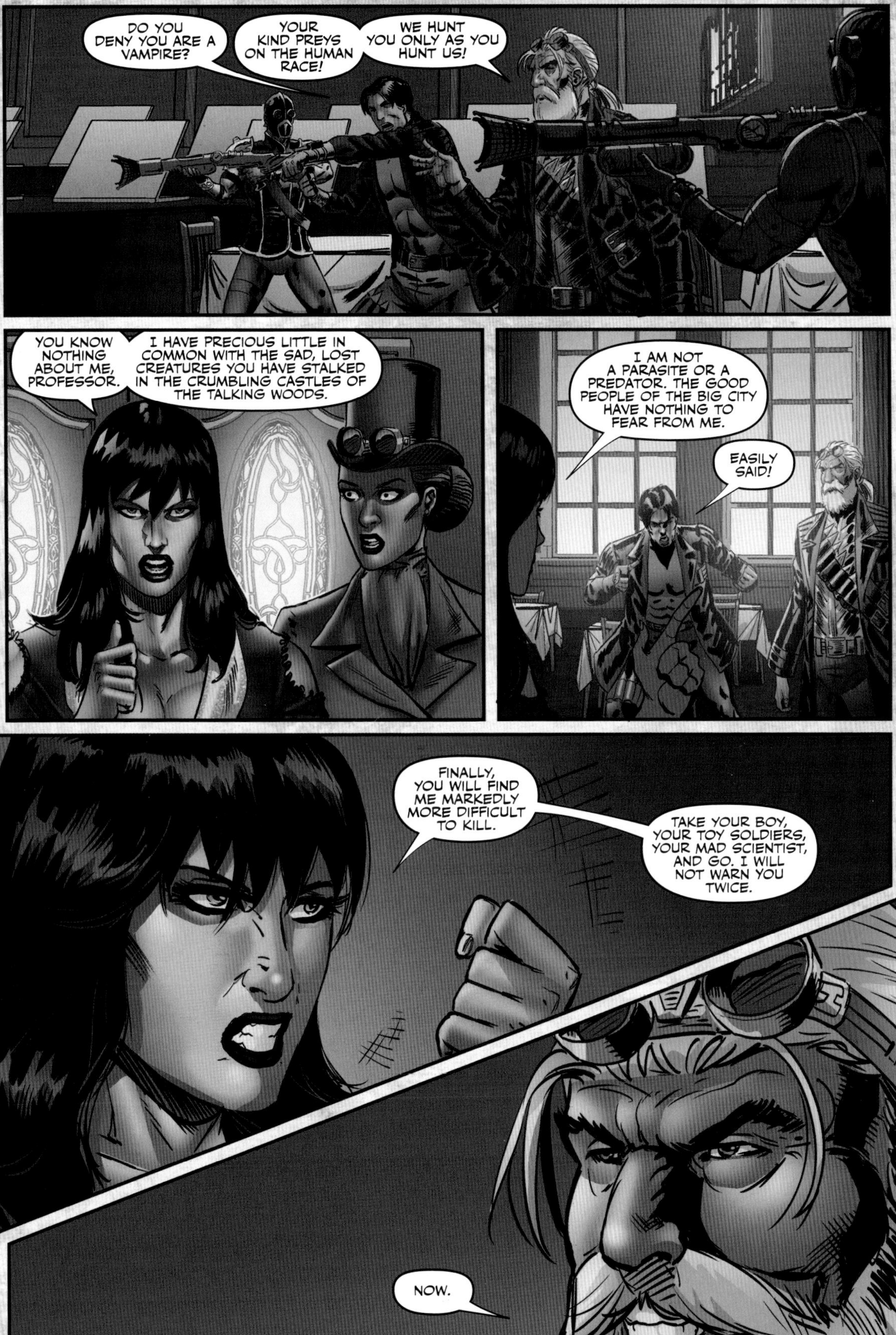
DO YOU DENY YOU ARE A VAMPIRE?
YOUR KIND PREYS ON THE HUMAN RACE!
WE HUNT YOU ONLY AS YOU HUNT US!
YOU KNOW NOTHING ABOUT ME, PROFESSOR.
I HAVE PRECIOUS LITTLE IN COMMON WITH THE SAD, LOST CREATURES YOU HAVE STALKED IN THE CRUMBLING CASTLES OF THE TALKING WOODS.
I AM NOT A PARASITE OR A PREDATOR. THE GOOD PEOPLE OF THE BIG CITY HAVE NOTHING TO FEAR FROM ME.
EASILY SAID!
FINALLY, YOU WILL FIND ME MARKEDLY MORE DIFFICULT TO KILL.
TAKE YOUR BOY, YOUR TOY SOLDIERS, YOUR MAD SCIENTIST, AND GO. I WILL NOT WARN YOU TWICE.
NOW.

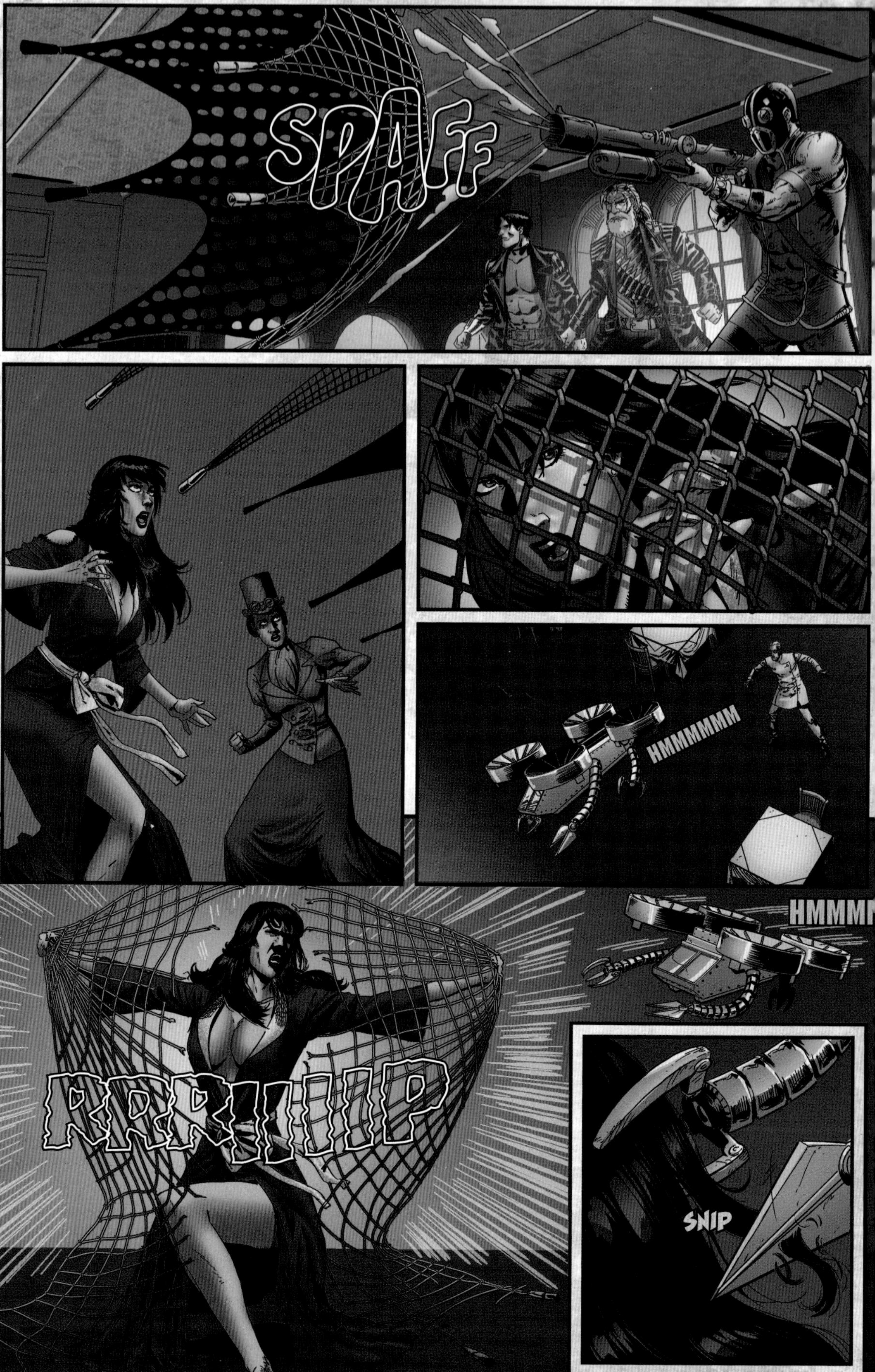
SPAFF
HMMMMMM
HMMMM
RRRIIIIP
SNIP

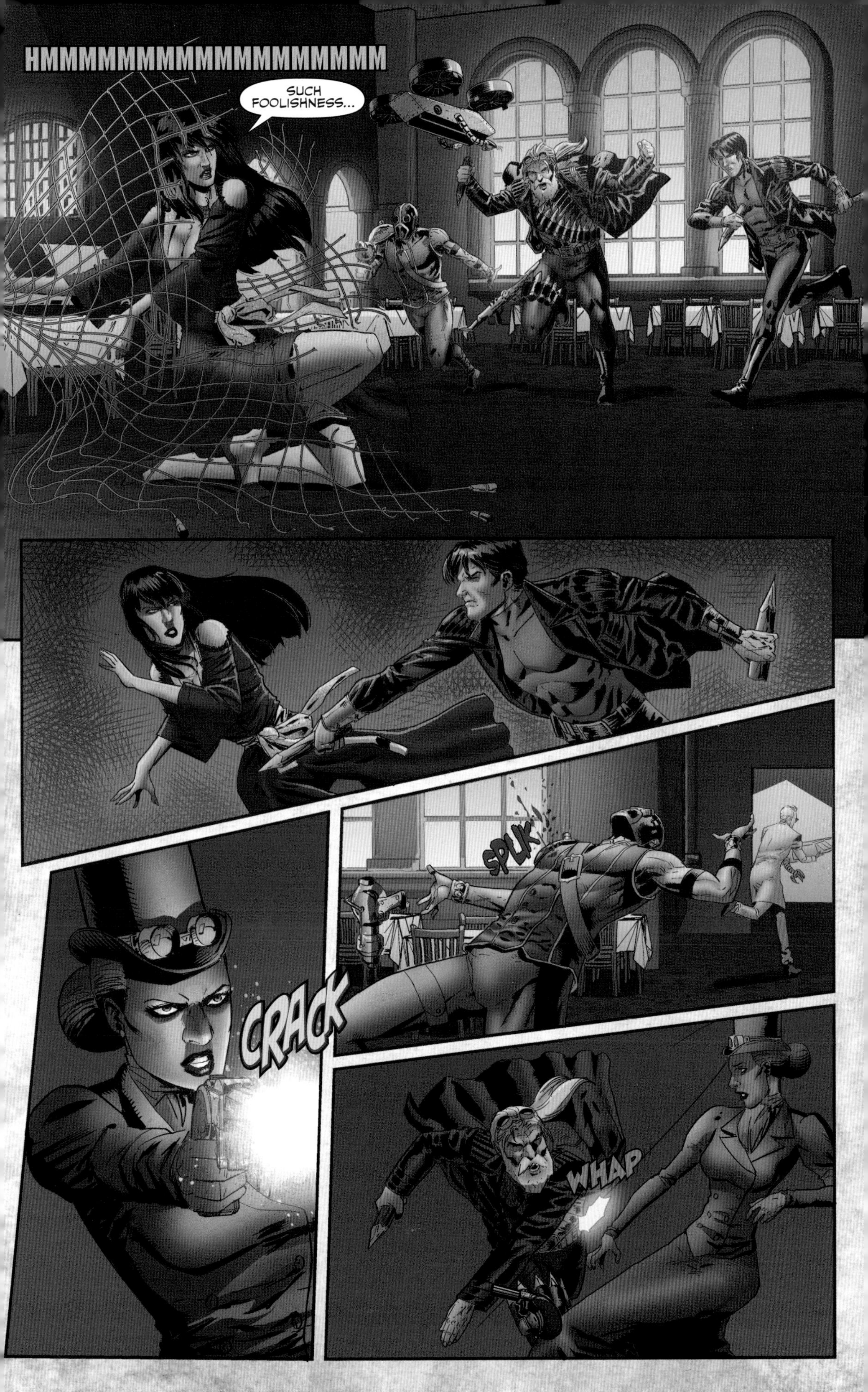
HMMMMMMMMMMMMMMMMMMMM
SUCH FOOLISHNESS...
SPLIK
CRACK
WHAP

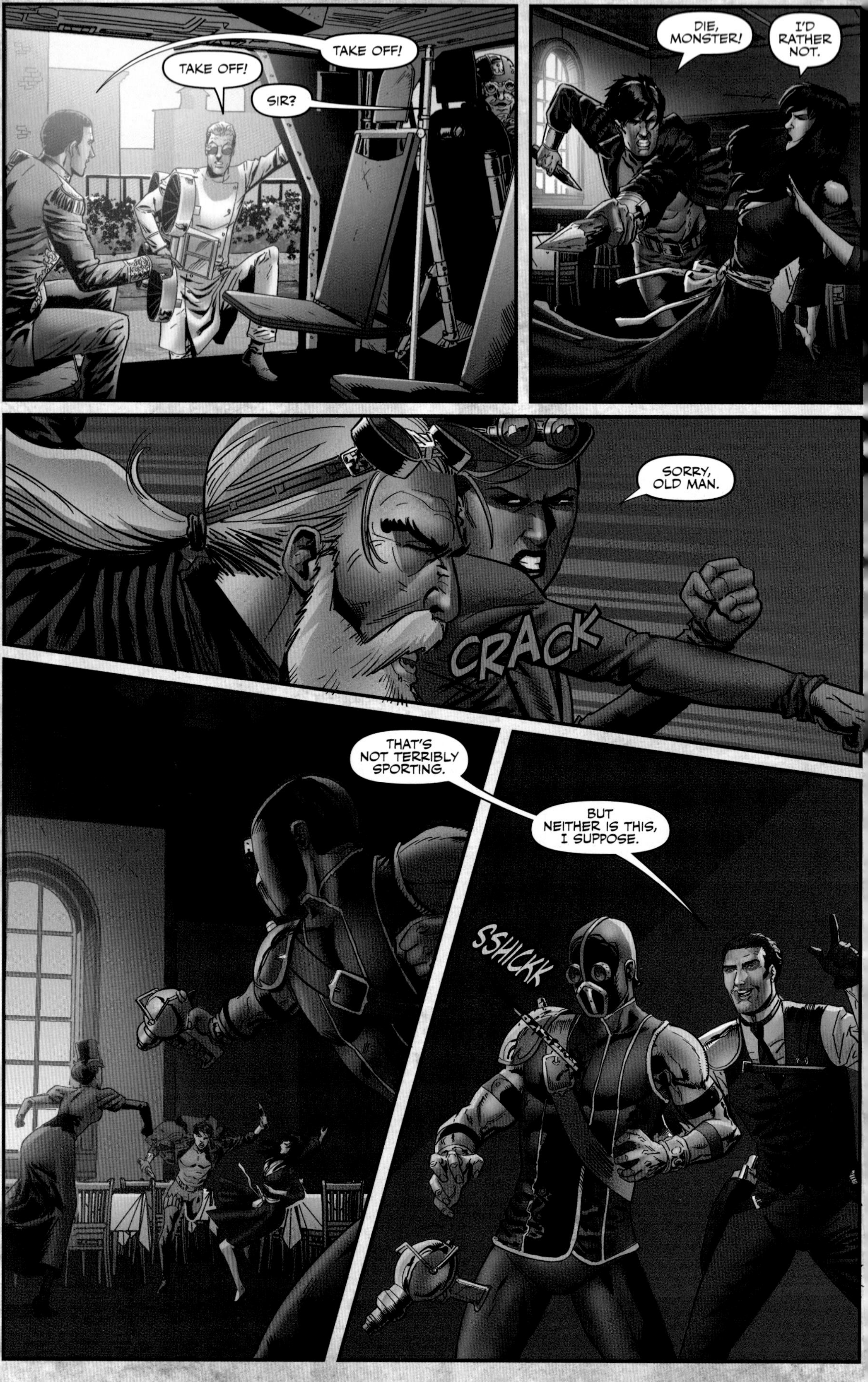

TAKE OFF!
TAKE OFF!
SIR?
DIE, MONSTER!
I'D RATHER NOT.
SORRY, OLD MAN.
CRACK
THAT'S NOT TERRIBLY SPORTING.
BUT NEITHER IS THIS, I SUPPOSE.
SSHICKK

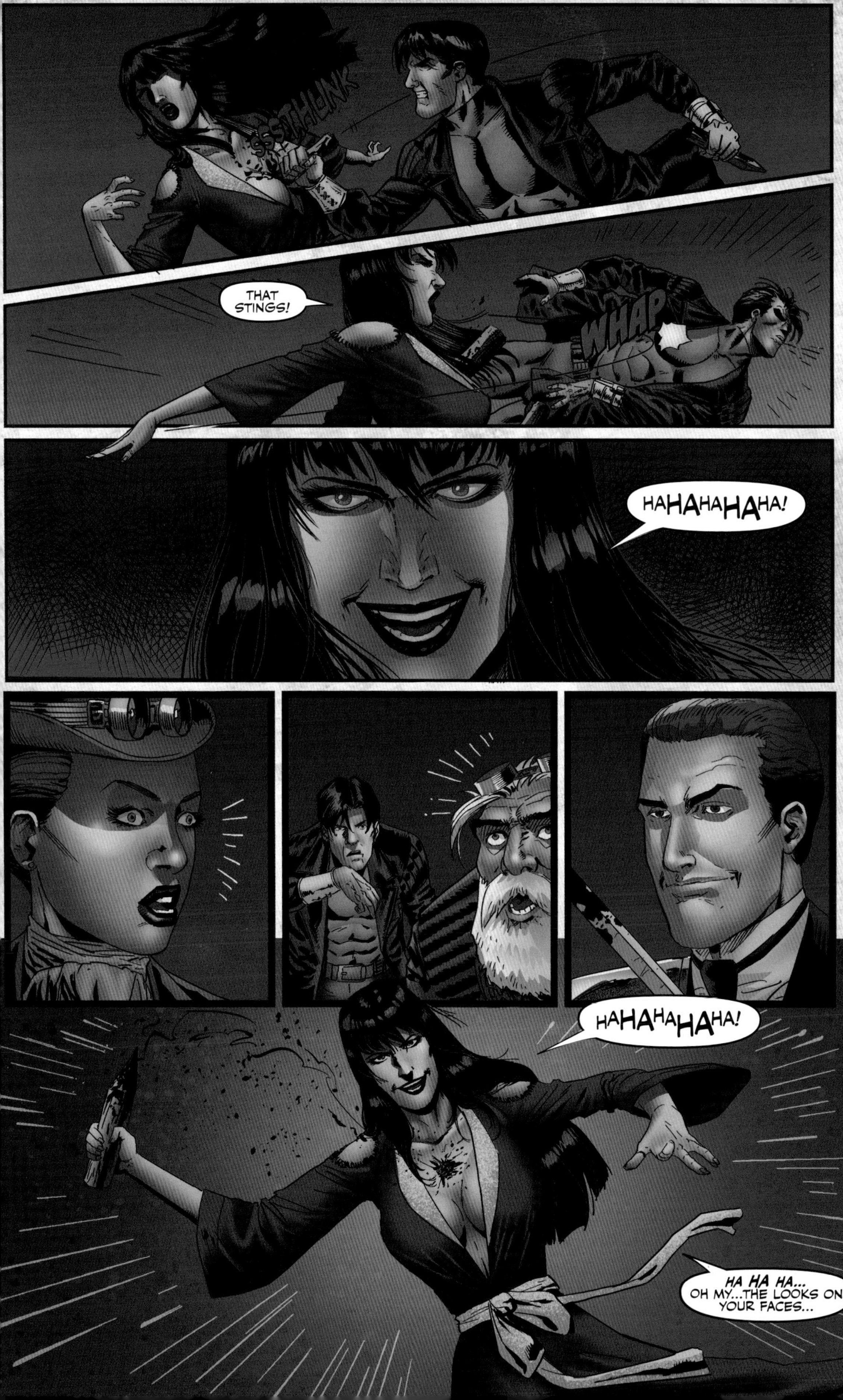

SSSTHUNK
THAT STINGS!
WHAP
HAHAHAHAHAHA!
HAHAHAHAHAHA!
HA HA HA... OH MY...THE LOOKS ON YOUR FACES...

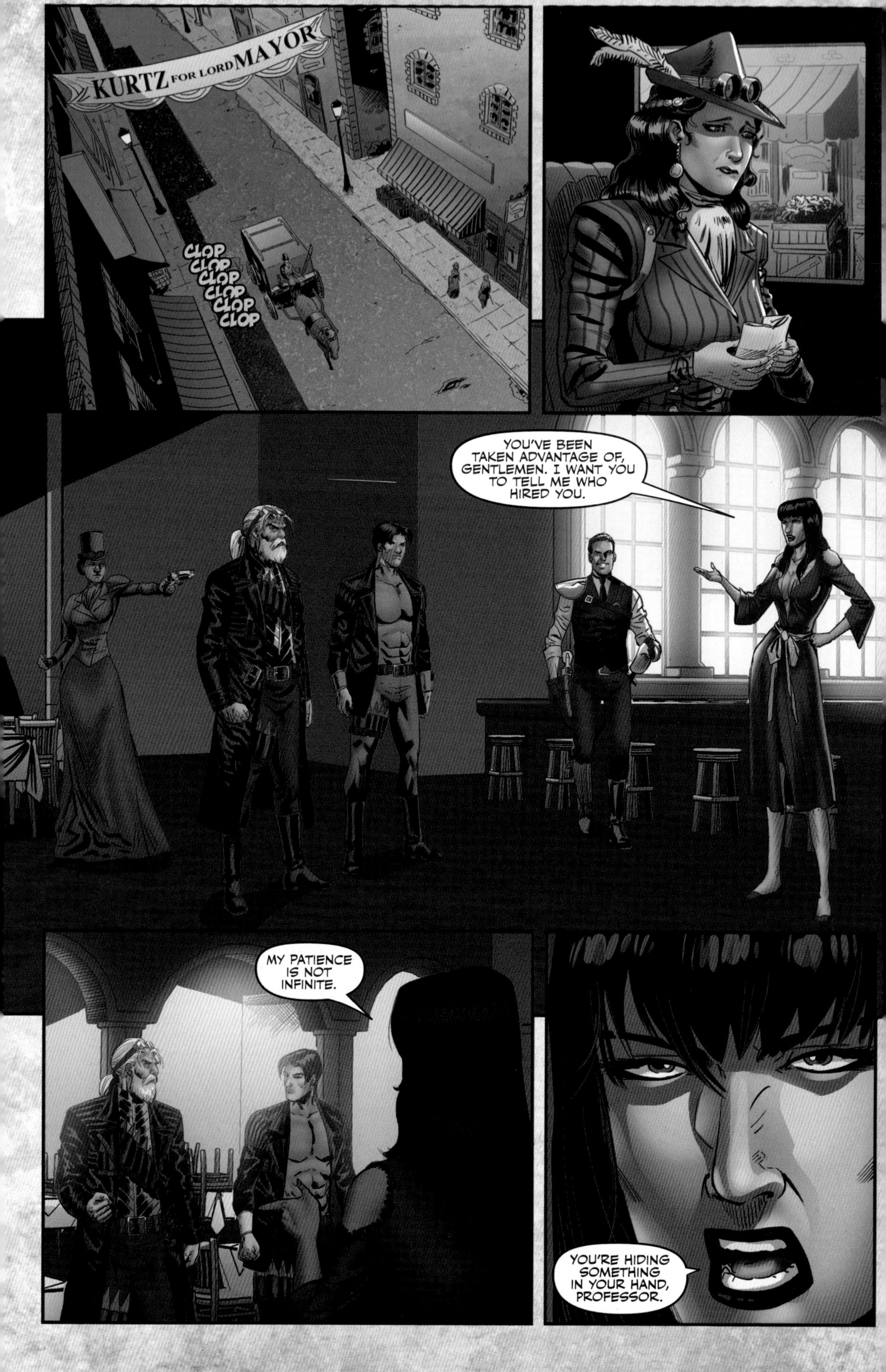
KURTZ FOR LORD MAYOR
CLOP CLOP CLOP CLOP CLOP CLOP
YOU'VE BEEN TAKEN ADVANTAGE OF, GENTLEMEN. I WANT YOU TO TELL ME WHO HIRED YOU.
MY PATIENCE IS NOT INFINITE.
YOU'RE HIDING SOMETHING IN YOUR HAND, PROFESSOR.

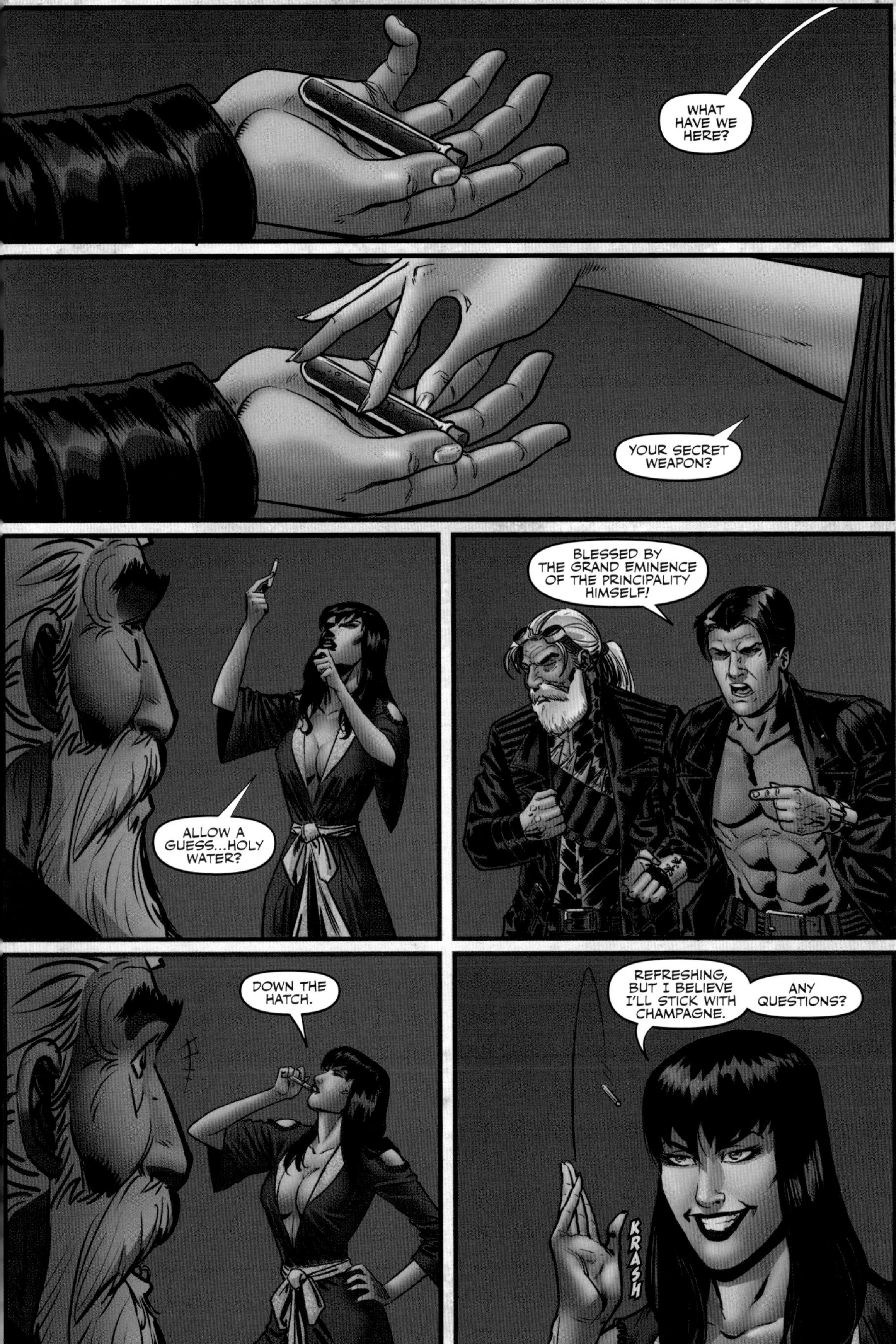
WHAT HAVE WE HERE?
YOUR SECRET WEAPON?
ALLOW A GUESS...HOLY WATER?
BLESSED BY THE GRAND EMINENCE OF THE PRINCIPALITY HIMSELF!
DOWN THE HATCH.
REFRESHING, BUT I BELIEVE I'LL STICK WITH CHAMPAGNE.
ANY QUESTIONS?
KRASH

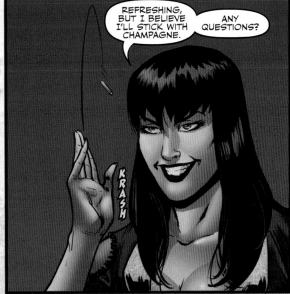

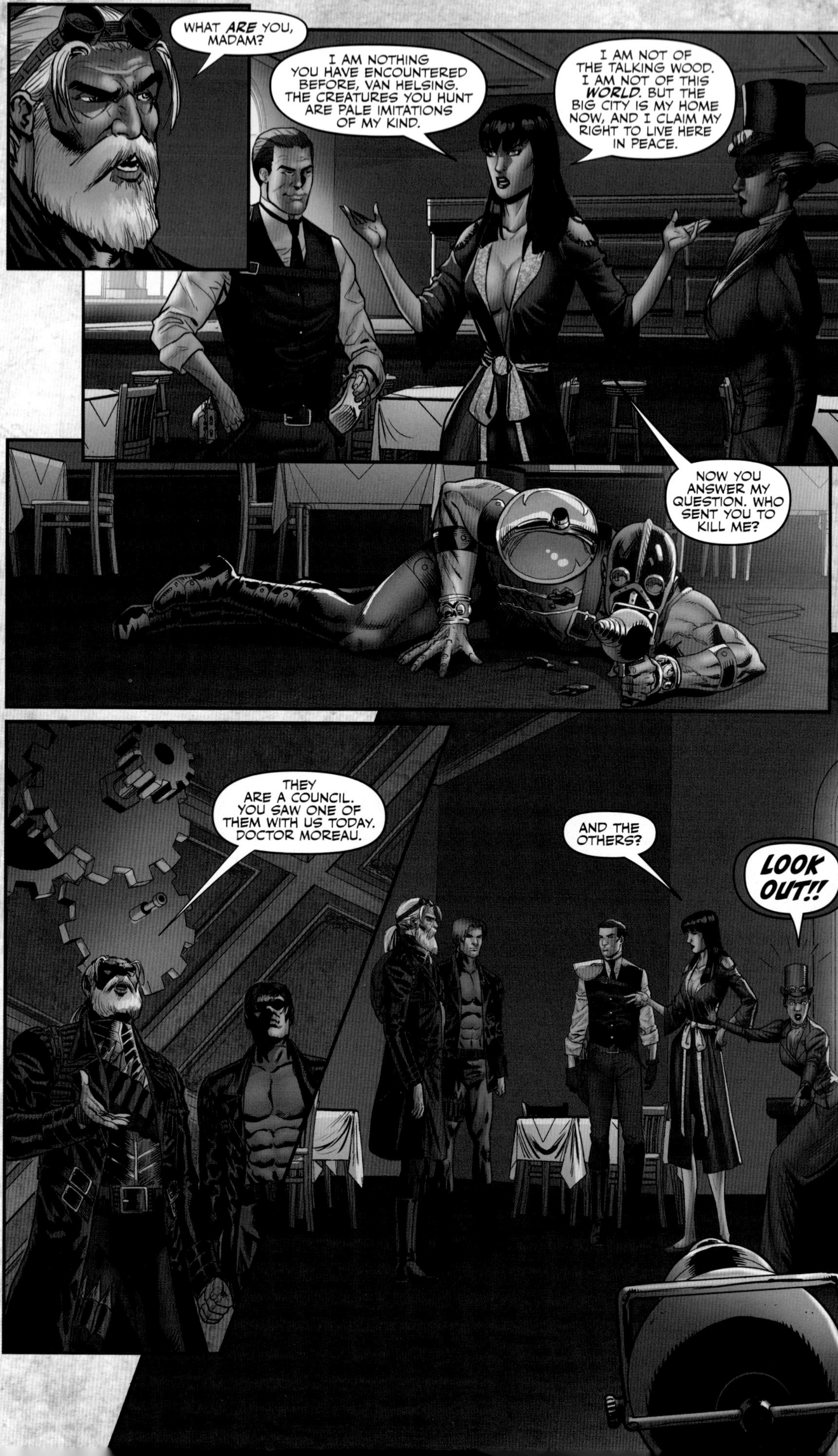
WHAT *ARE* YOU, MADAM?
I AM NOTHING YOU HAVE ENCOUNTERED BEFORE, VAN HELSING. THE CREATURES YOU HUNT ARE PALE IMITATIONS OF MY KIND.
I AM NOT OF THE TALKING WOOD. I AM NOT OF THIS *WORLD*. BUT THE BIG CITY IS MY HOME NOW, AND I CLAIM MY RIGHT TO LIVE HERE IN PEACE.
NOW YOU ANSWER MY QUESTION. WHO SENT YOU TO KILL ME?
THEY ARE A COUNCIL. YOU SAW ONE OF THEM WITH US TODAY. DOCTOR MOREAU.
AND THE OTHERS?
LOOK OUT!!

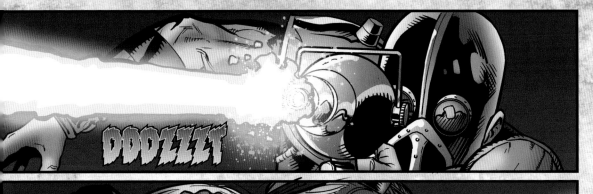

DDDZZZT

ZATCH

AAAGHH!

NO!!!

CRACKSH

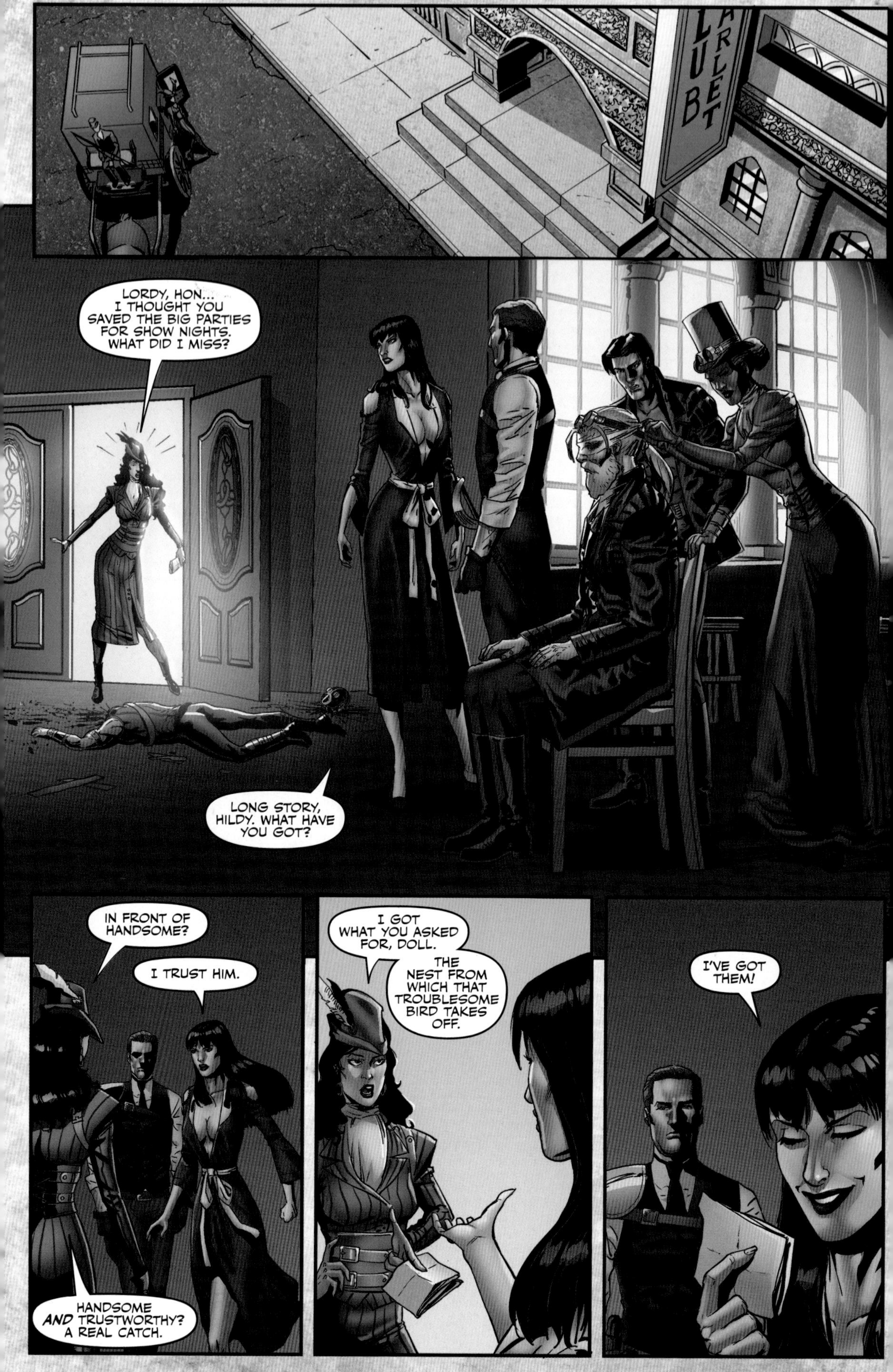
LORDY, HON... I THOUGHT YOU SAVED THE BIG PARTIES FOR SHOW NIGHTS. WHAT DID I MISS?
LONG STORY, HILDY. WHAT HAVE YOU GOT?
IN FRONT OF HANDSOME?
I TRUST HIM.
HANDSOME AND TRUSTWORTHY? A REAL CATCH.
I GOT WHAT YOU ASKED FOR, DOLL.
THE NEST FROM WHICH THAT TROUBLESOME BIRD TAKES OFF.
I'VE GOT THEM!

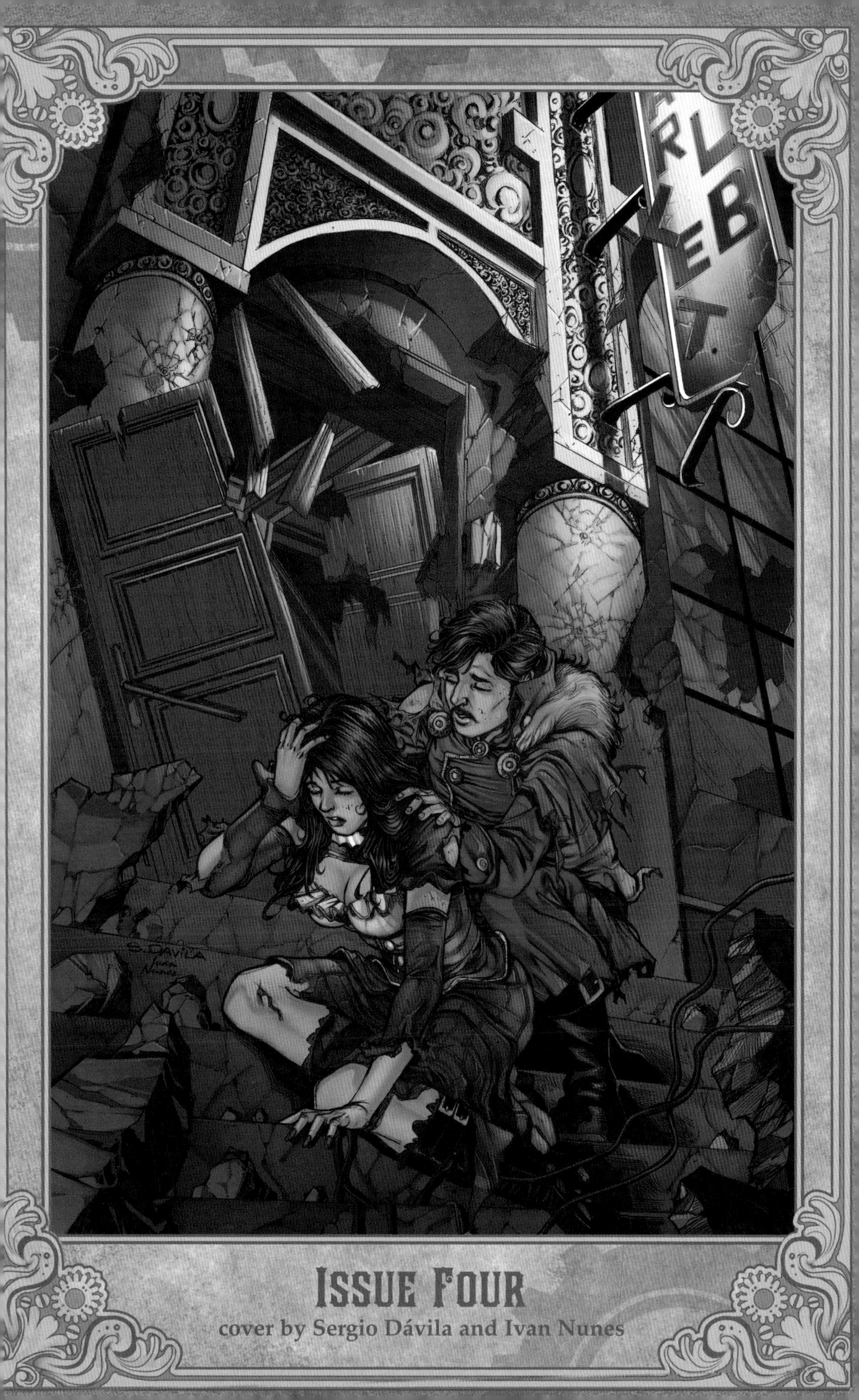
S.DAVILA
Ivan Nunes

ISSUE FOUR

cover by Sergio Dávila and Ivan Nunes

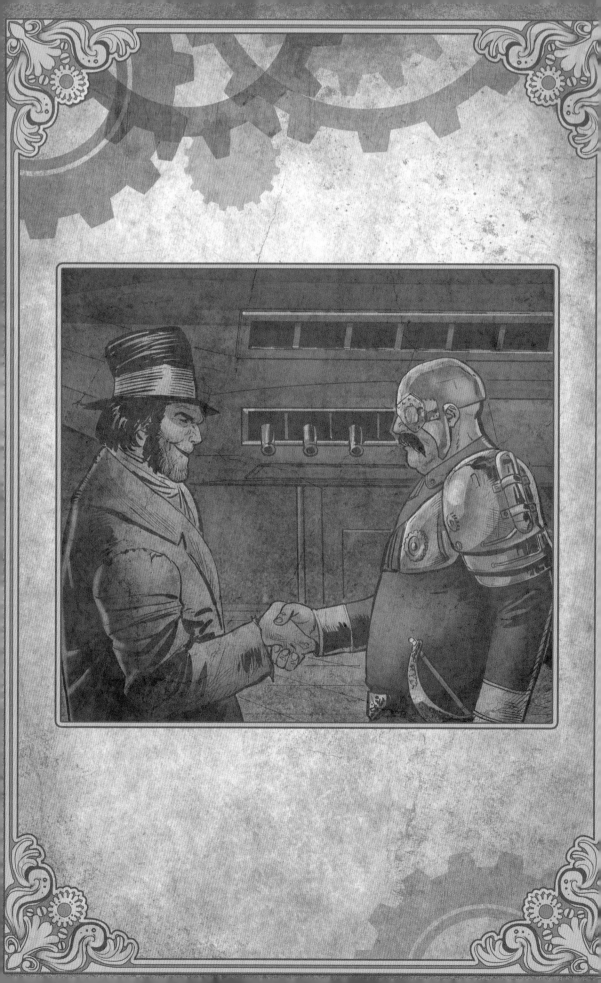

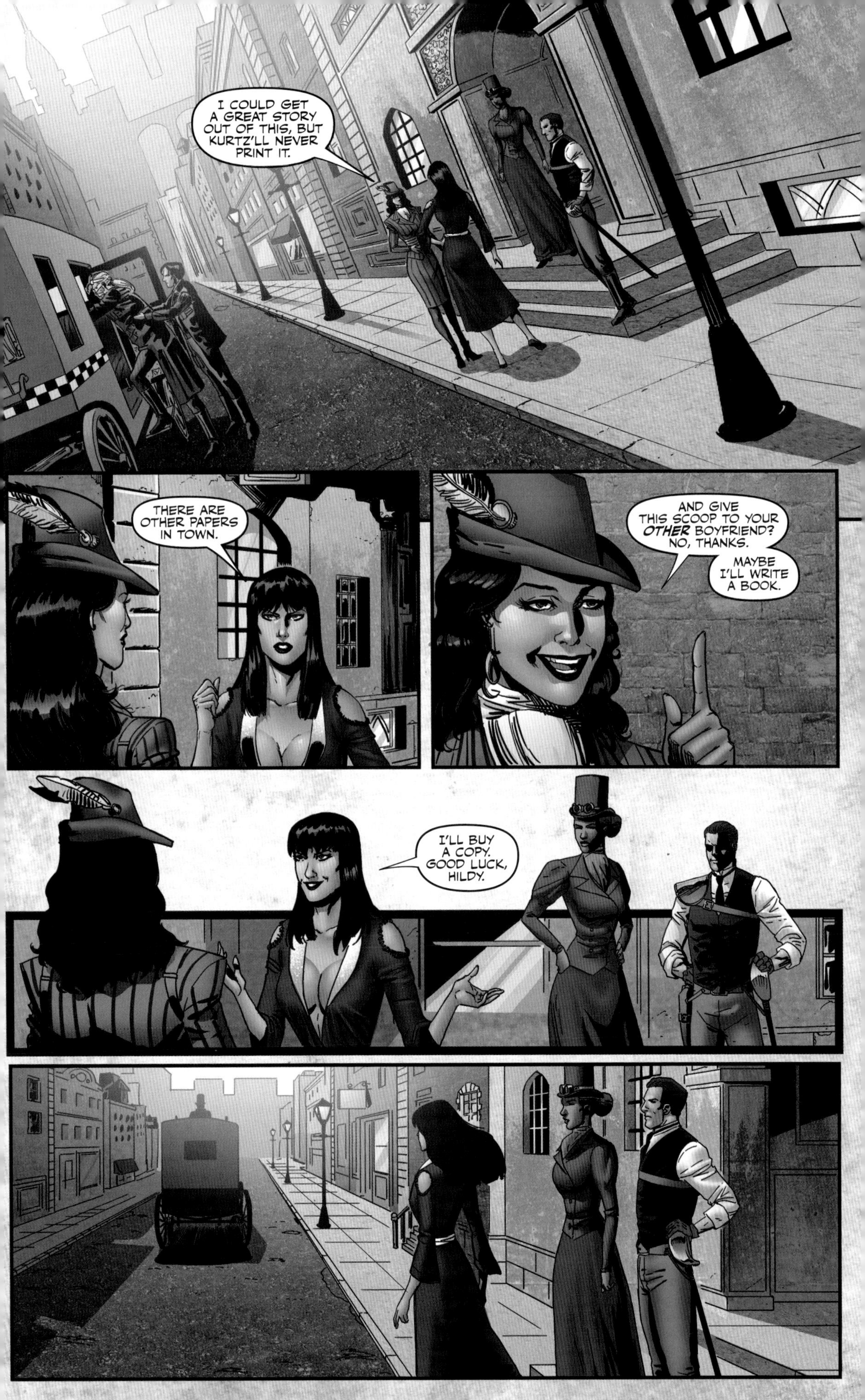
I COULD GET A GREAT STORY OUT OF THIS, BUT KURTZ'LL NEVER PRINT IT.
THERE ARE OTHER PAPERS IN TOWN.
AND GIVE THIS SCOOP TO YOUR *OTHER* BOYFRIEND? NO, THANKS.
MAYBE I'LL WRITE A BOOK.
I'LL BUY A COPY. GOOD LUCK, HILDY.

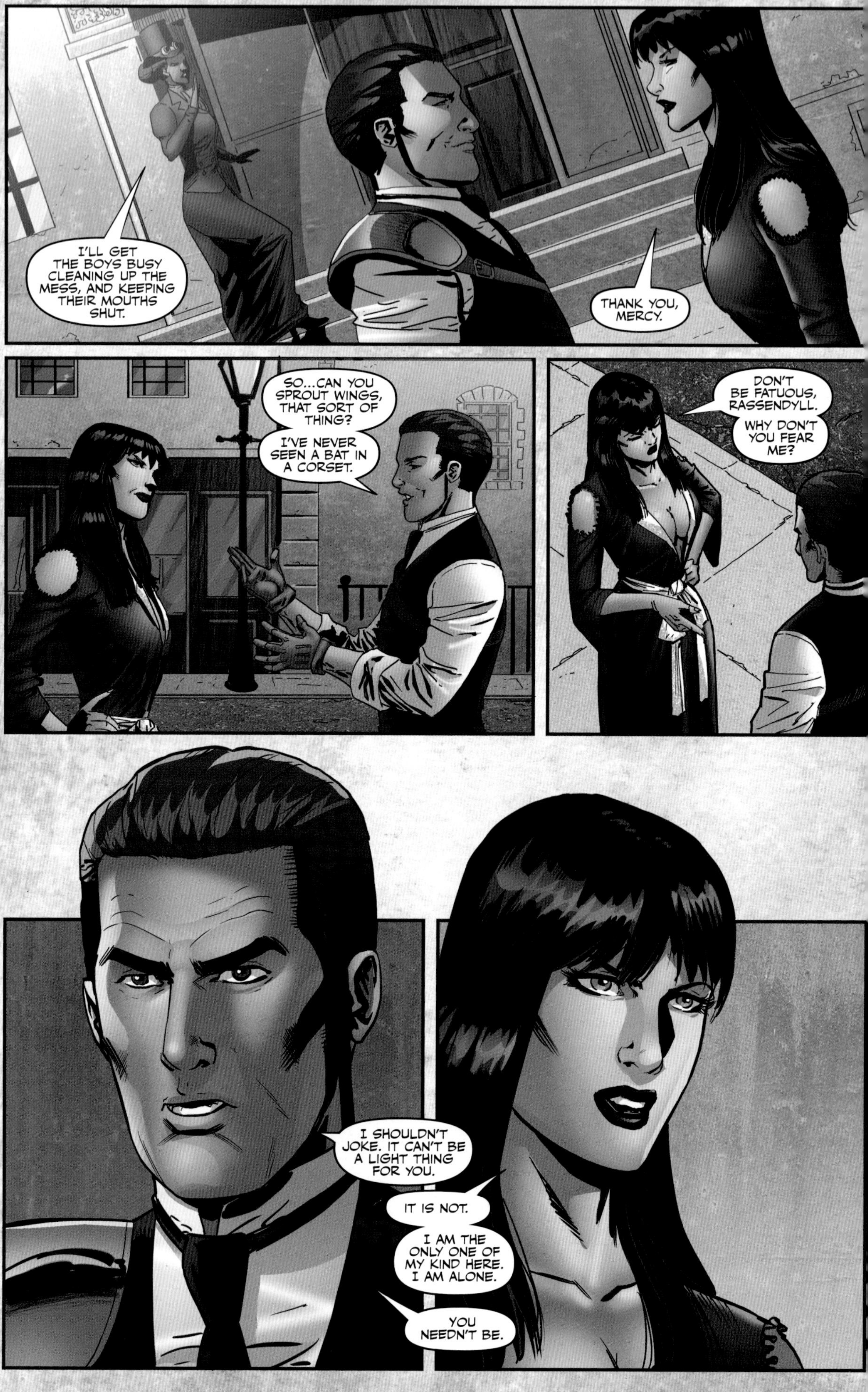
I'LL GET THE BOYS BUSY CLEANING UP THE MESS, AND KEEPING THEIR MOUTHS SHUT.
THANK YOU, MERCY.
SO...CAN YOU SPROUT WINGS, THAT SORT OF THING?
I'VE NEVER SEEN A BAT IN A CORSET.
DON'T BE FATUOUS, RASSENDYLL.
WHY DON'T YOU FEAR ME?
I SHOULDN'T JOKE. IT CAN'T BE A LIGHT THING FOR YOU.
IT IS NOT.
I AM THE ONLY ONE OF MY KIND HERE. I AM ALONE.
YOU NEEDN'T BE.

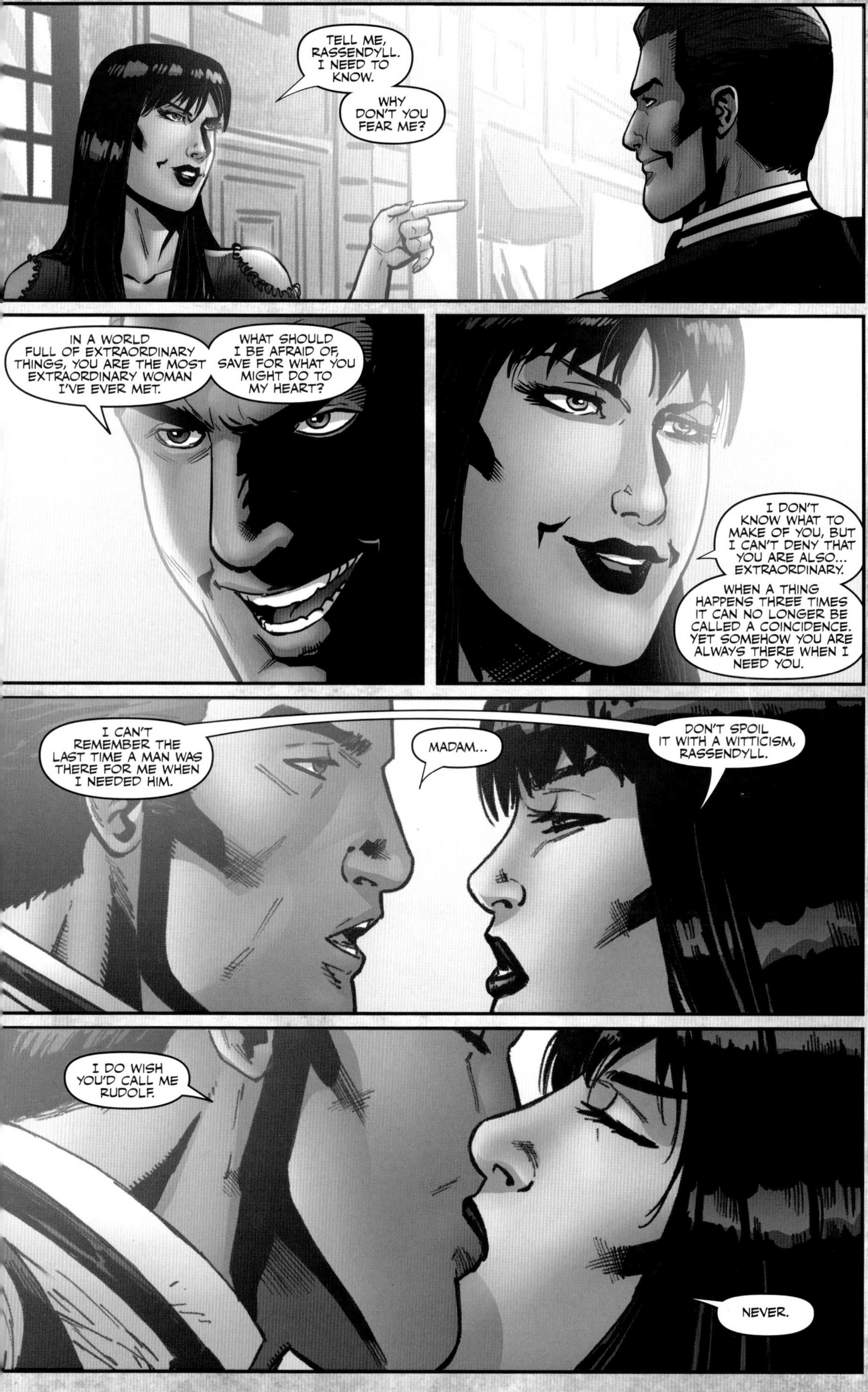
TELL ME, RASSENDYLL. I NEED TO KNOW.
WHY DON'T YOU FEAR ME?
IN A WORLD FULL OF EXTRAORDINARY THINGS, YOU ARE THE MOST EXTRAORDINARY WOMAN I'VE EVER MET.
WHAT SHOULD I BE AFRAID OF, SAVE FOR WHAT YOU MIGHT DO TO MY HEART?
I DON'T KNOW WHAT TO MAKE OF YOU, BUT I CAN'T DENY THAT YOU ARE ALSO... EXTRAORDINARY.
WHEN A THING HAPPENS THREE TIMES IT CAN NO LONGER BE CALLED A COINCIDENCE. YET SOMEHOW YOU ARE ALWAYS THERE WHEN I NEED YOU.
I CAN'T REMEMBER THE LAST TIME A MAN WAS THERE FOR ME WHEN I NEEDED HIM.
MADAM...
DON'T SPOIL IT WITH A WITTICISM, RASSENDYLL.
I DO WISH YOU'D CALL ME RUDOLF.
NEVER.

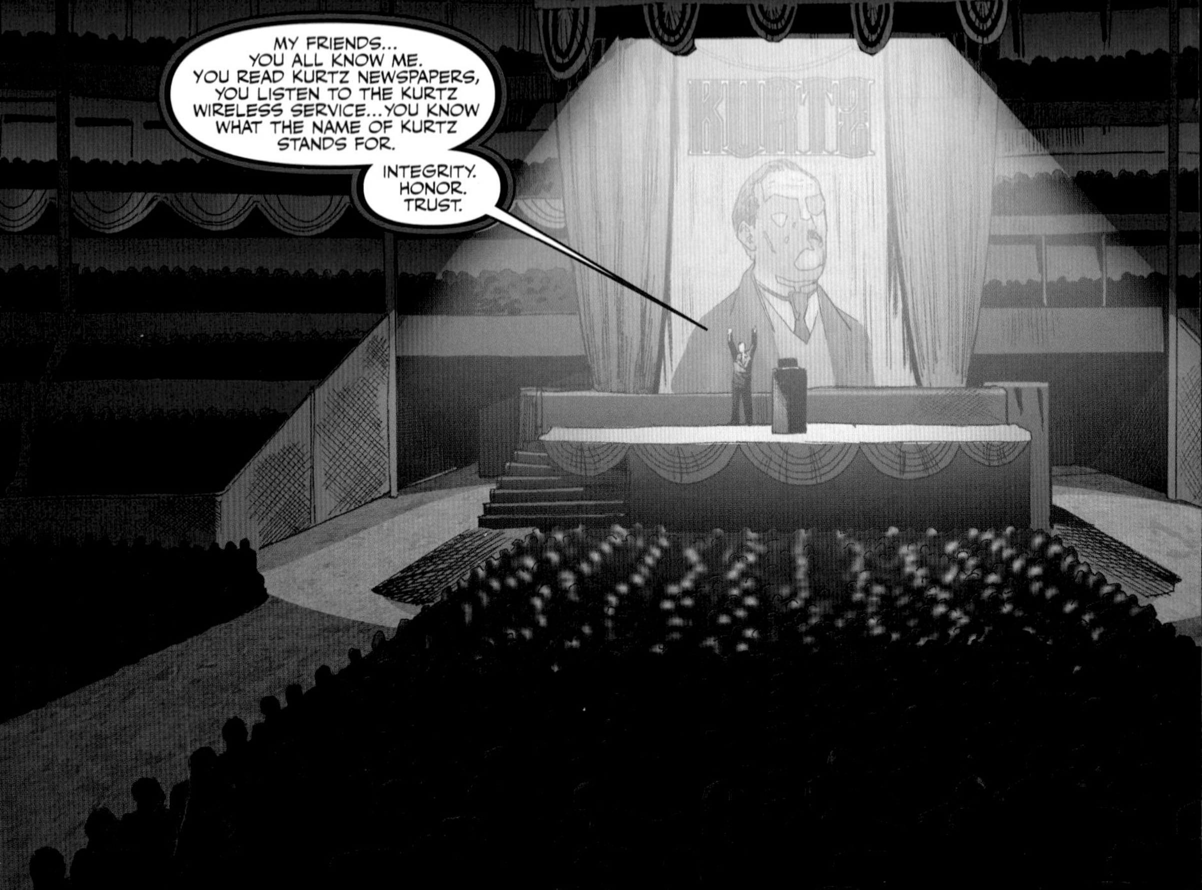
MY FRIENDS... YOU ALL KNOW ME. YOU READ KURTZ NEWSPAPERS, YOU LISTEN TO THE KURTZ WIRELESS SERVICE...YOU KNOW WHAT THE NAME OF KURTZ STANDS FOR.
INTEGRITY. HONOR. TRUST.
KURTZ

Chapter Four: Citizen Kurtz

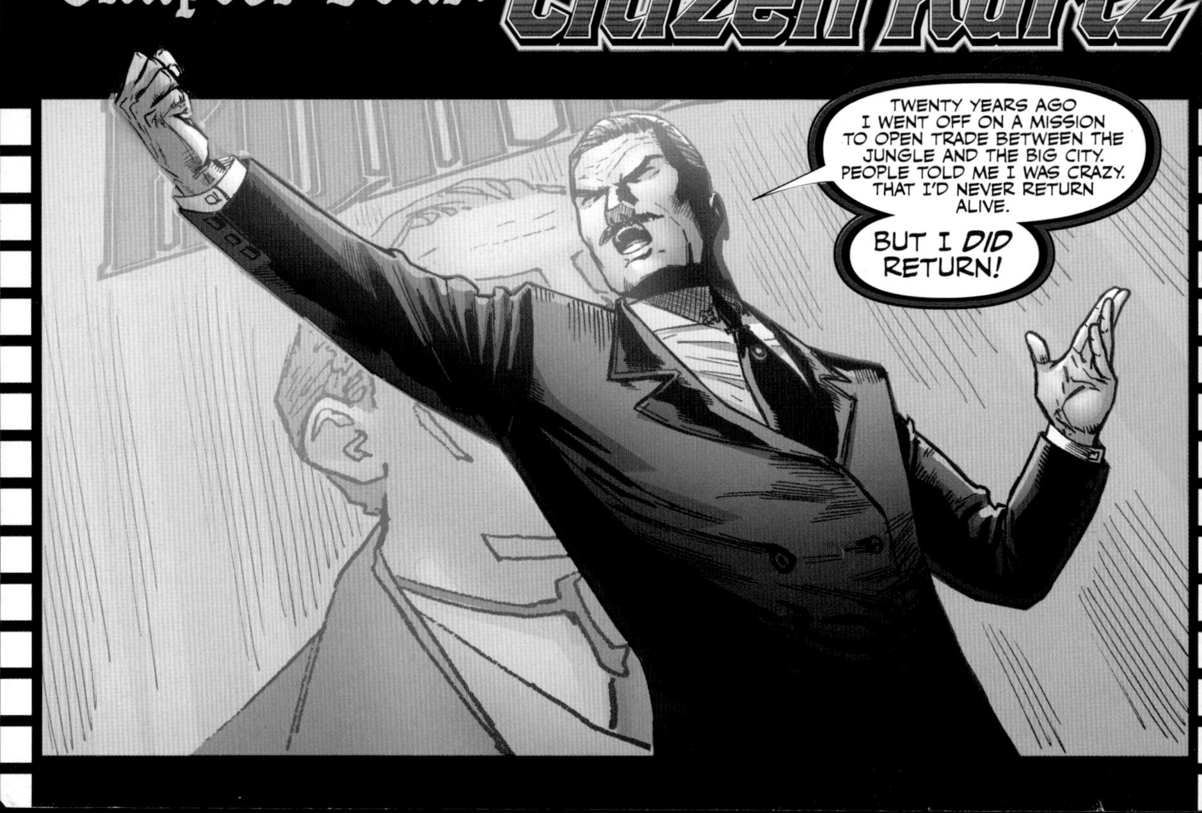
TWENTY YEARS AGO I WENT OFF ON A MISSION TO OPEN TRADE BETWEEN THE JUNGLE AND THE BIG CITY. PEOPLE TOLD ME I WAS CRAZY. THAT I'D NEVER RETURN ALIVE.
BUT I *DID* RETURN!

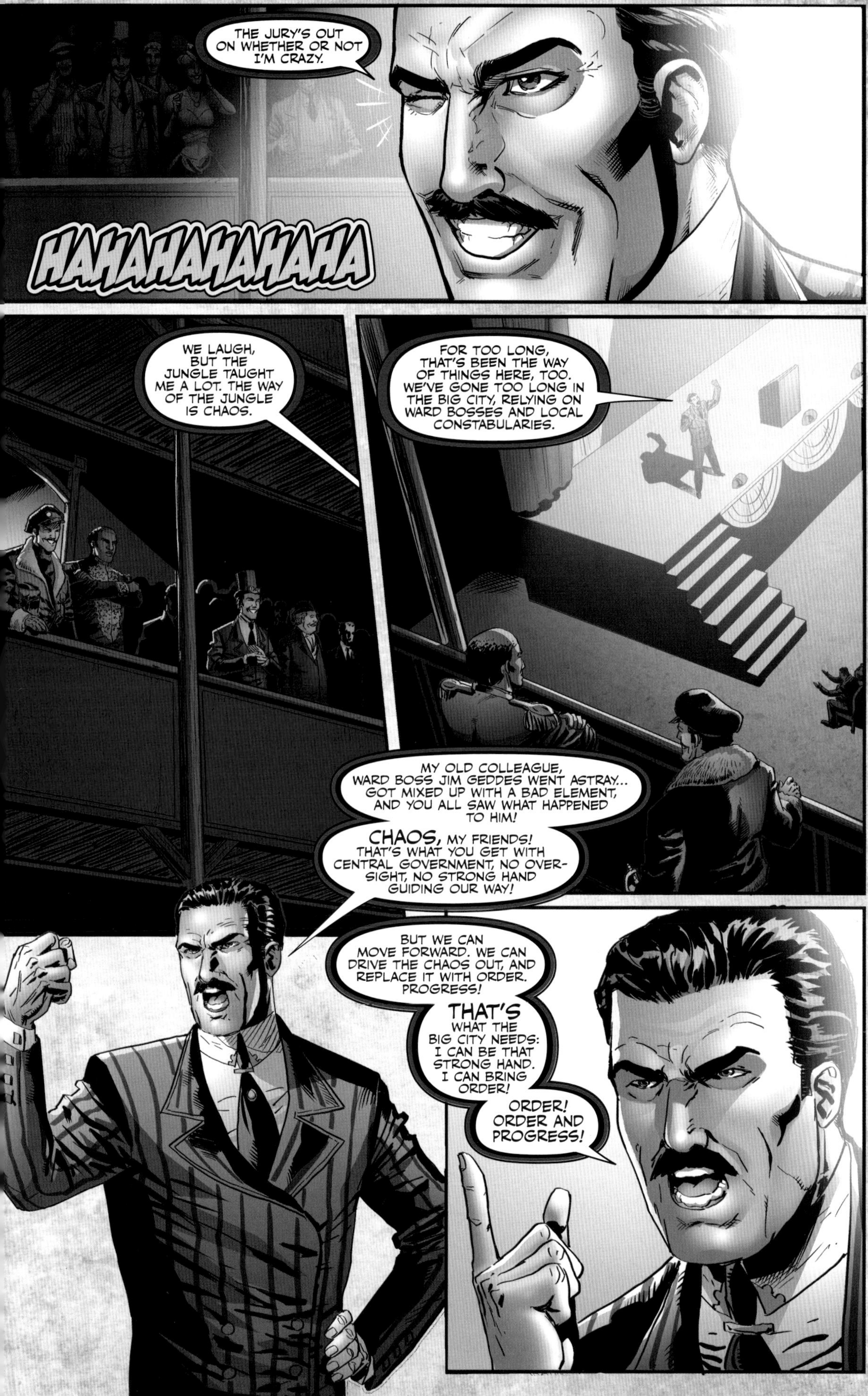
THE JURY'S OUT ON WHETHER OR NOT I'M CRAZY.
HAHAHAHAHAHA
WE LAUGH, BUT THE JUNGLE TAUGHT ME A LOT. THE WAY OF THE JUNGLE IS CHAOS.
FOR TOO LONG, THAT'S BEEN THE WAY OF THINGS HERE, TOO. WE'VE GONE TOO LONG IN THE BIG CITY, RELYING ON WARD BOSSES AND LOCAL CONSTABULARIES.
MY OLD COLLEAGUE, WARD BOSS JIM GEDDES WENT ASTRAY... GOT MIXED UP WITH A BAD ELEMENT, AND YOU ALL SAW WHAT HAPPENED TO HIM!
CHAOS, MY FRIENDS! THAT'S WHAT YOU GET WITH CENTRAL GOVERNMENT, NO OVER-SIGHT, NO STRONG HAND GUIDING OUR WAY!
BUT WE CAN MOVE FORWARD. WE CAN DRIVE THE CHAOS OUT, AND REPLACE IT WITH ORDER. PROGRESS!
THAT'S WHAT THE BIG CITY NEEDS: I CAN BE THAT STRONG HAND. I CAN BRING ORDER!
ORDER! ORDER AND PROGRESS!

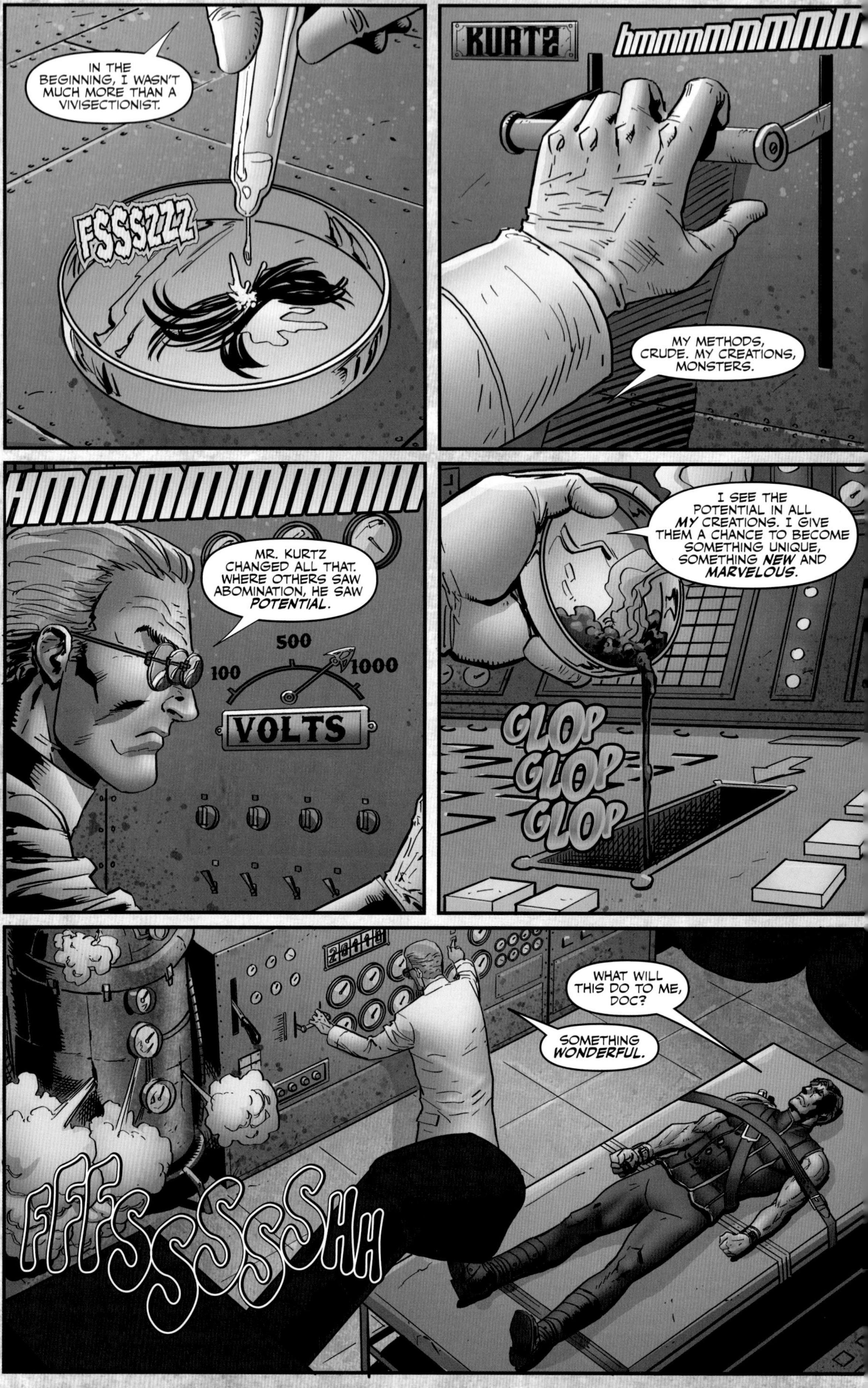
IN THE BEGINNING, I WASN'T MUCH MORE THAN A VIVISECTIONIST.
FSSSZZZ
KURTZ
hmmmmmmmm
MY METHODS, CRUDE. MY CREATIONS, MONSTERS.
HMMMMMMMM
MR. KURTZ CHANGED ALL THAT. WHERE OTHERS SAW ABOMINATION, HE SAW *POTENTIAL*.
500
100
1000
VOLTS
I SEE THE POTENTIAL IN ALL *MY* CREATIONS. I GIVE THEM A CHANCE TO BECOME SOMETHING UNIQUE, SOMETHING ***NEW*** AND ***MARVELOUS***.
GLOP
GLOP
GLOP
WHAT WILL THIS DO TO ME, DOC?
SOMETHING ***WONDERFUL***.
FFFSSSSSSHH

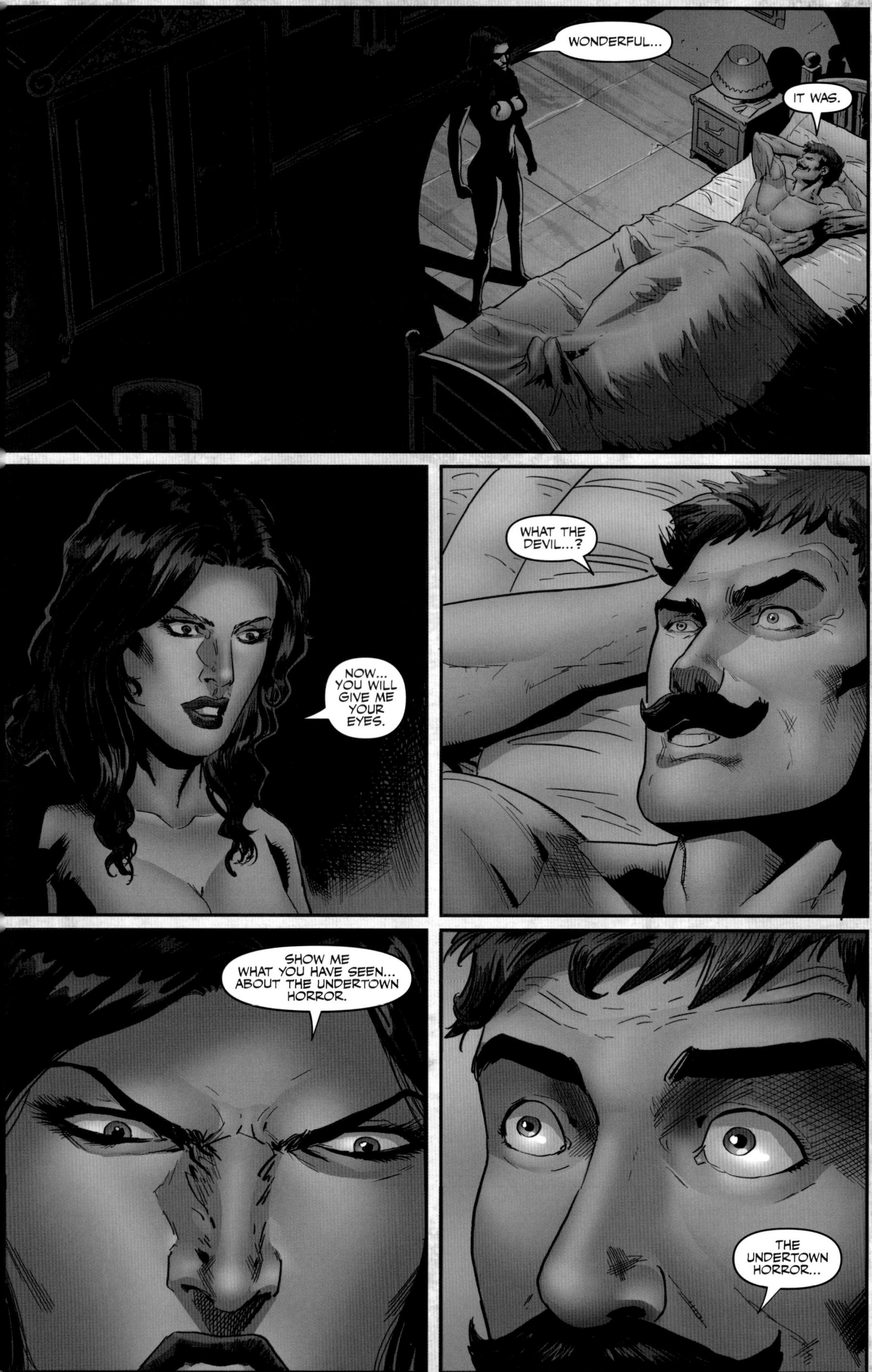
WONDERFUL...
IT WAS.
NOW... YOU WILL GIVE ME YOUR EYES.
WHAT THE DEVIL...?
SHOW ME WHAT YOU HAVE SEEN... ABOUT THE UNDERTOWN HORROR.
THE UNDERTOWN HORROR...

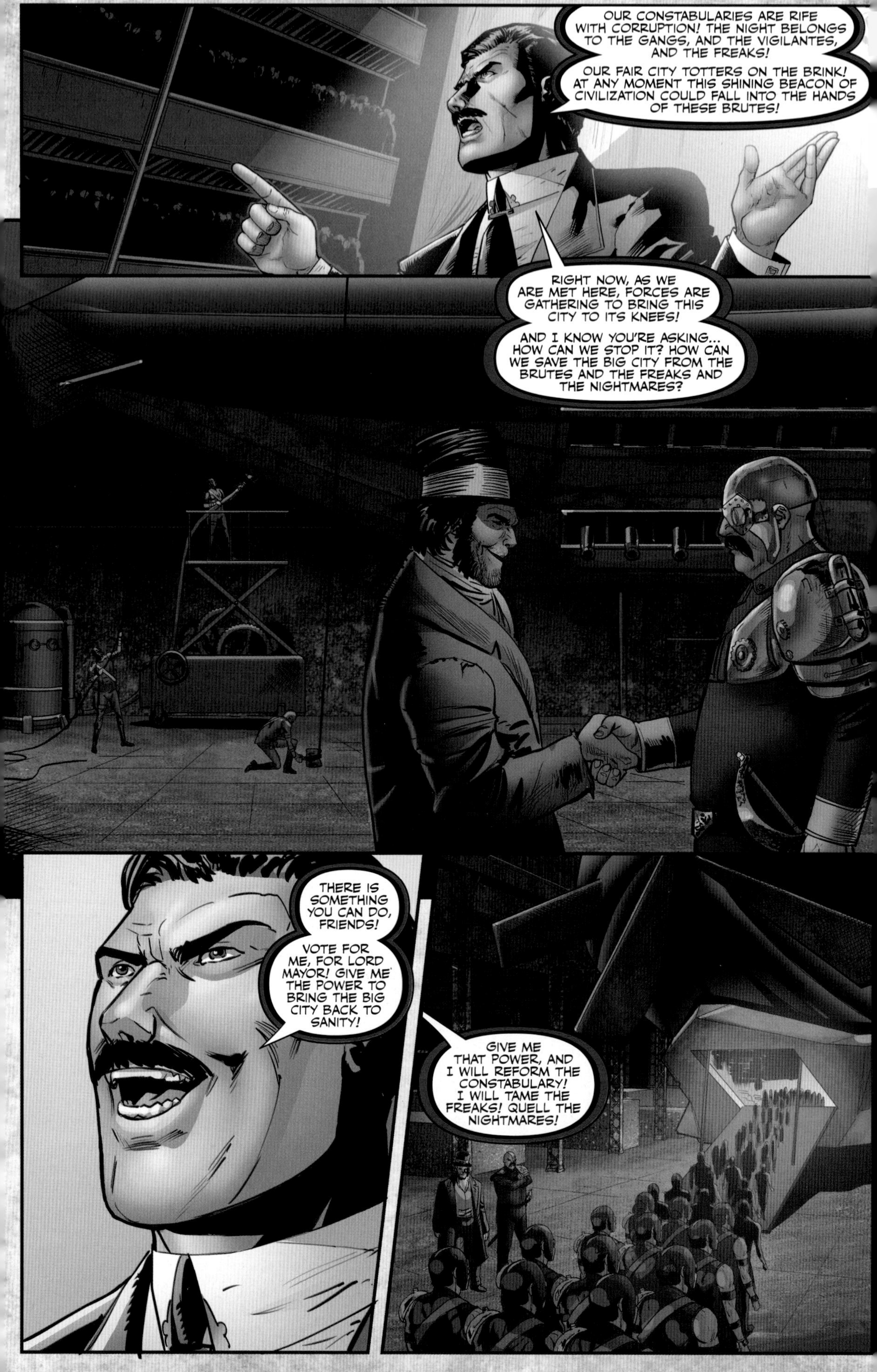
OUR CONSTABULARIES ARE RIFE WITH CORRUPTION! THE NIGHT BELONGS TO THE GANGS, AND THE VIGILANTES, AND THE FREAKS!
OUR FAIR CITY TOTTERS ON THE BRINK! AT ANY MOMENT THIS SHINING BEACON OF CIVILIZATION COULD FALL INTO THE HANDS OF THESE BRUTES!
RIGHT NOW, AS WE ARE MET HERE, FORCES ARE GATHERING TO BRING THIS CITY TO ITS KNEES!
AND I KNOW YOU'RE ASKING... HOW CAN WE STOP IT? HOW CAN WE SAVE THE BIG CITY FROM THE BRUTES AND THE FREAKS AND THE NIGHTMARES?
THERE IS SOMETHING YOU CAN DO, FRIENDS!
VOTE FOR ME, FOR LORD MAYOR! GIVE ME THE POWER TO BRING THE BIG CITY BACK TO SANITY!
GIVE ME THAT POWER, AND I WILL REFORM THE CONSTABULARY! I WILL TAME THE FREAKS! QUELL THE NIGHTMARES!

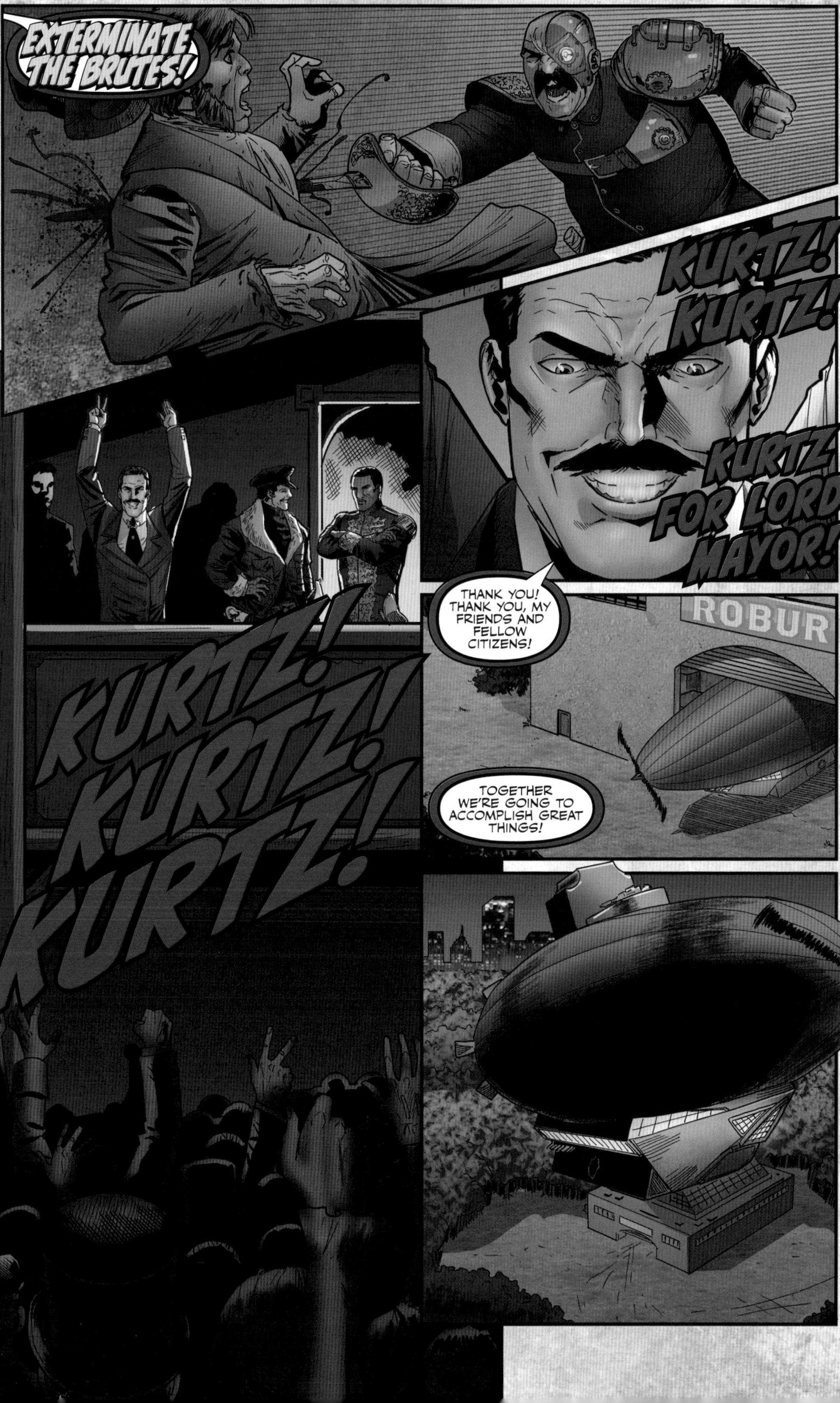
EXTERMINATE THE BRUTES!
KURTZ! KURTZ!
KURTZ FOR LORD MAYOR!
KURTZ! KURTZ! KURTZ!
THANK YOU! THANK YOU, MY FRIENDS AND FELLOW CITIZENS!
ROBUR
TOGETHER WE'RE GOING TO ACCOMPLISH GREAT THINGS!

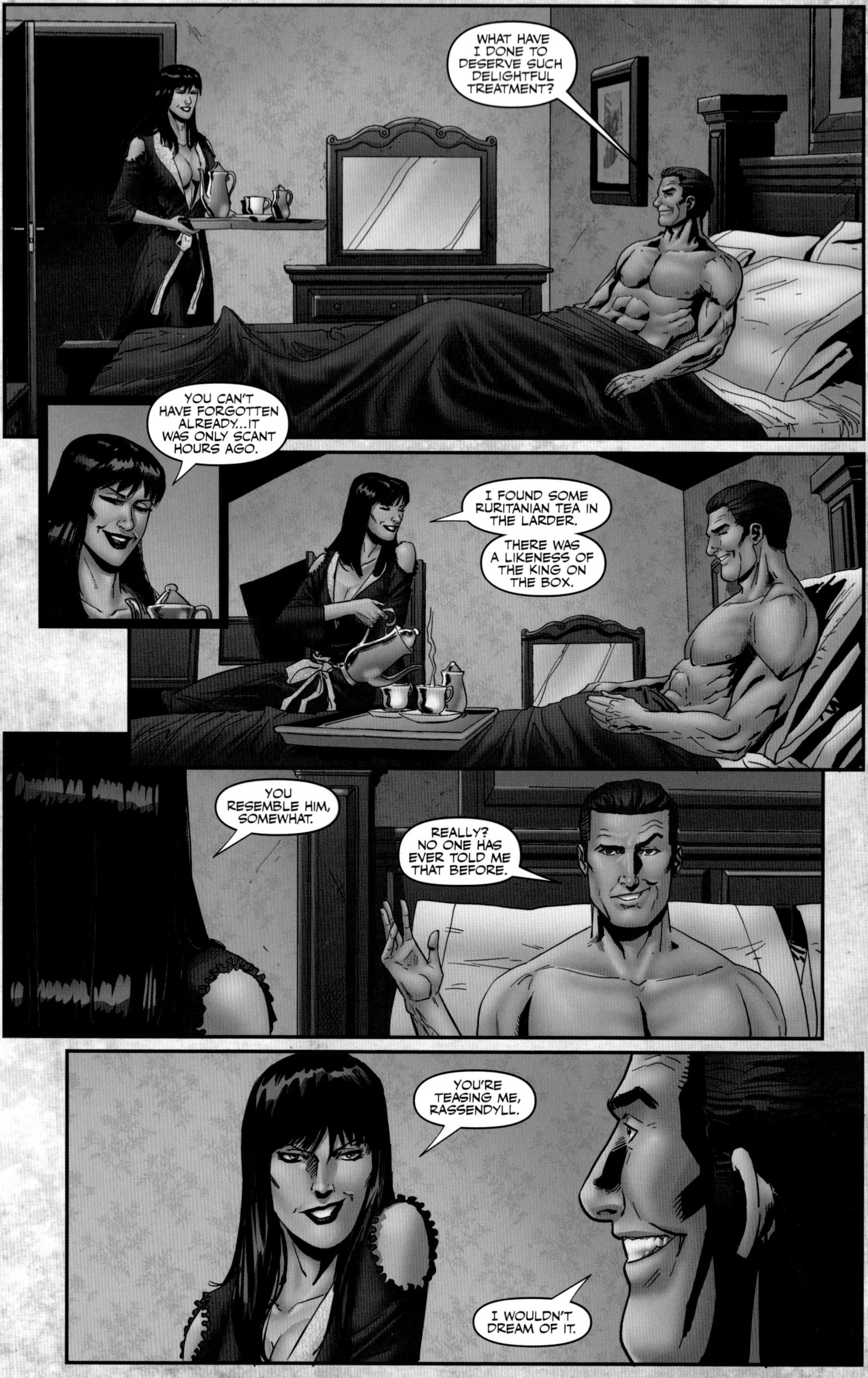
WHAT HAVE I DONE TO DESERVE SUCH DELIGHTFUL TREATMENT?
YOU CAN'T HAVE FORGOTTEN ALREADY...IT WAS ONLY SCANT HOURS AGO.
I FOUND SOME RURITANIAN TEA IN THE LARDER.
THERE WAS A LIKENESS OF THE KING ON THE BOX.
YOU RESEMBLE HIM, SOMEWHAT.
REALLY? NO ONE HAS EVER TOLD ME THAT BEFORE.
YOU'RE TEASING ME, RASSENDYLL.
I WOULDN'T DREAM OF IT.

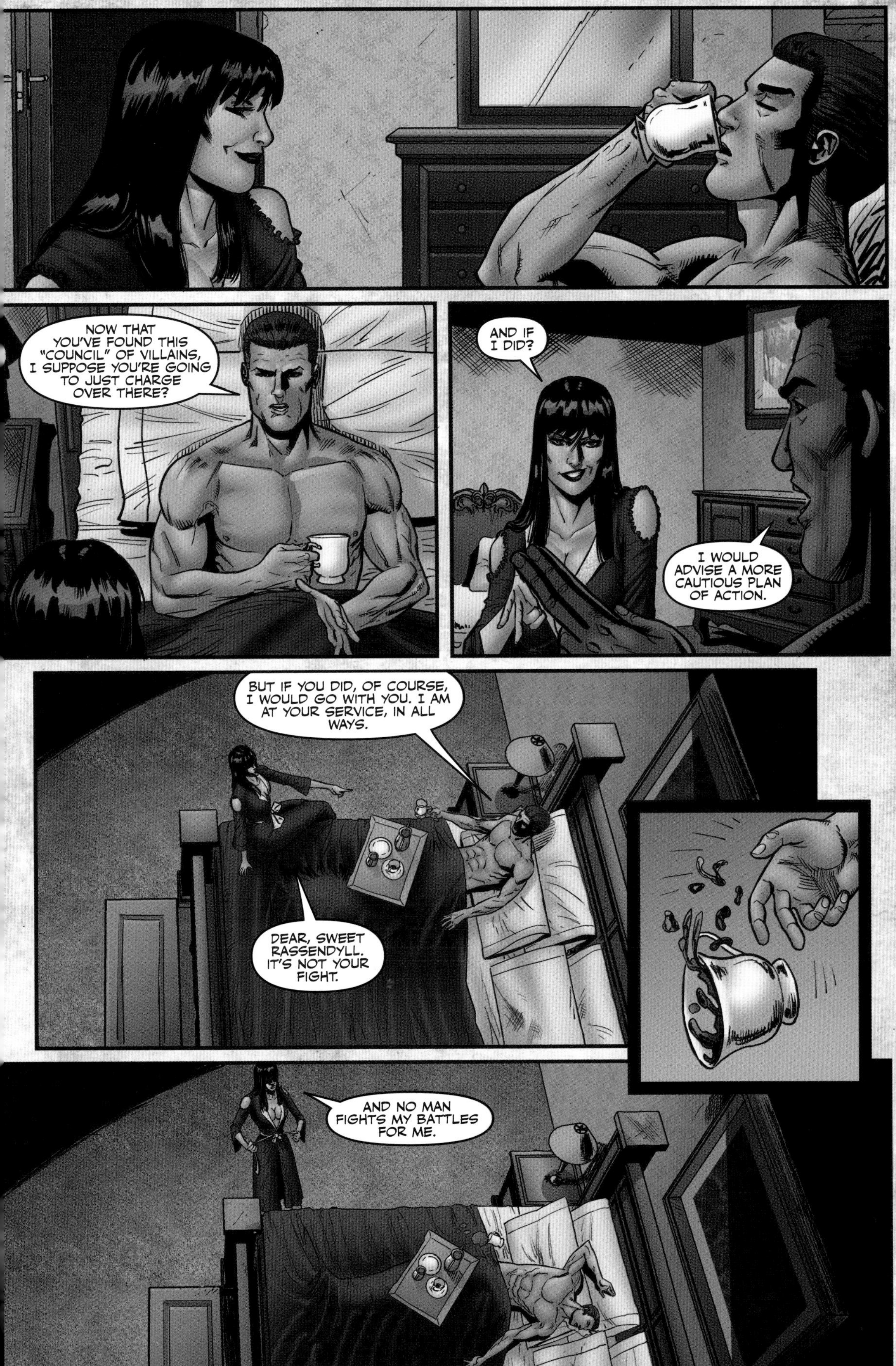
NOW THAT YOU'VE FOUND THIS "COUNCIL" OF VILLAINS, I SUPPOSE YOU'RE GOING TO JUST CHARGE OVER THERE?
AND IF I DID?
I WOULD ADVISE A MORE CAUTIOUS PLAN OF ACTION.
BUT IF YOU DID, OF COURSE, I WOULD GO WITH YOU. I AM AT YOUR SERVICE, IN ALL WAYS.
DEAR, SWEET RASSENDYLL. IT'S NOT YOUR FIGHT.
AND NO MAN FIGHTS MY BATTLES FOR ME.

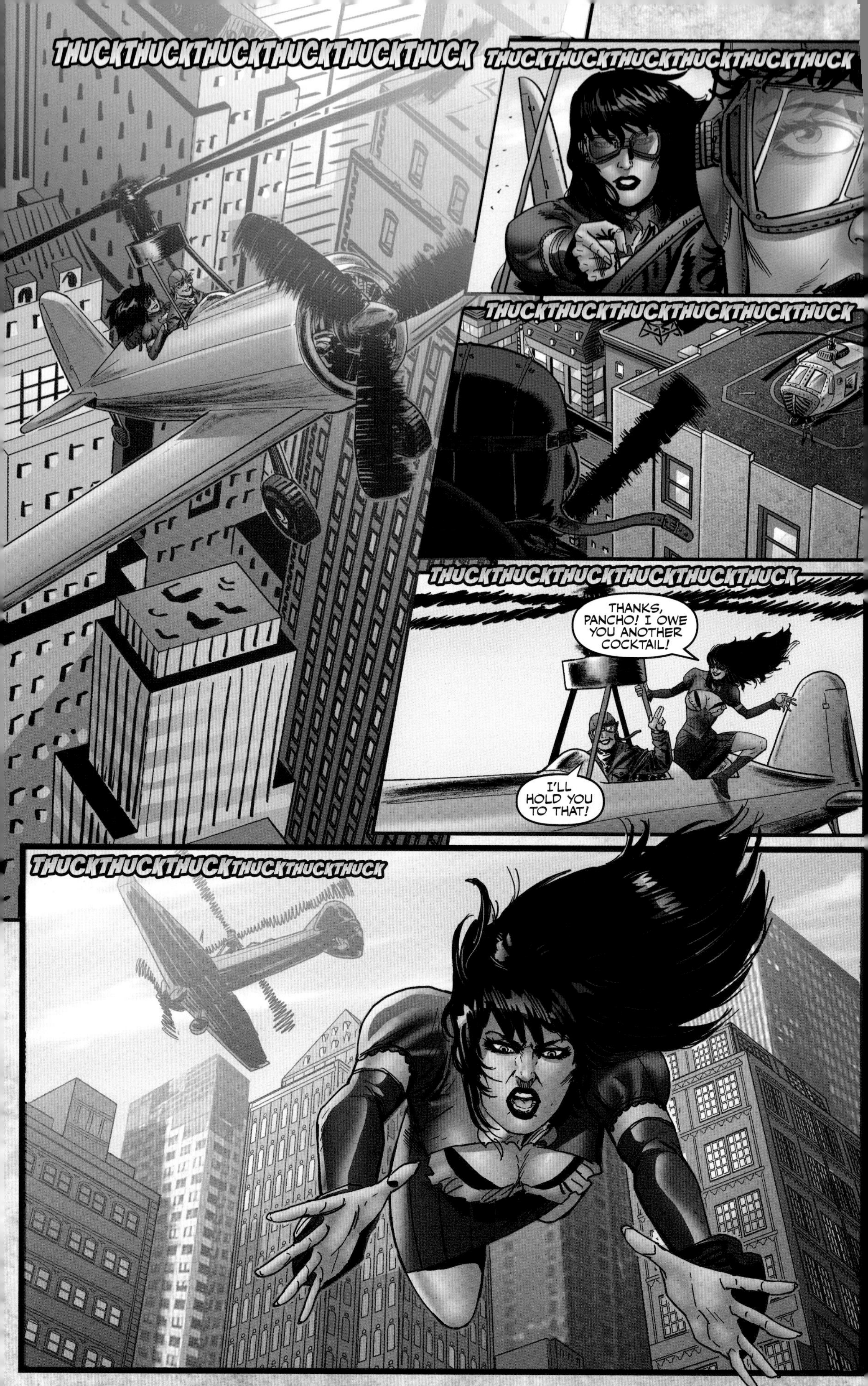
THUCKTHUCKTHUCKTHUCKTHUCKTHUCK
THUCKTHUCKTHUCKTHUCKTHUCKTHUCK
THUCKTHUCKTHUCKTHUCKTHUCKTHUCK
THUCKTHUCKTHUCKTHUCKTHUCKTHUCK
THANKS, PANCHO! I OWE YOU ANOTHER COCKTAIL!
I'LL HOLD YOU TO THAT!
THUCKTHUCKTHUCKTHUCKTHUCKTHUCK

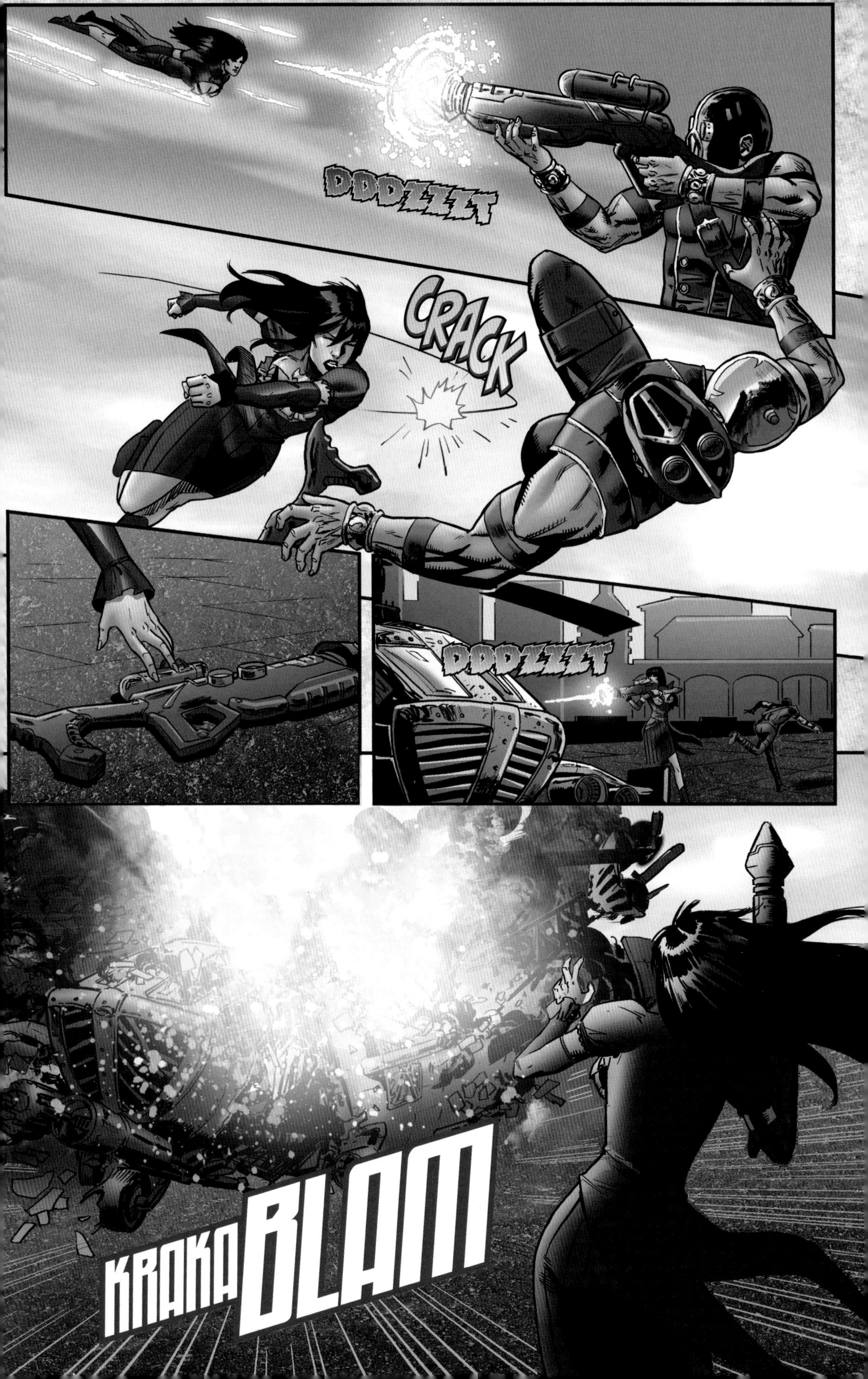
DDDZZZT
CRACK
DDDZZZT
KRAKA BLAM

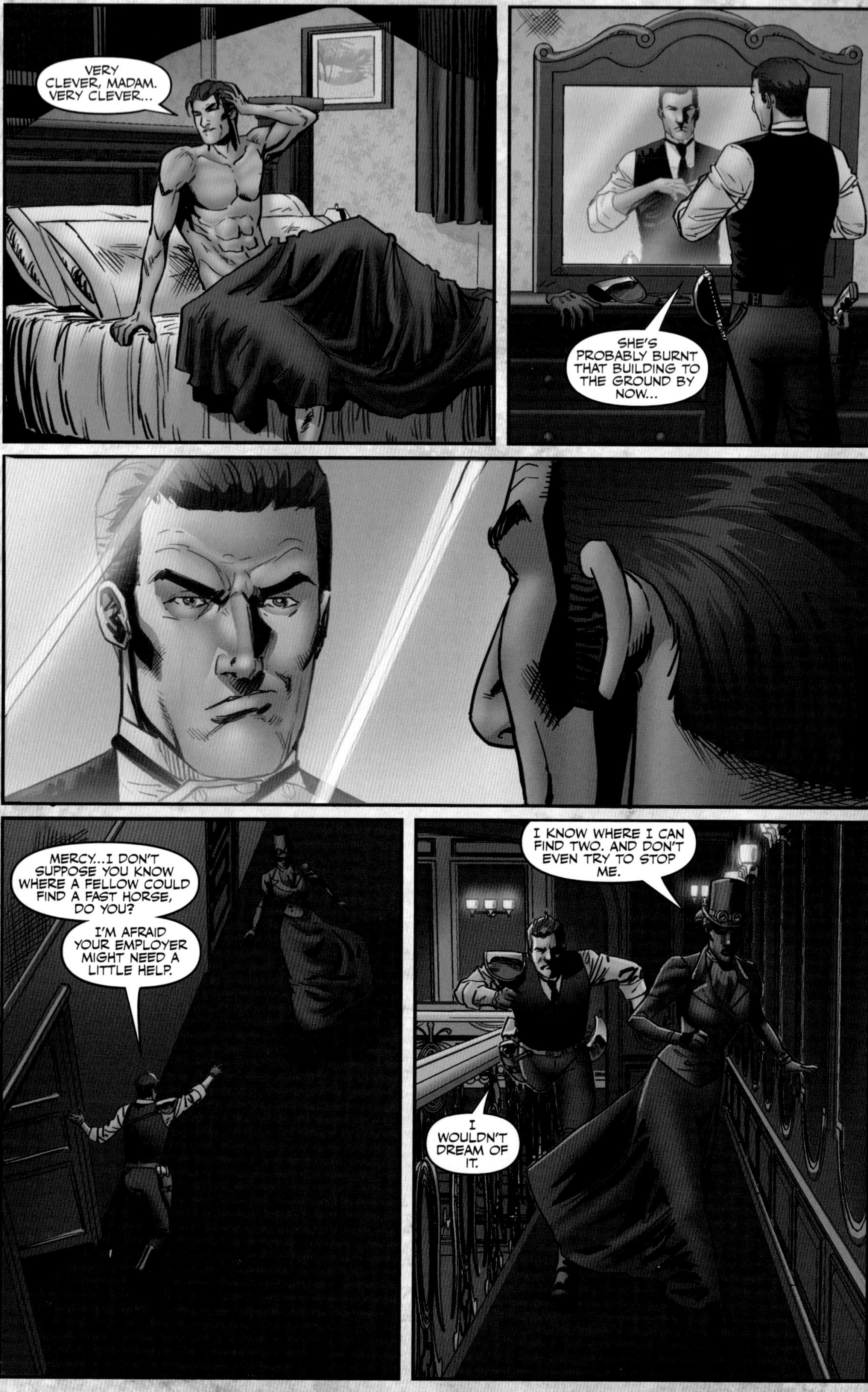

VERY CLEVER, MADAM. VERY CLEVER...
SHE'S PROBABLY BURNT THAT BUILDING TO THE GROUND BY NOW...
MERCY...I DON'T SUPPOSE YOU KNOW WHERE A FELLOW COULD FIND A FAST HORSE, DO YOU?
I'M AFRAID YOUR EMPLOYER MIGHT NEED A LITTLE HELP.
I KNOW WHERE I CAN FIND TWO. AND DON'T EVEN TRY TO STOP ME.
I WOULDN'T DREAM OF IT.

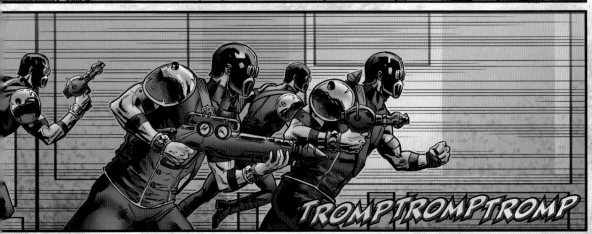

TROMPTROMPTROMP

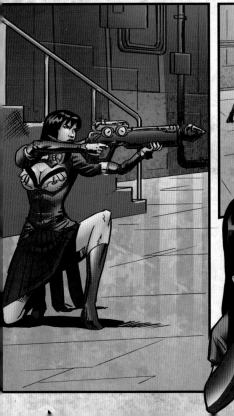

DDDZZZT

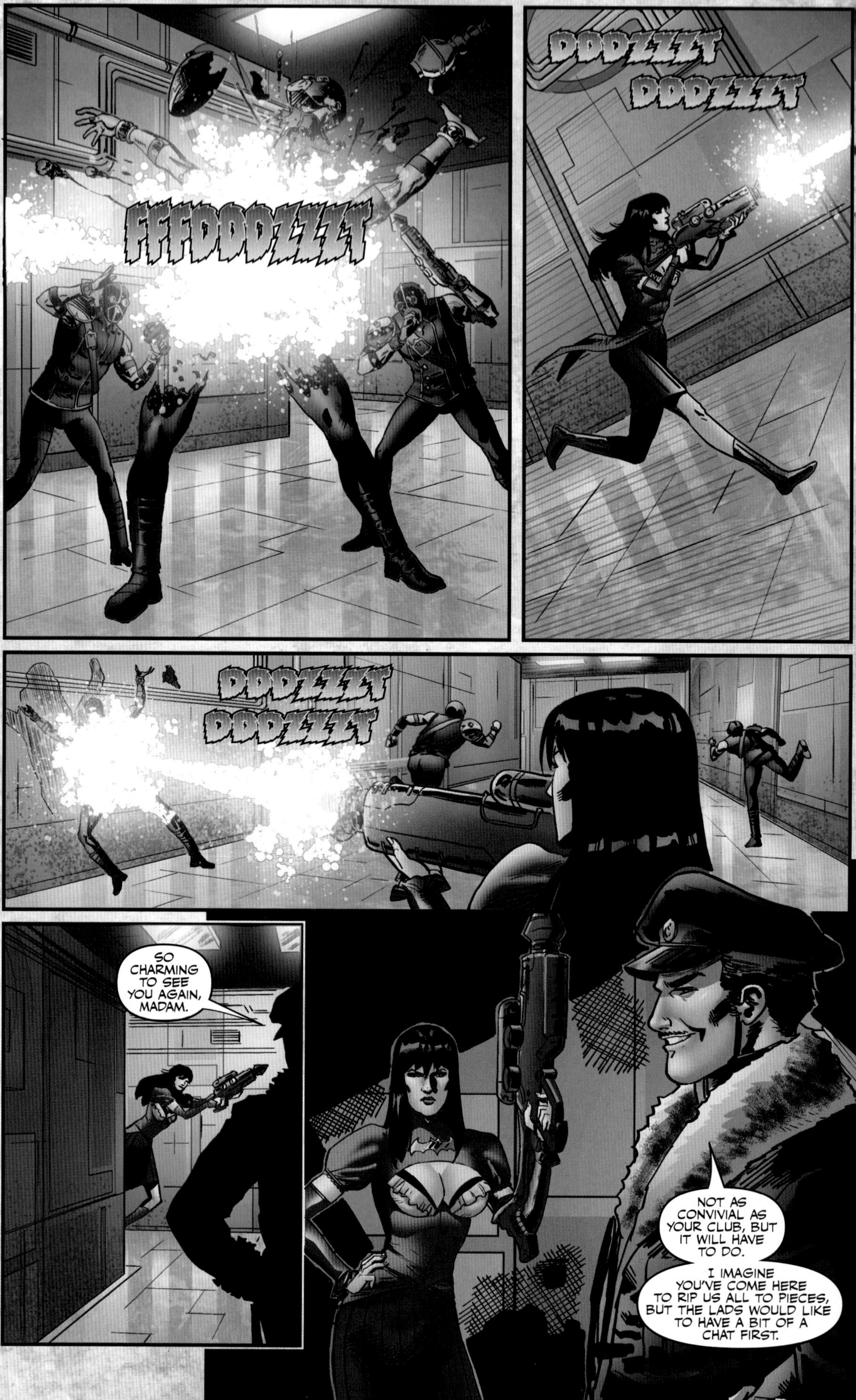
FFFDDDZZZZT
DDDZZZZT
DDDZZZZT
DDDZZZZT
DDDZZZZT
SO CHARMING TO SEE YOU AGAIN, MADAM.
NOT AS CONVIVIAL AS YOUR CLUB, BUT IT WILL HAVE TO DO.
I IMAGINE YOU'VE COME HERE TO RIP US ALL TO PIECES, BUT THE LADS WOULD LIKE TO HAVE A BIT OF A CHAT FIRST.

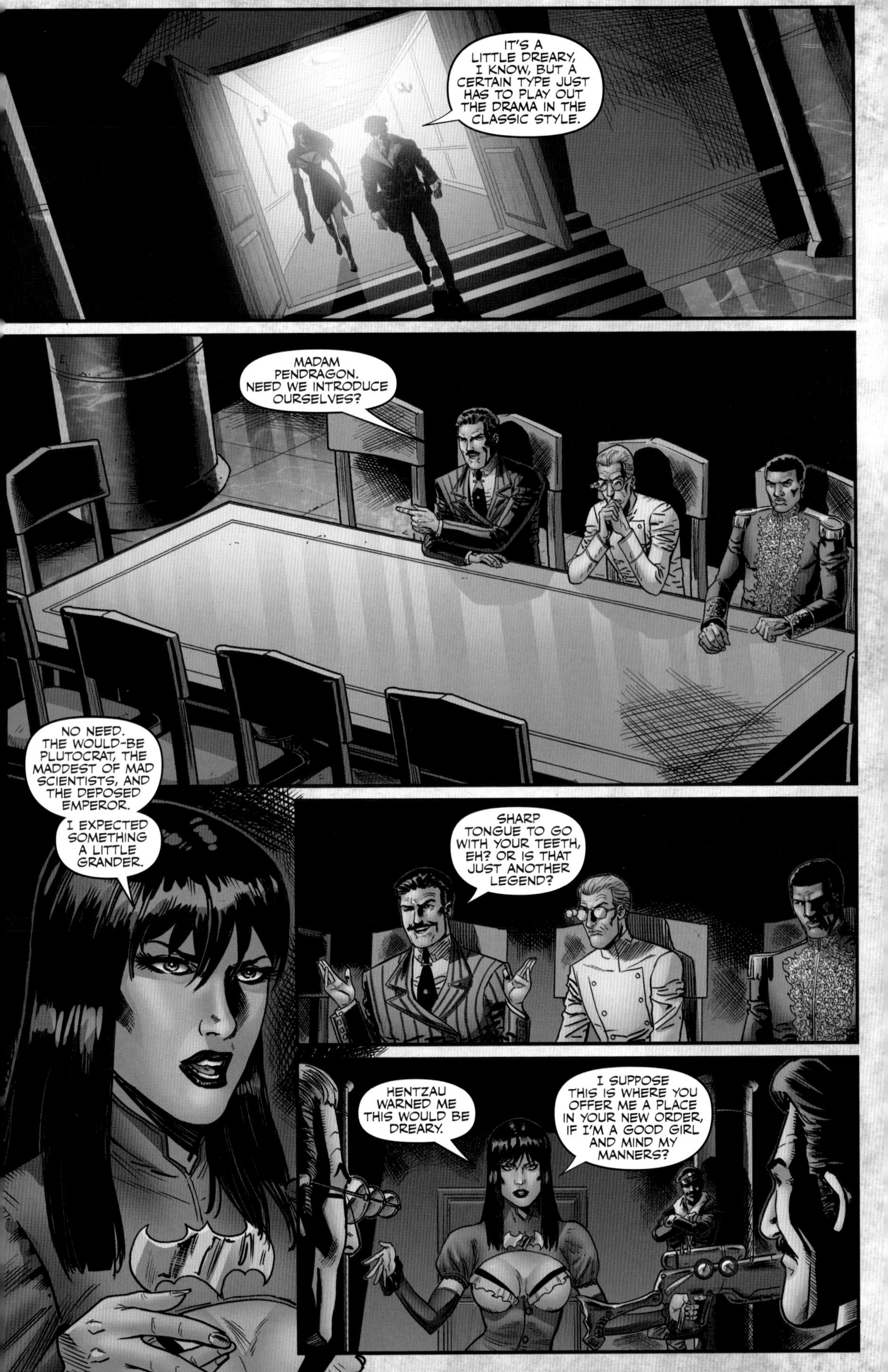
IT'S A LITTLE DREARY, I KNOW, BUT A CERTAIN TYPE JUST HAS TO PLAY OUT THE DRAMA IN THE CLASSIC STYLE.
MADAM PENDRAGON. NEED WE INTRODUCE OURSELVES?
NO NEED. THE WOULD-BE PLUTOCRAT, THE MADDEST OF MAD SCIENTISTS, AND THE DEPOSED EMPEROR.
I EXPECTED SOMETHING A LITTLE GRANDER.
SHARP TONGUE TO GO WITH YOUR TEETH, EH? OR IS THAT JUST ANOTHER LEGEND?
HENTZAU WARNED ME THIS WOULD BE DREARY.
I SUPPOSE THIS IS WHERE YOU OFFER ME A PLACE IN YOUR NEW ORDER, IF I'M A GOOD GIRL AND MIND MY MANNERS?

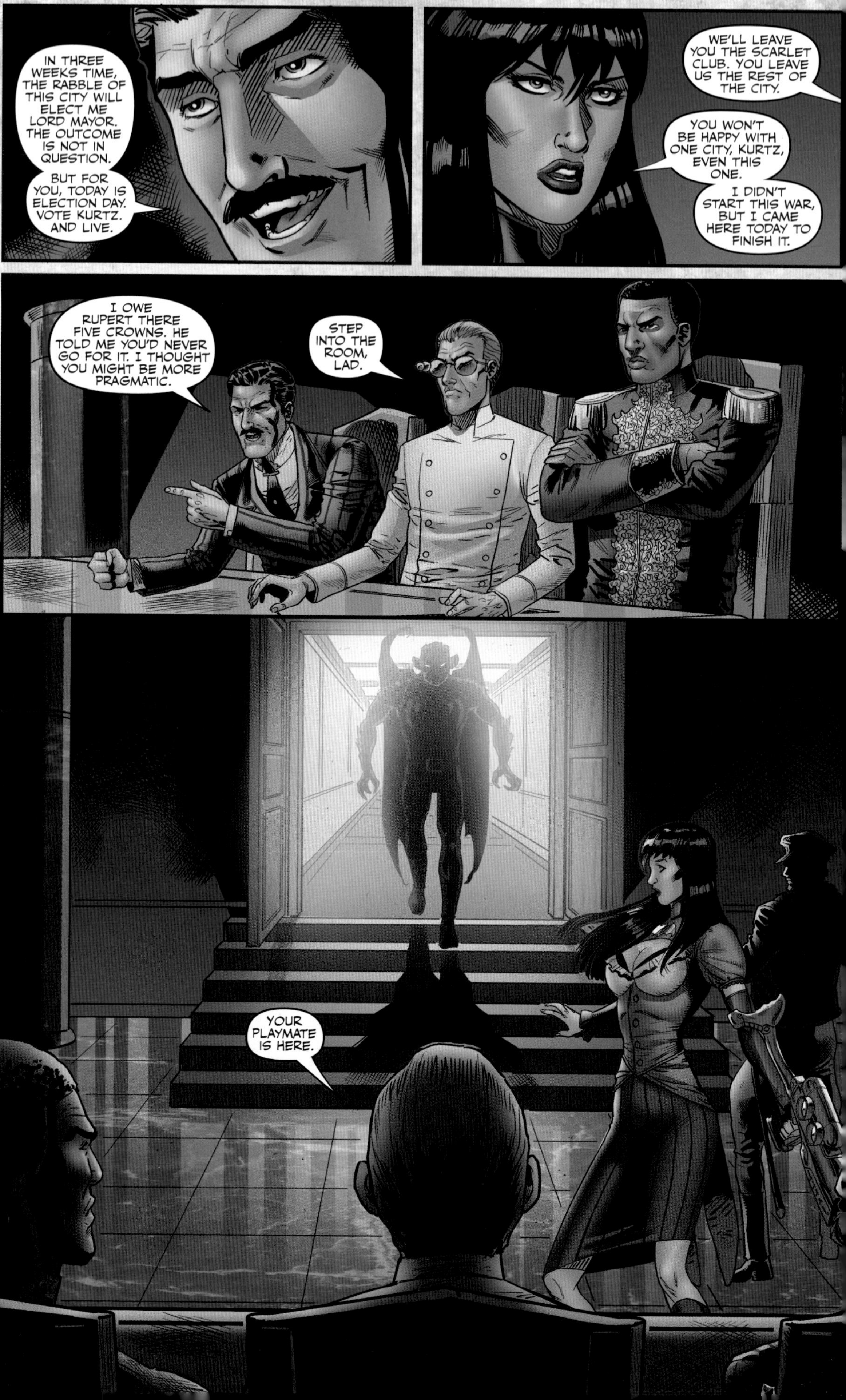
IN THREE WEEKS TIME, THE RABBLE OF THIS CITY WILL ELECT ME LORD MAYOR. THE OUTCOME IS NOT IN QUESTION.
BUT FOR YOU, TODAY IS ELECTION DAY. VOTE KURTZ. AND LIVE.
WE'LL LEAVE YOU THE SCARLET CLUB. YOU LEAVE US THE REST OF THE CITY.
YOU WON'T BE HAPPY WITH ONE CITY, KURTZ, EVEN THIS ONE.
I DIDN'T START THIS WAR, BUT I CAME HERE TODAY TO FINISH IT.
I OWE RUPERT THERE FIVE CROWNS. HE TOLD ME YOU'D NEVER GO FOR IT. I THOUGHT YOU MIGHT BE MORE PRAGMATIC.
STEP INTO THE ROOM, LAD.
YOUR PLAYMATE IS HERE.

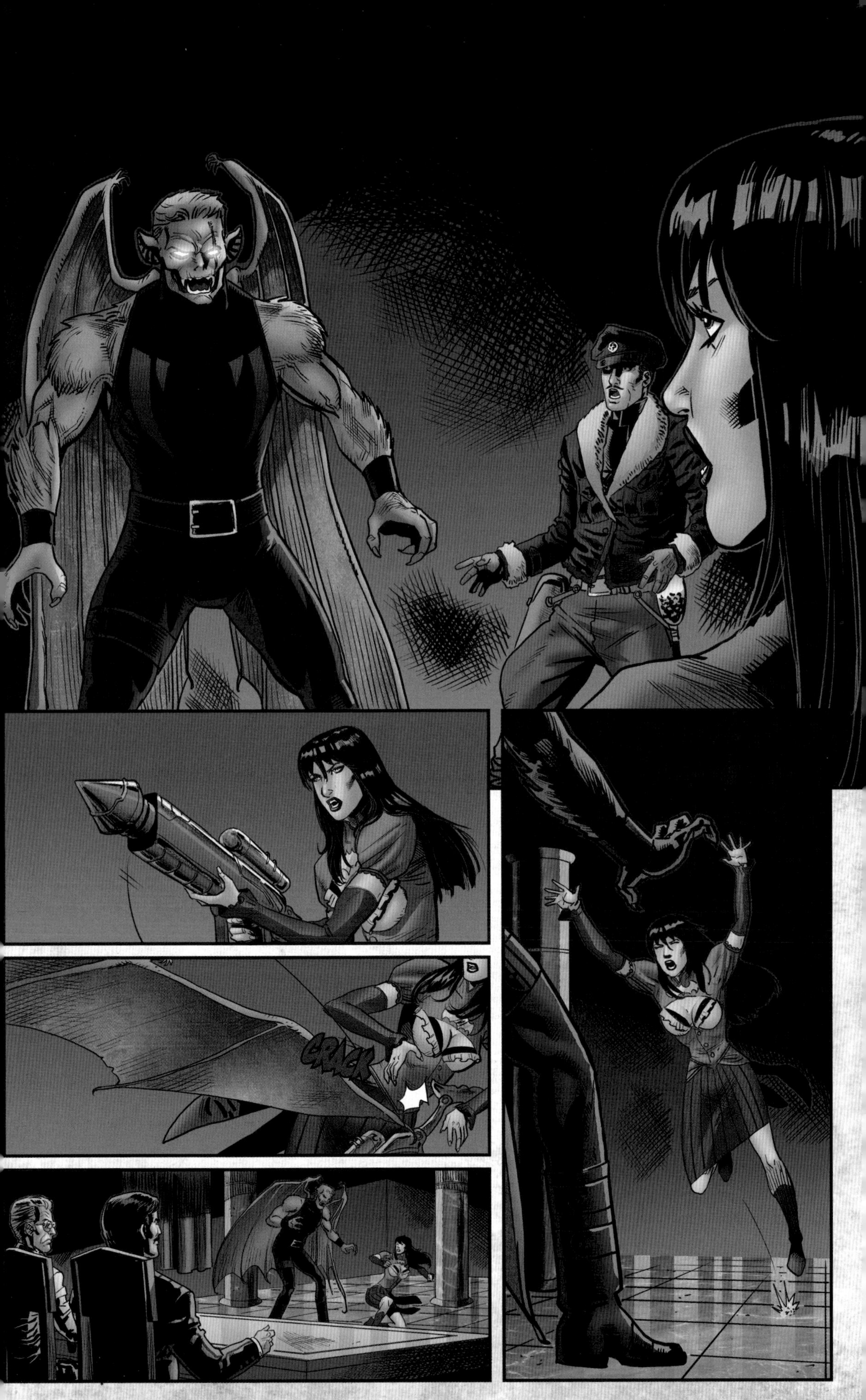
CRACK

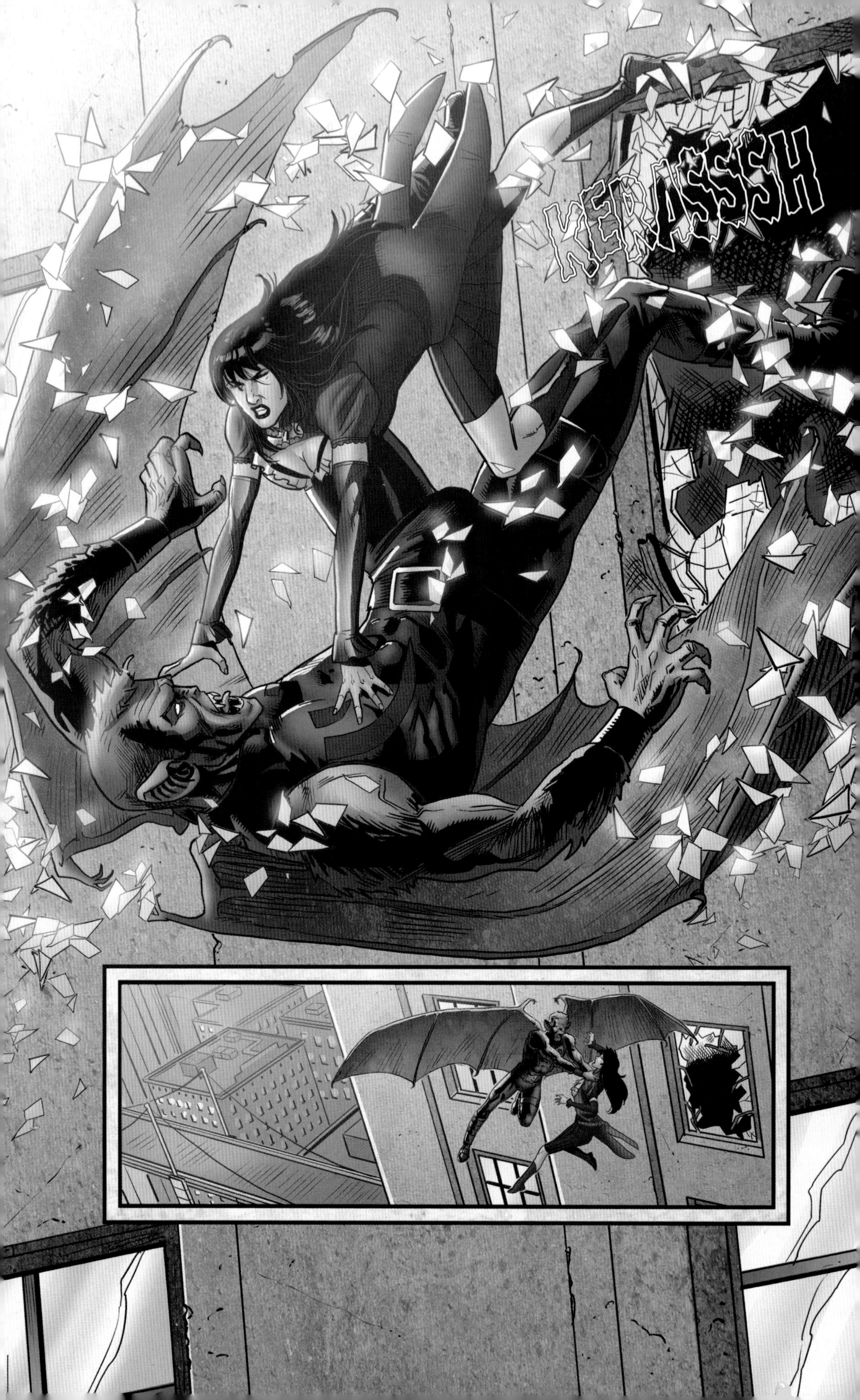
KERASSSH

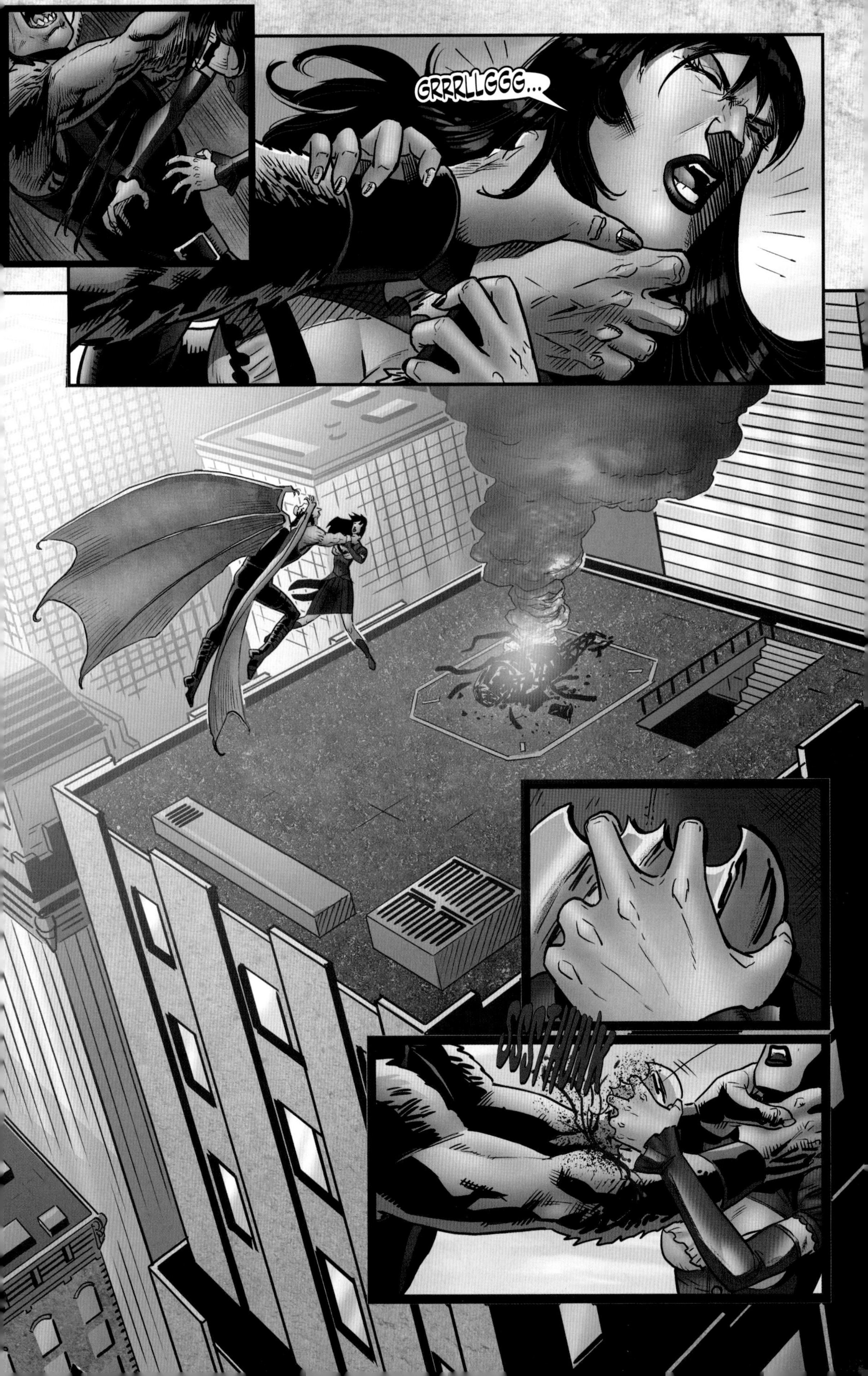
GRRRLLGGG...
SSSTHUNK

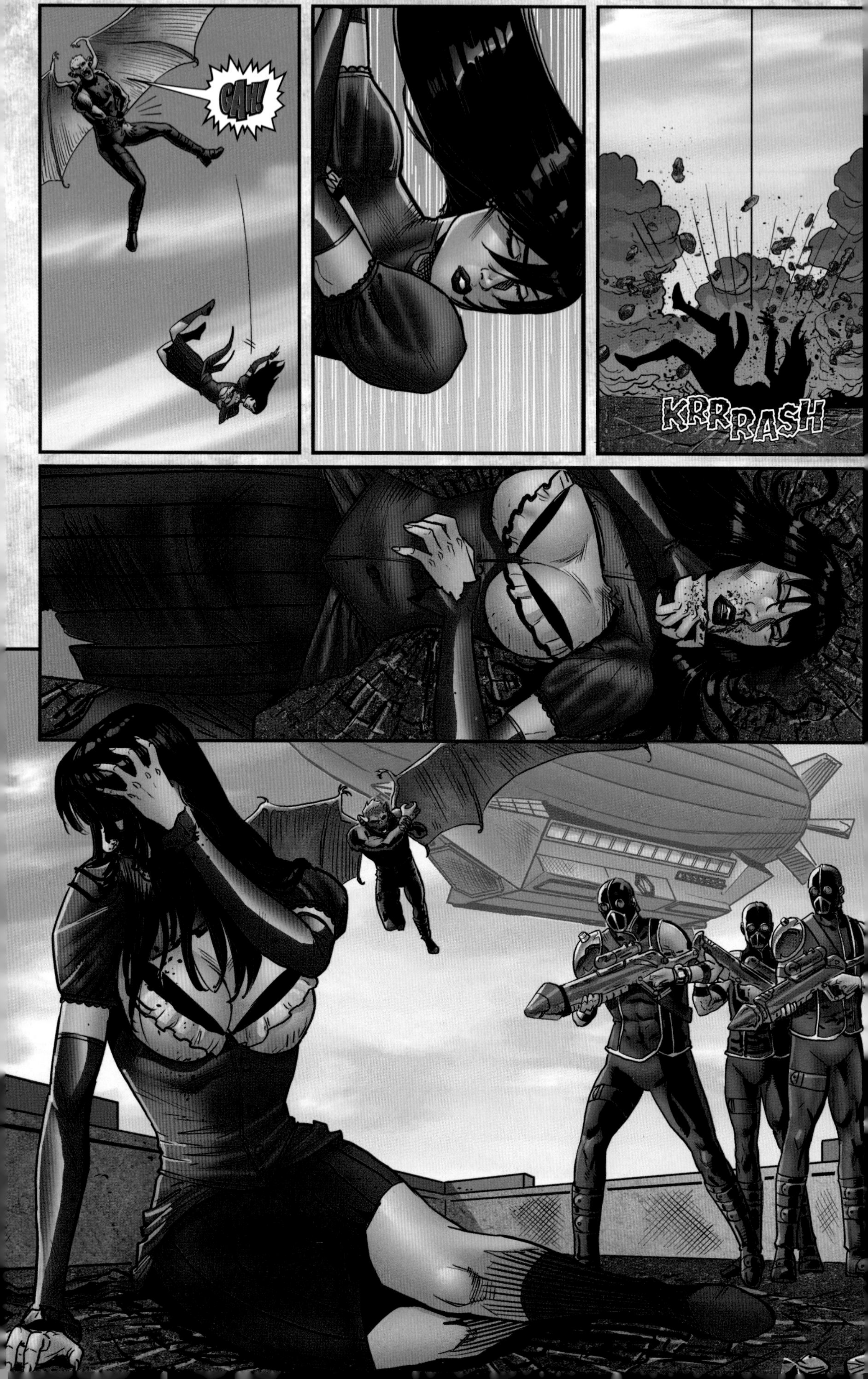
GAH!
KRRRASH

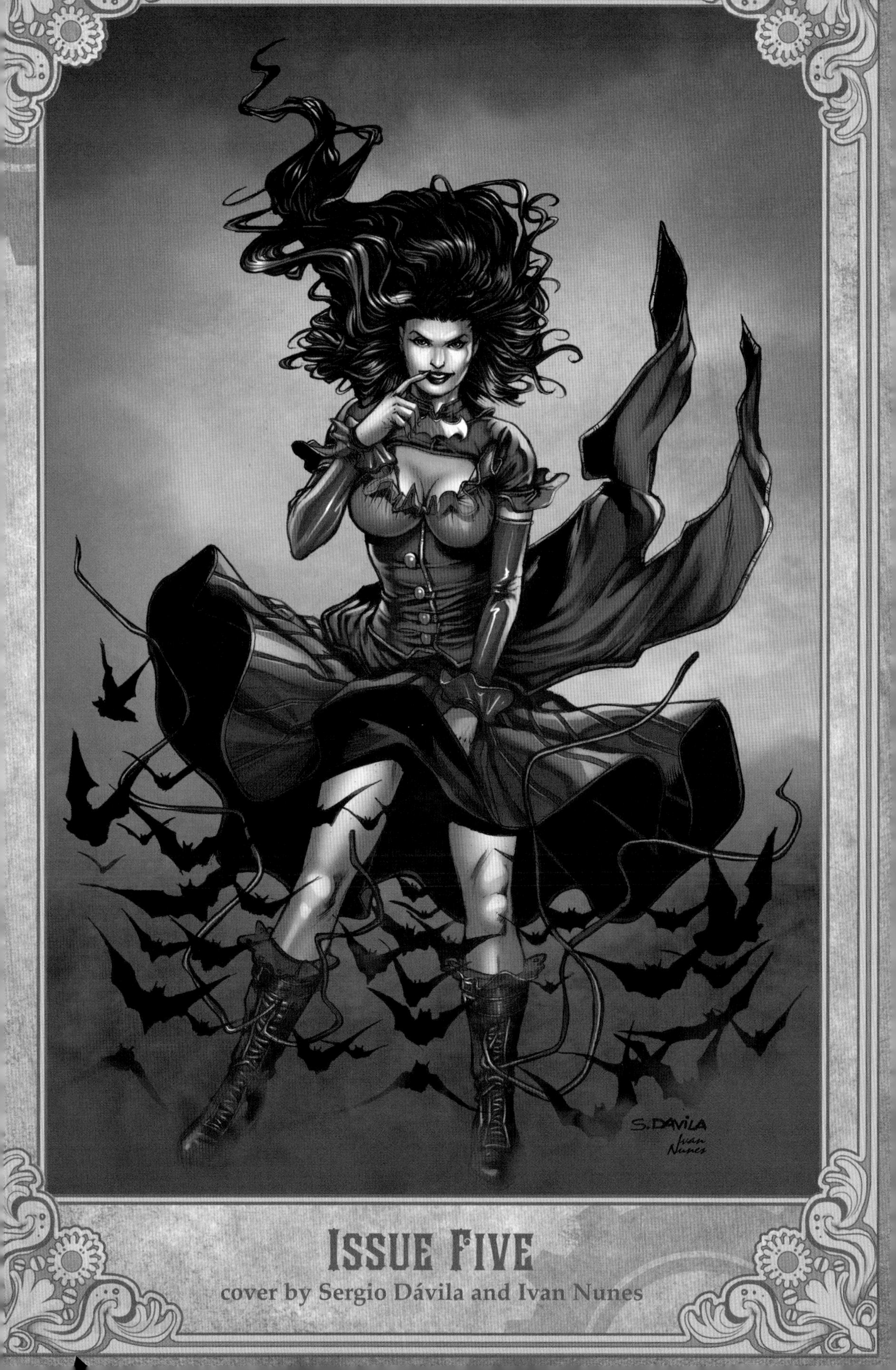
S. DAVILA
Ivan Nunes

Issue Five

cover by Sergio Dávila and Ivan Nunes

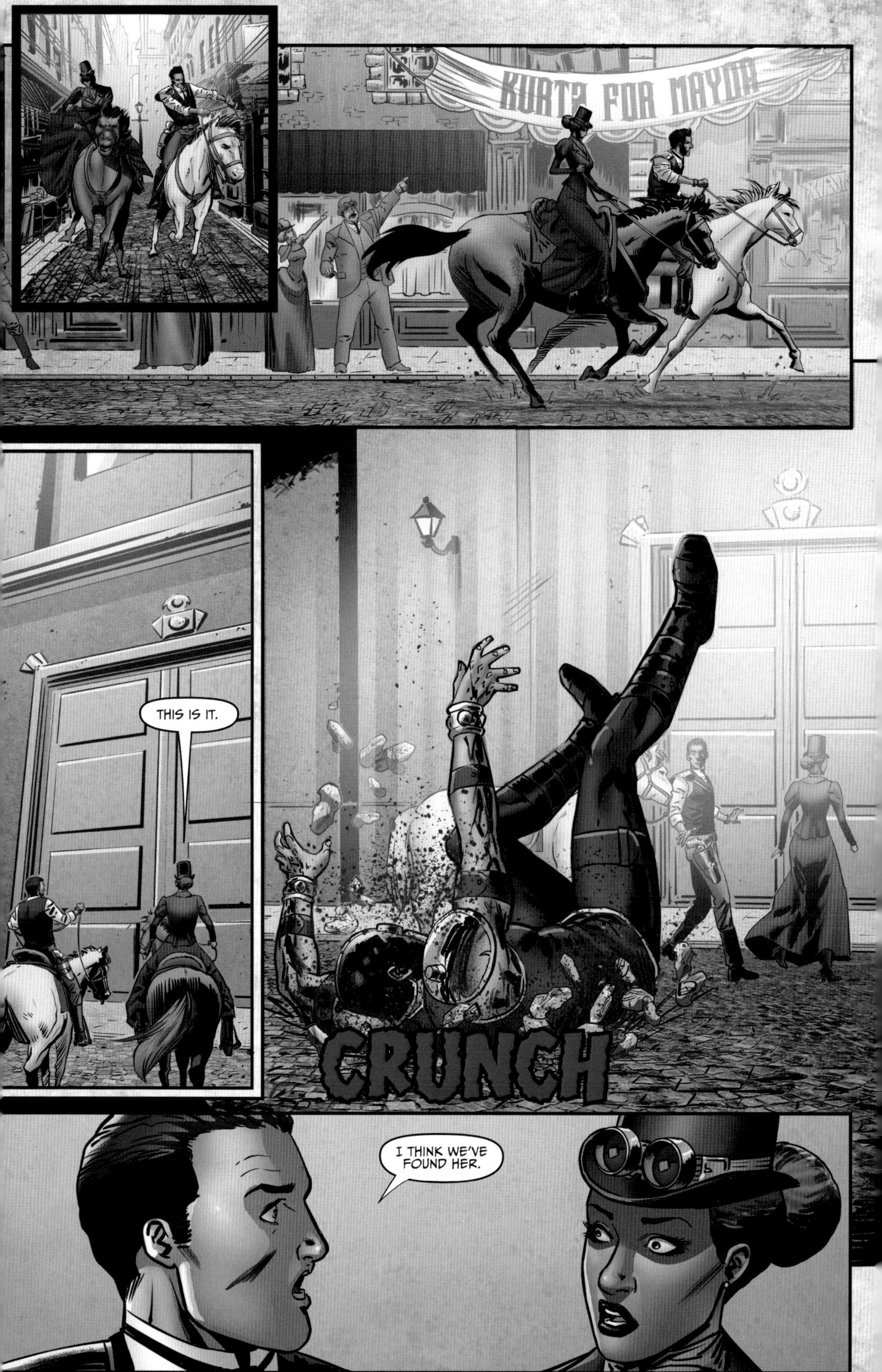
KURTZ FOR MAYOR
THIS IS IT.
CRUNCH
I THINK WE'VE FOUND HER.

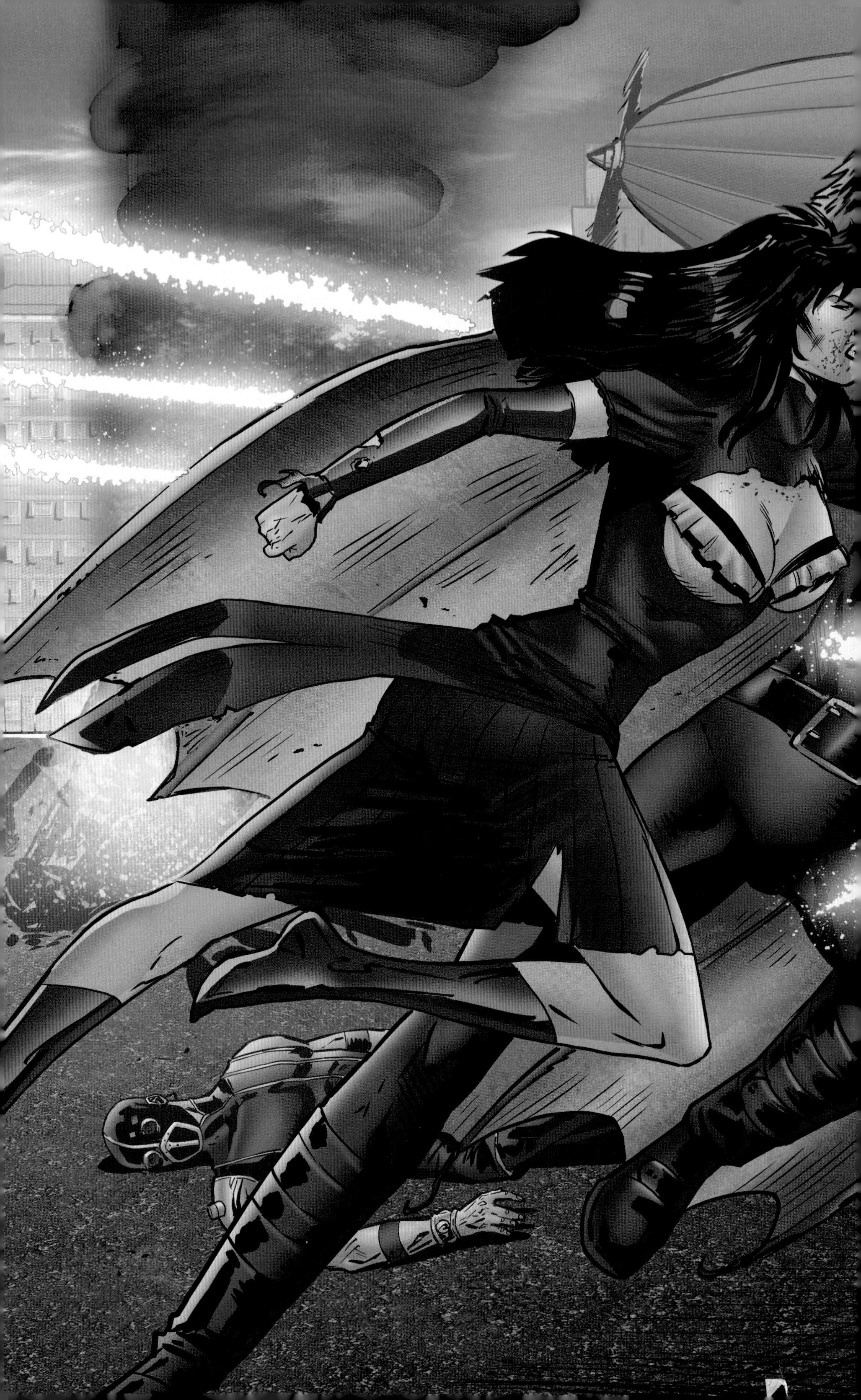

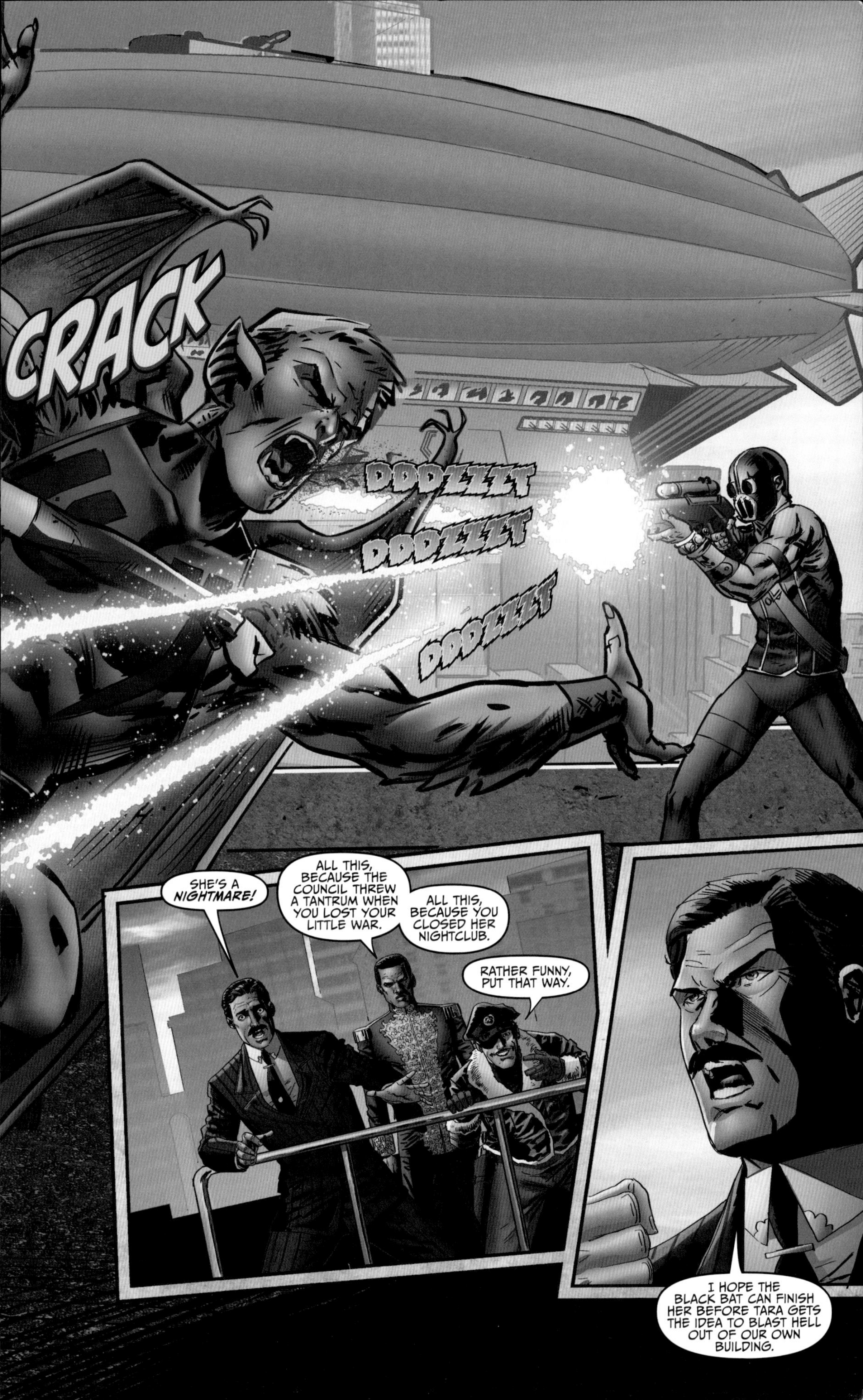
CRACK
DDDZZZT
DDDZZZT
DDDZZZT
SHE'S A *NIGHTMARE!*
ALL THIS, BECAUSE THE COUNCIL THREW A TANTRUM WHEN YOU LOST YOUR LITTLE WAR.
ALL THIS, BECAUSE YOU CLOSED HER NIGHTCLUB.
RATHER FUNNY, PUT THAT WAY.
I HOPE THE BLACK BAT CAN FINISH HER BEFORE TARA GETS THE IDEA TO BLAST HELL OUT OF OUR OWN BUILDING.

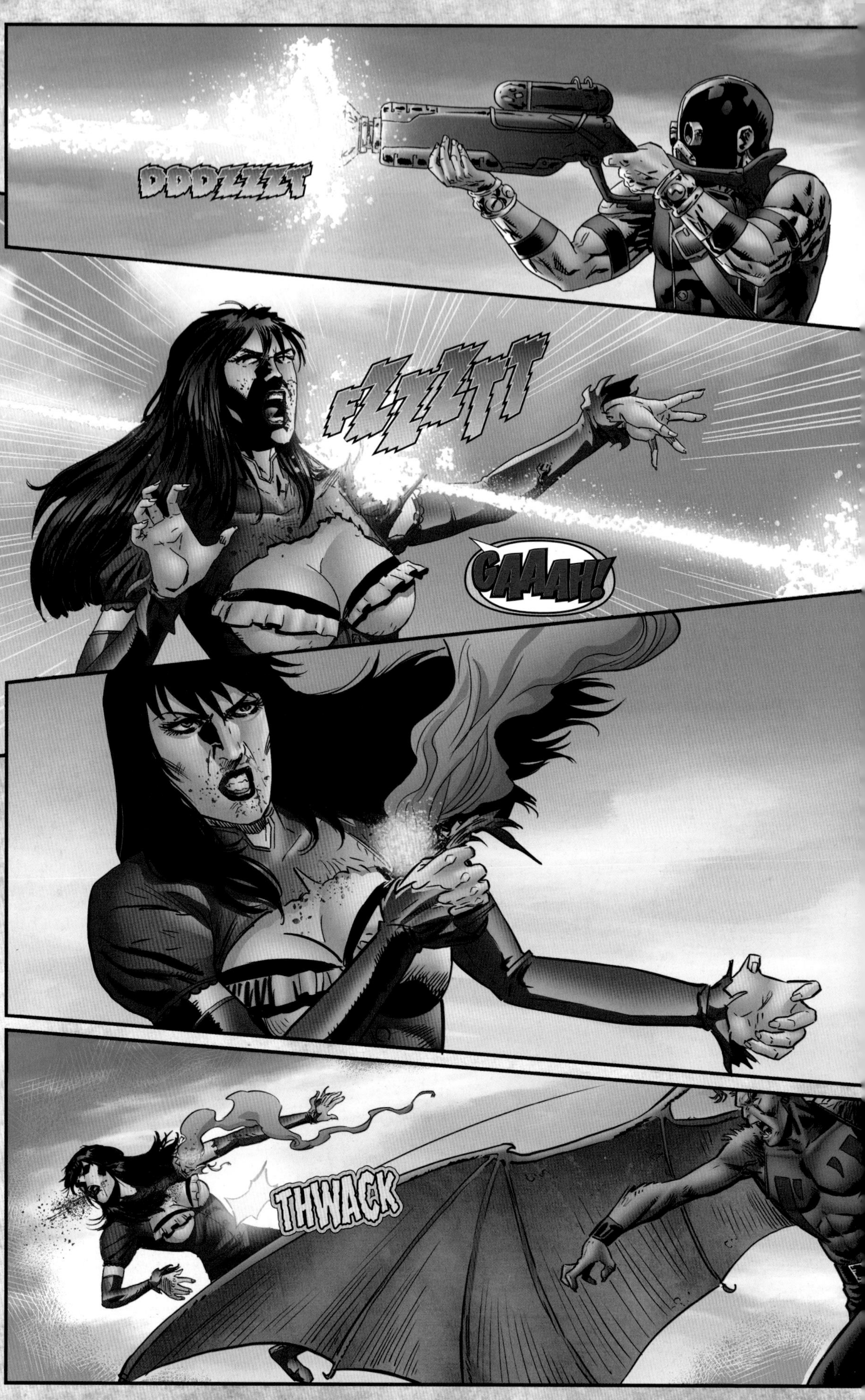
DDDZZZT
FZZZTT
GAAAH!
THWACK

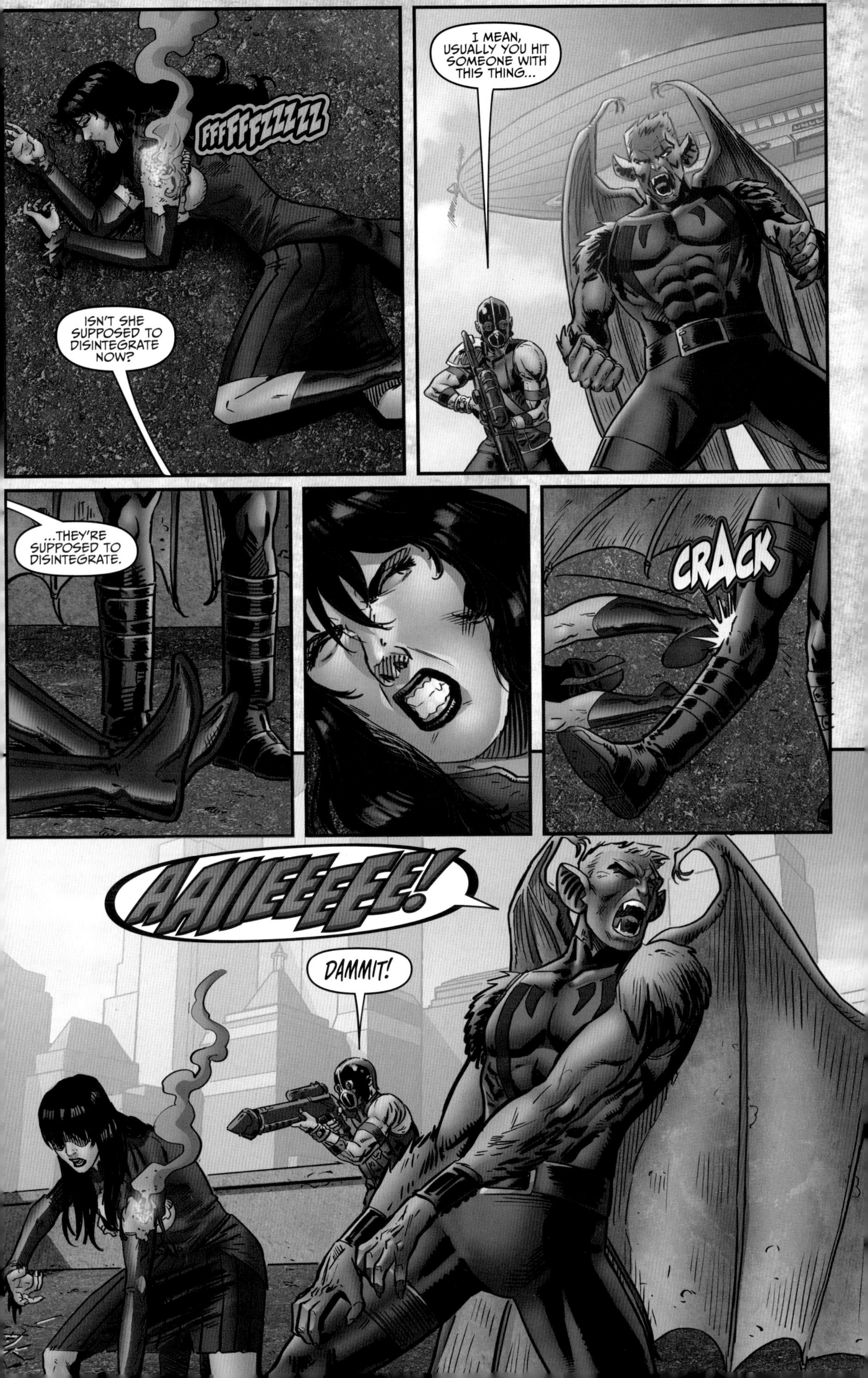
FFFFFFZZZZZZ
ISN'T SHE SUPPOSED TO DISINTEGRATE NOW?
I MEAN, USUALLY YOU HIT SOMEONE WITH THIS THING...
...THEY'RE SUPPOSED TO DISINTEGRATE.
CRACK
AAIIEEEEEE!
DAMMIT!

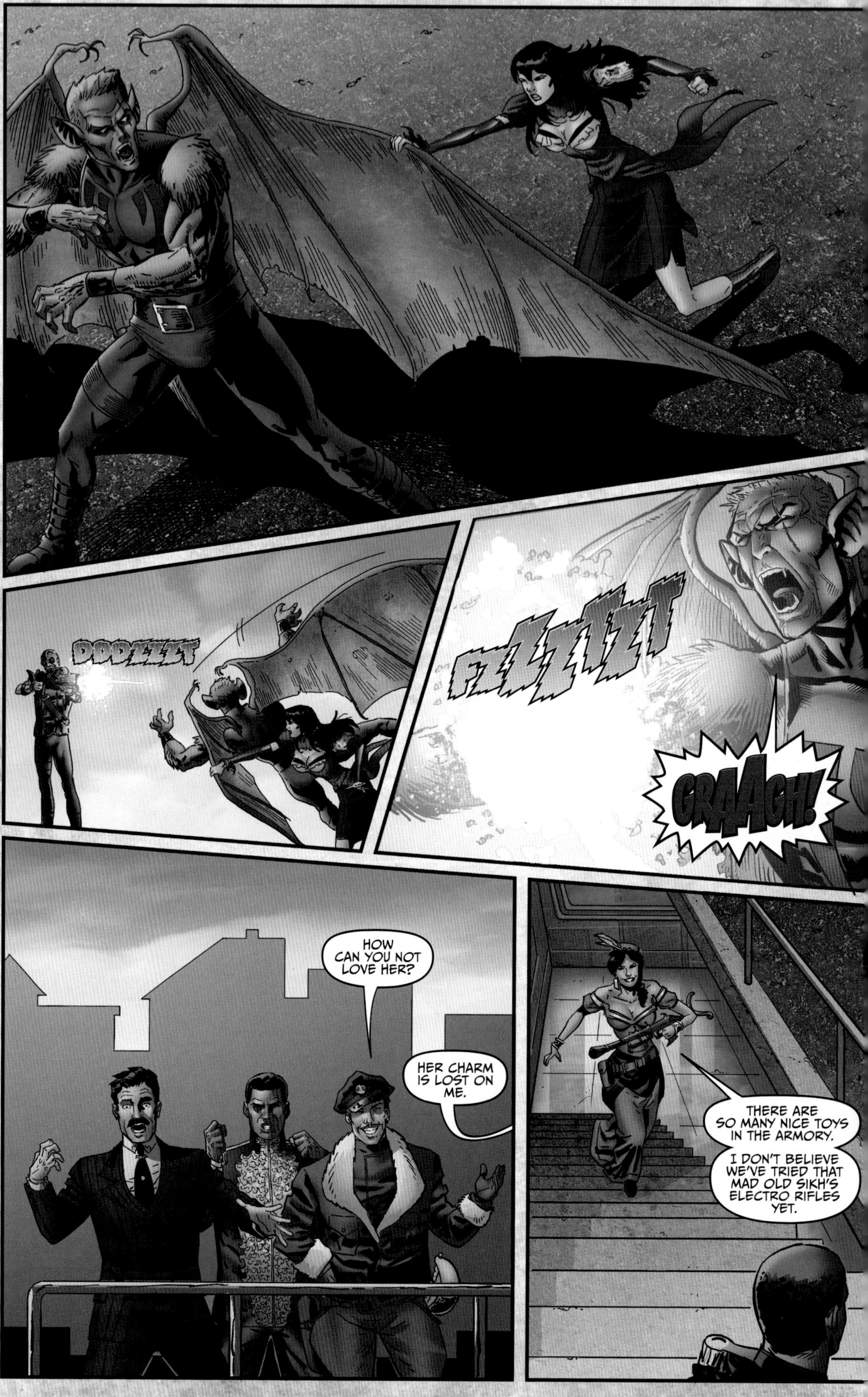
DOOZZZT
FZZZZZT
GRAAACH!
HOW CAN YOU NOT LOVE HER?
HER CHARM IS LOST ON ME.
THERE ARE SO MANY NICE TOYS IN THE ARMORY.
I DON'T BELIEVE WE'VE TRIED THAT MAD OLD SIKH'S ELECTRO RIFLES YET.

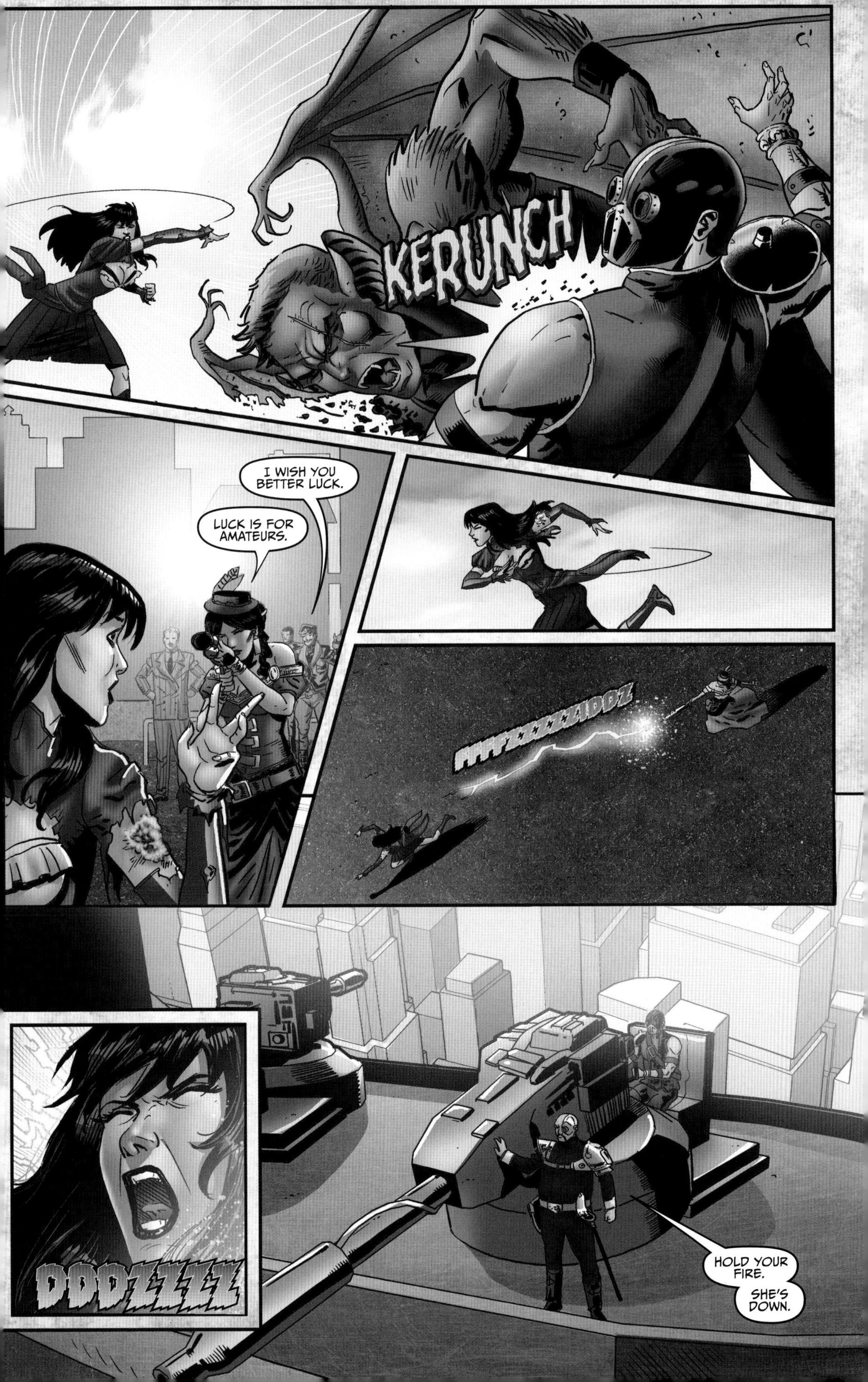
KERUNCH
I WISH YOU BETTER LUCK.
LUCK IS FOR AMATEURS.
FFFZZZZZIDDZ
DDDZZZZZ
HOLD YOUR FIRE.
SHE'S DOWN.

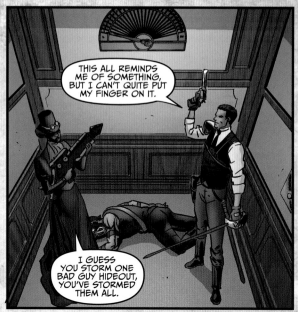

THIS ALL REMINDS ME OF SOMETHING, BUT I CAN'T QUITE PUT MY FINGER ON IT.

I GUESS YOU STORM ONE BAD GUY HIDEOUT, YOU'VE STORMED THEM ALL.

IS BLACKMASS WITH YOU?

THAT'S MY THANKS FOR TAKING DOWN PENDRAGON?

BETWEEN THE BLACK BAT AND THE DEMOLECULORIZER BEAM, THERE WASN'T MUCH LEFT OF HER WHEN YOU GOT HERE.

WHAT MAKES YOU SO SURE I'VE DONE THIS SORT OF THING BEFORE?

YOU WANT TO TELL ME WHY RUPERT OF HENTZAU HATES YOU SO MUCH?

TOUCHÉ.

MY ERSTWHILE HUSBAND WENT ON A BIT OF A SPREE. YANKED THE LIVING SOULS OUT OF A FEW CITIZENS, BUT HE HASN'T STRUCK AGAIN IN DAYS.

I BELIEVE HE HAS LEFT THE BIG CITY.

PERHAPS THAT'S FOR THE BEST...

NOT YOUR FIRST TIME AT THE CIRCUS EITHER I IMAGINE.

MISTER, I'VE BEEN DEALING WITH CLOWNS MY WHOLE LIFE.

I'VE JUST CONCEIVED A CUNNING NEW DRAMATIC TABLEAU WHICH SHOULD PROVE HIGHLY ENTERTAINING AND PROFITABLE FOR US ALL.

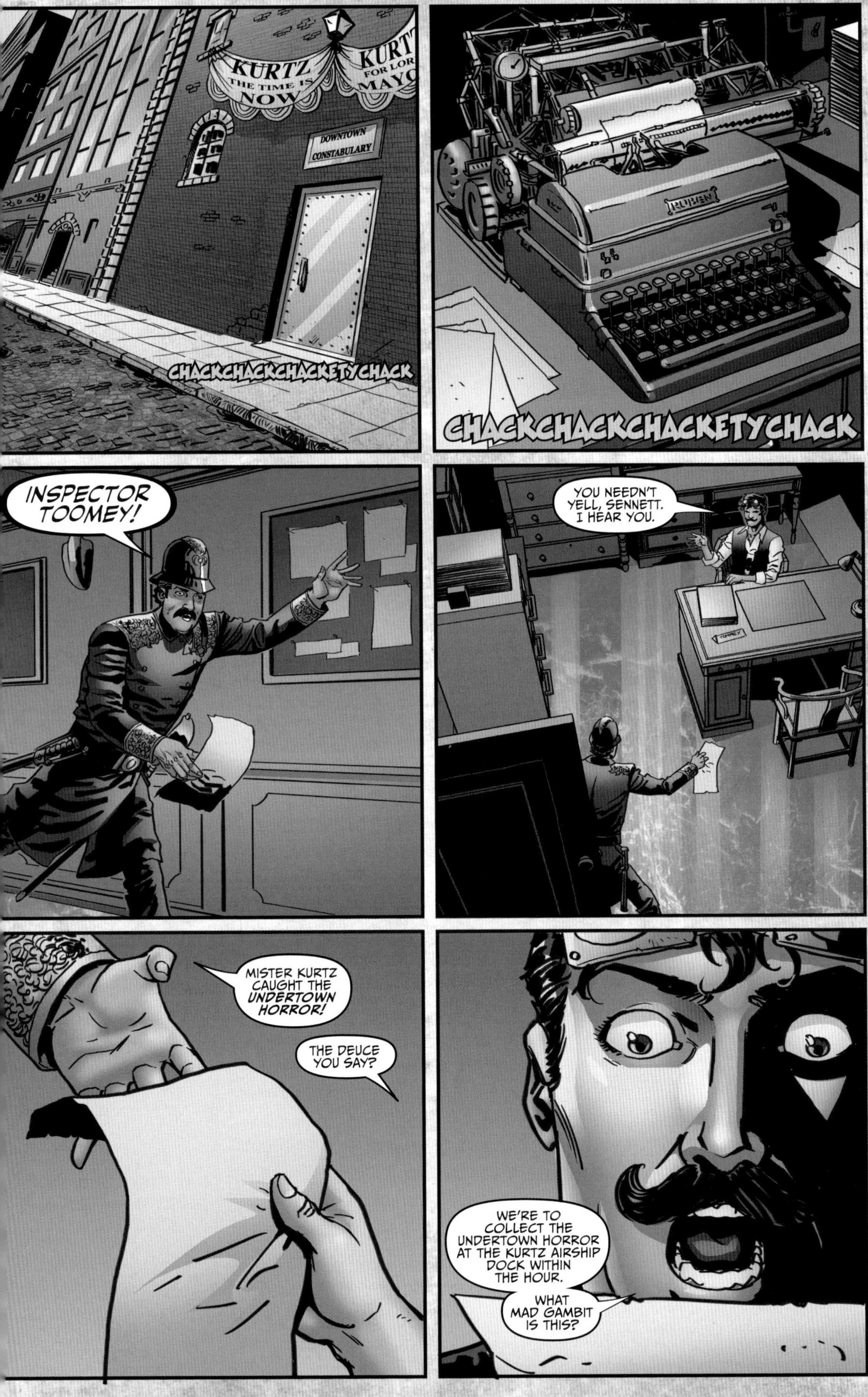
KURTZ THE TIME IS NOW
KURTZ FOR LOR MAYO
DOWNTOWN CONSTABULARY
CHACKCHACKCHACKETYCHACK
CHACKCHACKCHACKETYCHACK
INSPECTOR TOOMEY!
YOU NEEDN'T YELL, SENNETT. I HEAR YOU.
MISTER KURTZ CAUGHT THE *UNDERTOWN HORROR!*
THE DEUCE YOU SAY?
WE'RE TO COLLECT THE UNDERTOWN HORROR AT THE KURTZ AIRSHIP DOCK WITHIN THE HOUR.
WHAT MAD GAMBIT IS THIS?

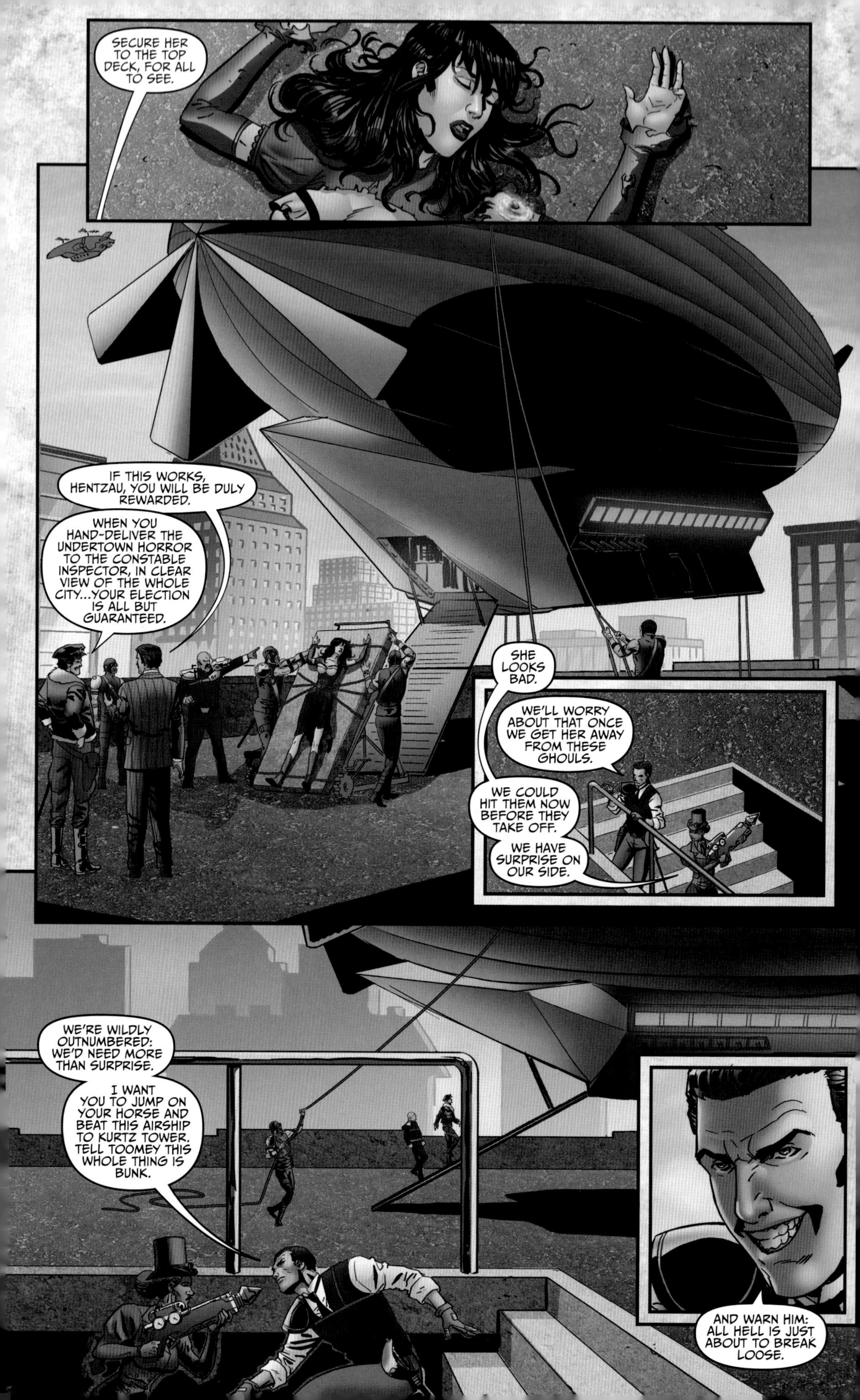
SECURE HER TO THE TOP DECK, FOR ALL TO SEE.
IF THIS WORKS, HENTZAU, YOU WILL BE DULY REWARDED.
WHEN YOU HAND-DELIVER THE UNDERTOWN HORROR TO THE CONSTABLE INSPECTOR, IN CLEAR VIEW OF THE WHOLE CITY...YOUR ELECTION IS ALL BUT GUARANTEED.
SHE LOOKS BAD.
WE'LL WORRY ABOUT THAT ONCE WE GET HER AWAY FROM THESE GHOULS.
WE COULD HIT THEM NOW BEFORE THEY TAKE OFF.
WE HAVE SURPRISE ON OUR SIDE.
WE'RE WILDLY OUTNUMBERED: WE'D NEED MORE THAN SURPRISE.
I WANT YOU TO JUMP ON YOUR HORSE AND BEAT THIS AIRSHIP TO KURTZ TOWER. TELL TOOMEY THIS WHOLE THING IS BUNK.
AND WARN HIM: ALL HELL IS JUST ABOUT TO BREAK LOOSE.

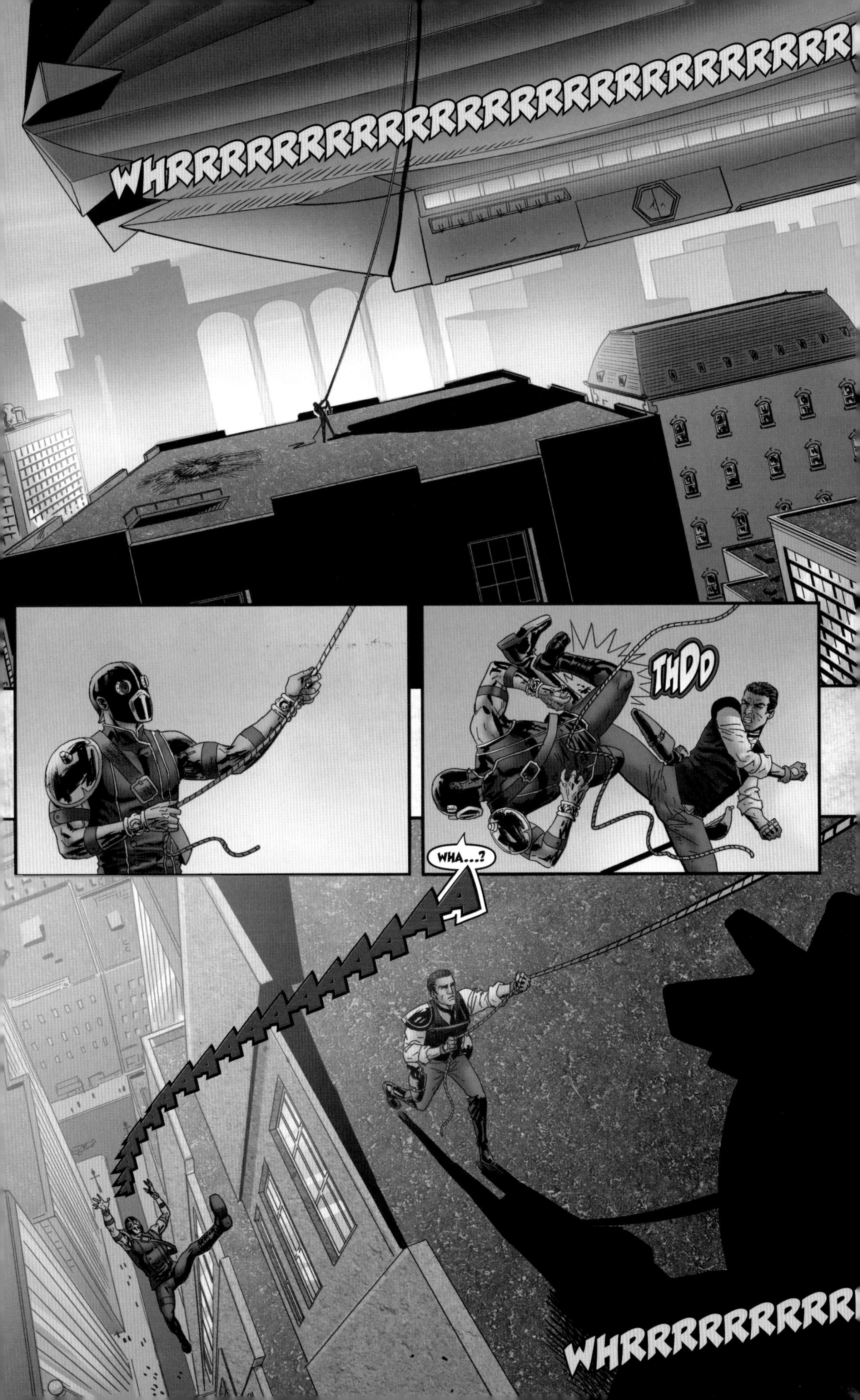
WHRRRRRRRRRRRRRRRRRRRRRRRRRRRR
THDD
WHA...?
AAAAAAAAAAAAAAAAA
WHRRRRRRRRRR

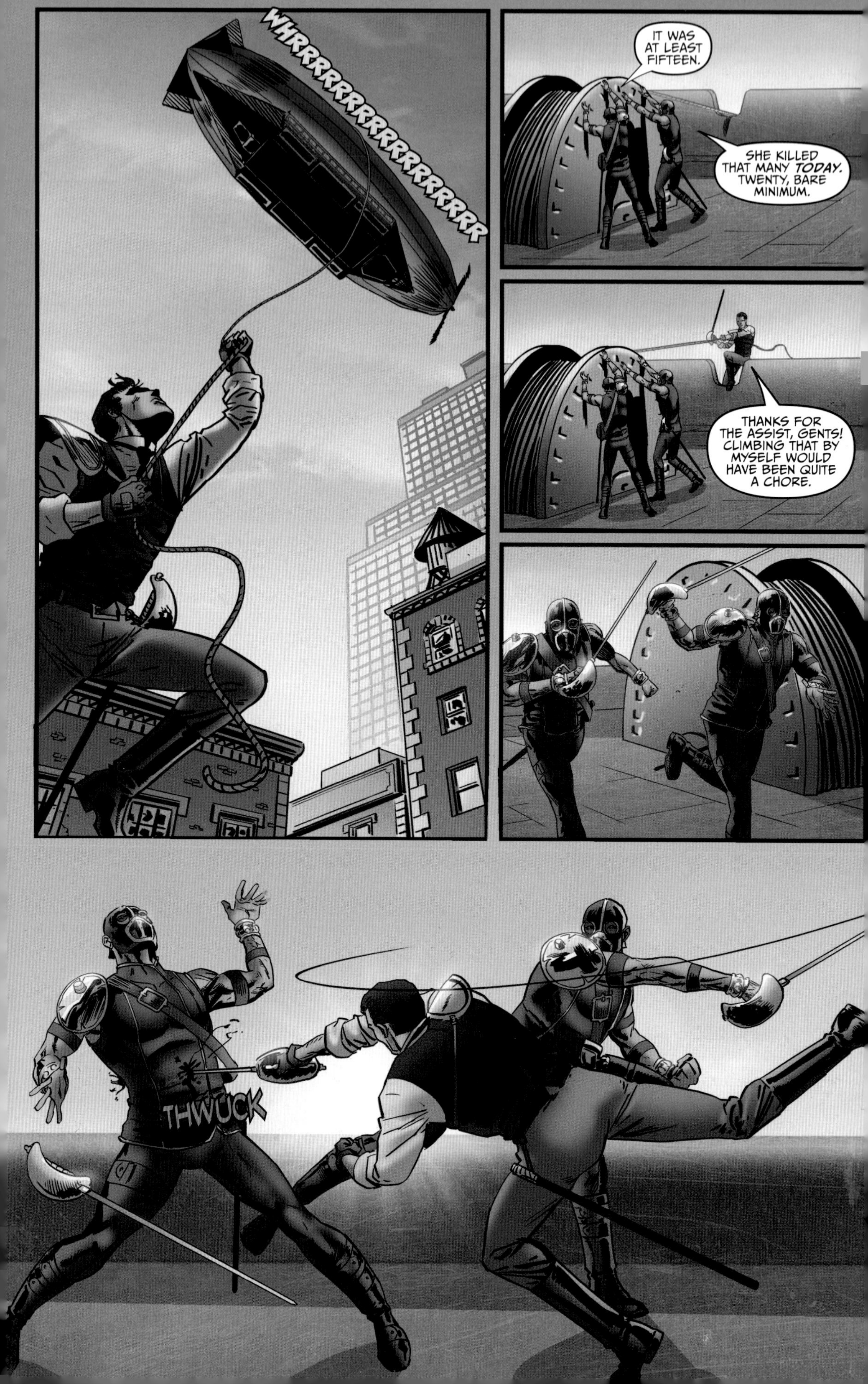
WHRRRRRRRRRRRRRRRRRR
IT WAS AT LEAST FIFTEEN.
SHE KILLED THAT MANY *TODAY.* TWENTY, BARE MINIMUM.
THANKS FOR THE ASSIST, GENTS! CLIMBING THAT BY MYSELF WOULD HAVE BEEN QUITE A CHORE.
THWUCK

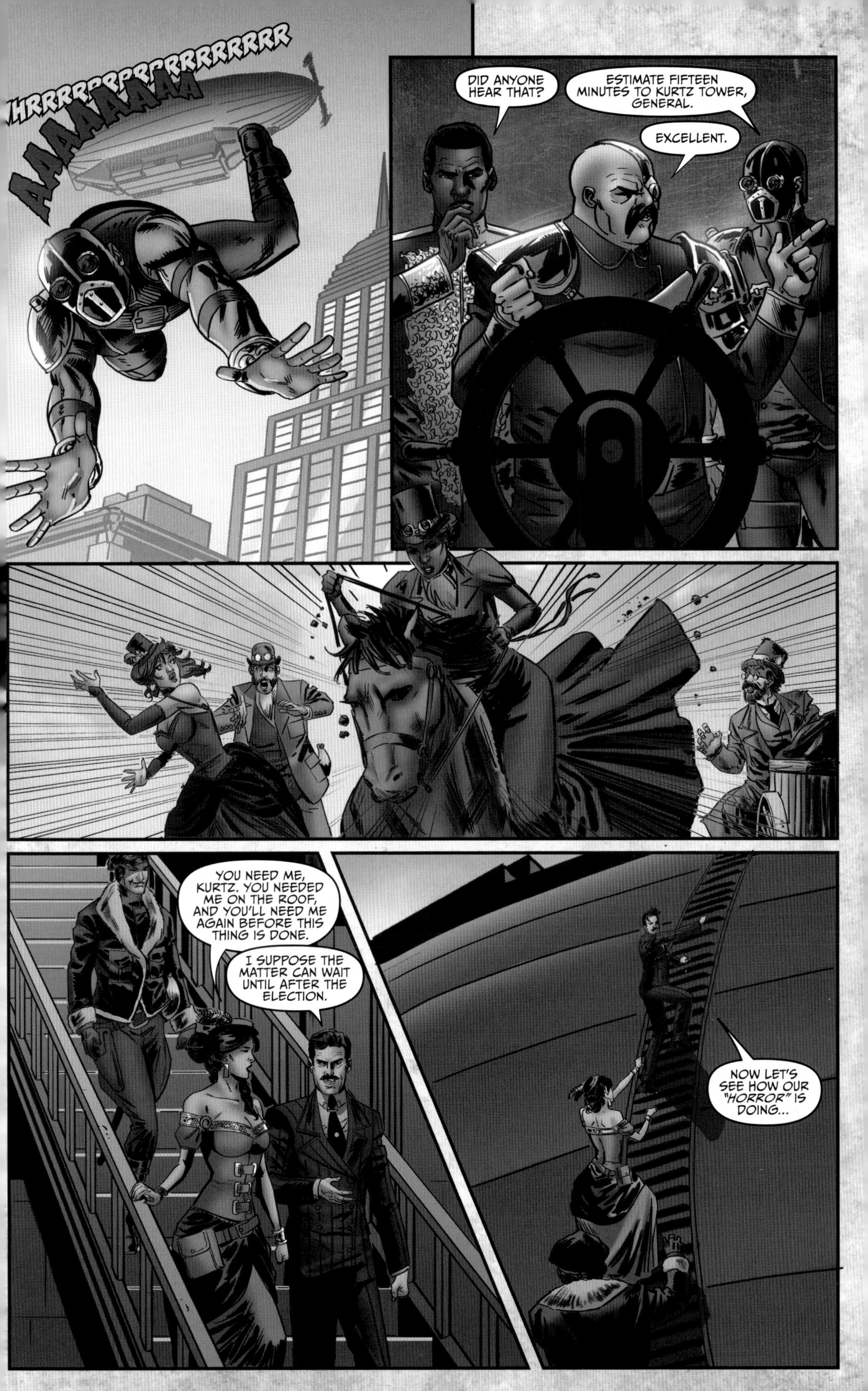
WHRRRRRRRRRRRRRRRRRR
AAAAAAAAAA
DID ANYONE HEAR THAT?
ESTIMATE FIFTEEN MINUTES TO KURTZ TOWER, GENERAL.
EXCELLENT.
YOU NEED ME, KURTZ. YOU NEEDED ME ON THE ROOF, AND YOU'LL NEED ME AGAIN BEFORE THIS THING IS DONE.
I SUPPOSE THE MATTER CAN WAIT UNTIL AFTER THE ELECTION.
NOW LET'S SEE HOW OUR "HORROR" IS DOING...

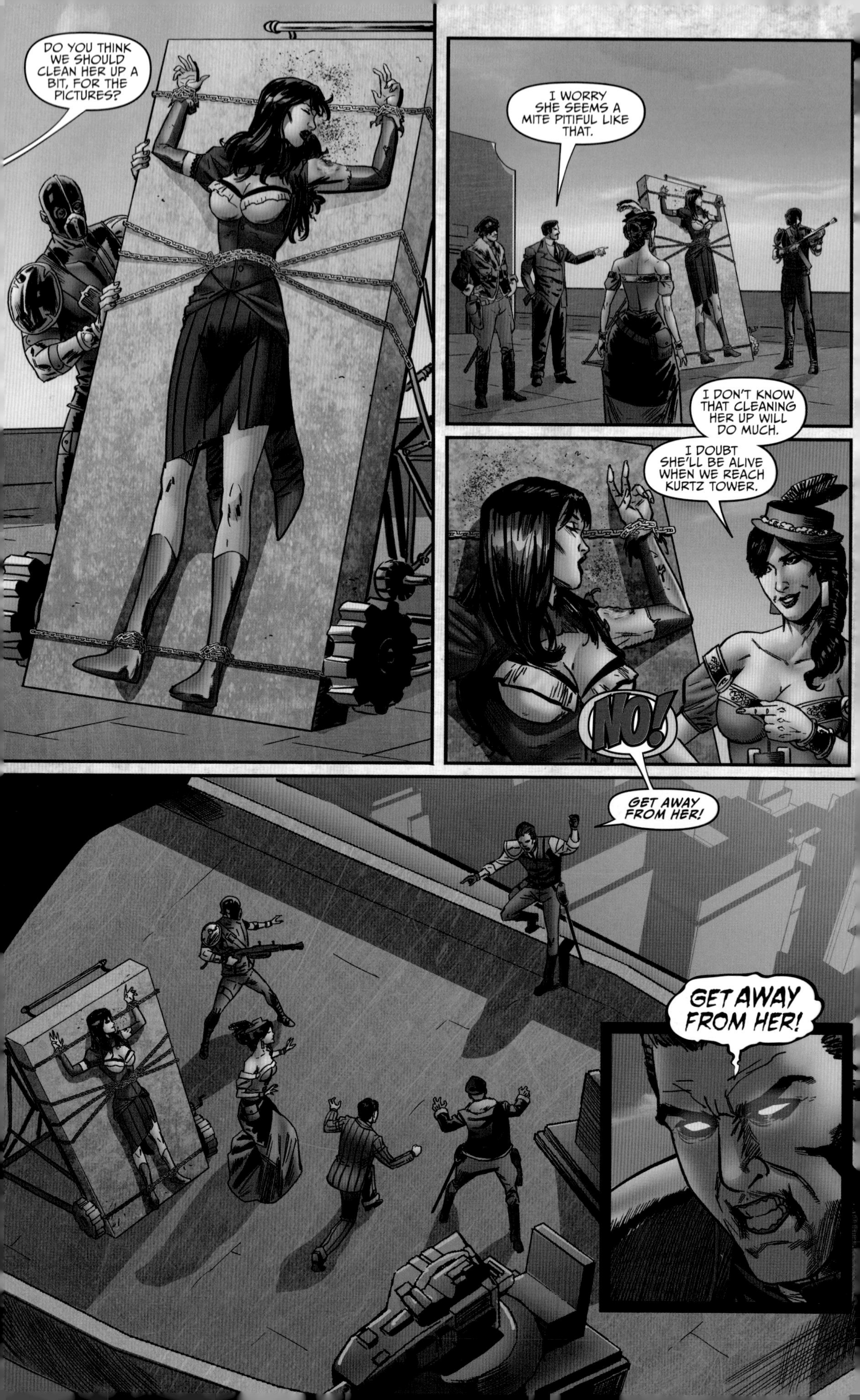
DO YOU THINK WE SHOULD CLEAN HER UP A BIT, FOR THE PICTURES?
I WORRY SHE SEEMS A MITE PITIFUL LIKE THAT.
I DON'T KNOW THAT CLEANING HER UP WILL DO MUCH.
I DOUBT SHE'LL BE ALIVE WHEN WE REACH KURTZ TOWER.
NO!
GET AWAY FROM HER!
GET AWAY FROM HER!

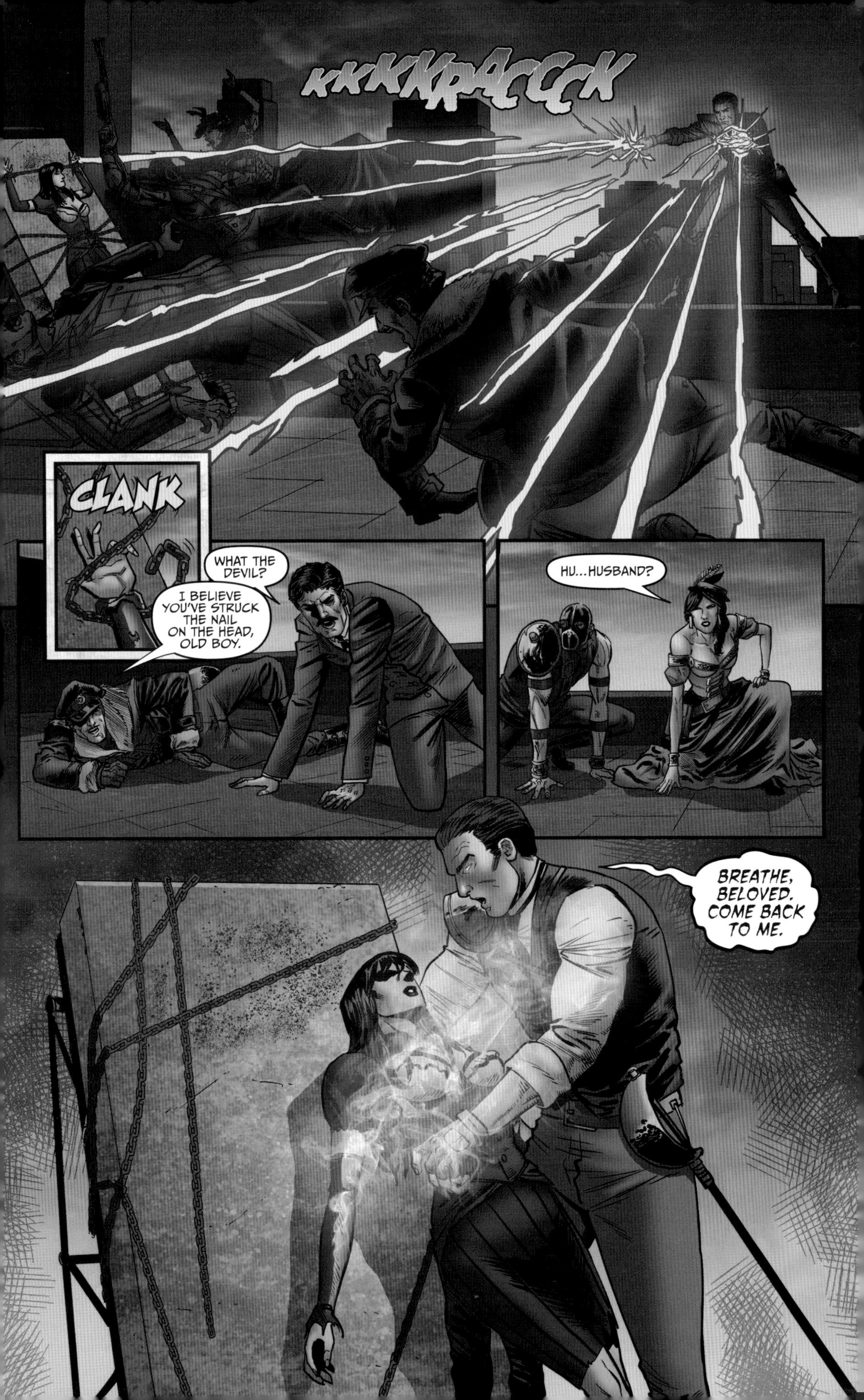
KKKKKRACCCK
CLANK
WHAT THE DEVIL?
I BELIEVE YOU'VE STRUCK THE NAIL ON THE HEAD, OLD BOY.
HU...HUSBAND?
BREATHE, BELOVED. COME BACK TO ME.

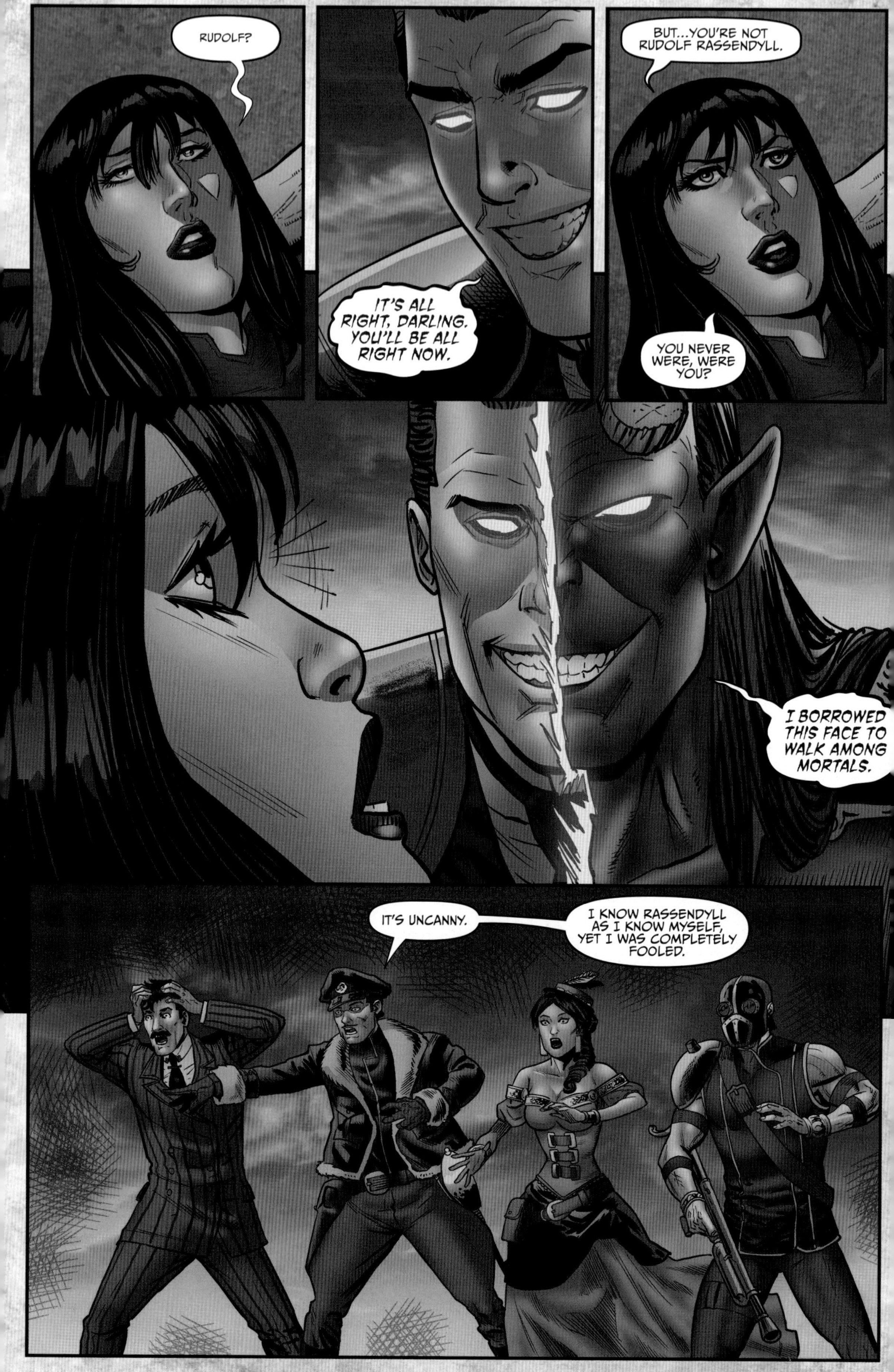
RUDOLF?
IT'S ALL RIGHT, DARLING. YOU'LL BE ALL RIGHT NOW.
BUT...YOU'RE NOT RUDOLF RASSENDYLL.
YOU NEVER WERE, WERE YOU?
I BORROWED THIS FACE TO WALK AMONG MORTALS.
IT'S UNCANNY.
I KNOW RASSENDYLL AS I KNOW MYSELF, YET I WAS COMPLETELY FOOLED.

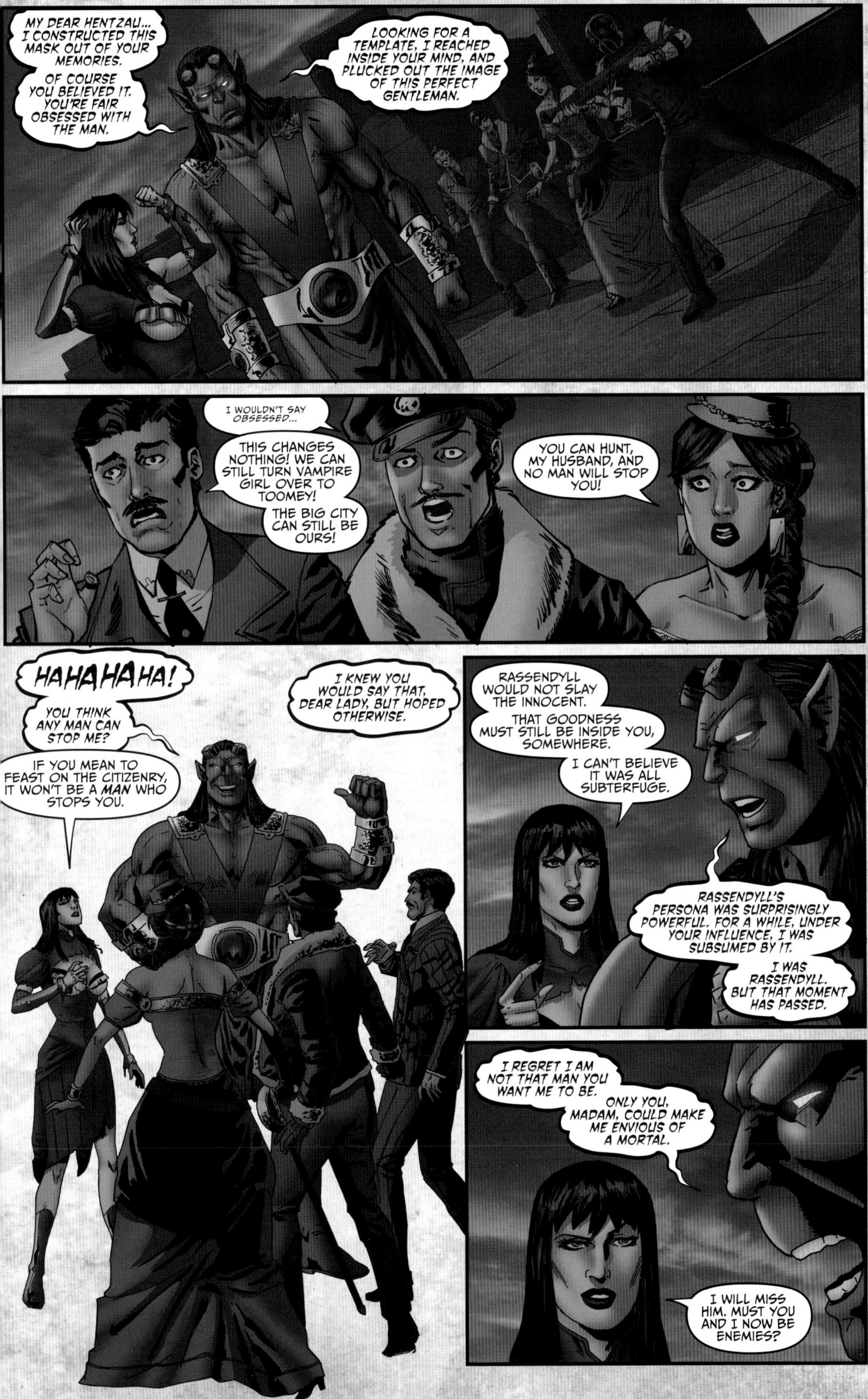
MY DEAR HENTZAU... I CONSTRUCTED THIS MASK OUT OF YOUR MEMORIES.
OF COURSE YOU BELIEVED IT. YOU'RE FAIR OBSESSED WITH THE MAN.
LOOKING FOR A TEMPLATE, I REACHED INSIDE YOUR MIND, AND PLUCKED OUT THE IMAGE OF THIS PERFECT GENTLEMAN.
I WOULDN'T SAY OBSESSED...
THIS CHANGES NOTHING! WE CAN STILL TURN VAMPIRE GIRL OVER TO TOOMEY!
THE BIG CITY CAN STILL BE OURS!
YOU CAN HUNT, MY HUSBAND, AND NO MAN WILL STOP YOU!
HAHAHAHAHA!
YOU THINK ANY MAN CAN STOP ME?
IF YOU MEAN TO FEAST ON THE CITIZENRY, IT WON'T BE A MAN WHO STOPS YOU.
I KNEW YOU WOULD SAY THAT, DEAR LADY, BUT HOPED OTHERWISE.
RASSENDYLL WOULD NOT SLAY THE INNOCENT.
THAT GOODNESS MUST STILL BE INSIDE YOU, SOMEWHERE.
I CAN'T BELIEVE IT WAS ALL SUBTERFUGE.
RASSENDYLL'S PERSONA WAS SURPRISINGLY POWERFUL. FOR A WHILE, UNDER YOUR INFLUENCE, I WAS SUBSUMED BY IT.
I WAS RASSENDYLL. BUT THAT MOMENT HAS PASSED.
I REGRET I AM NOT THAT MAN YOU WANT ME TO BE.
ONLY YOU, MADAM, COULD MAKE ME ENVIOUS OF A MORTAL.
I WILL MISS HIM. MUST YOU AND I NOW BE ENEMIES?

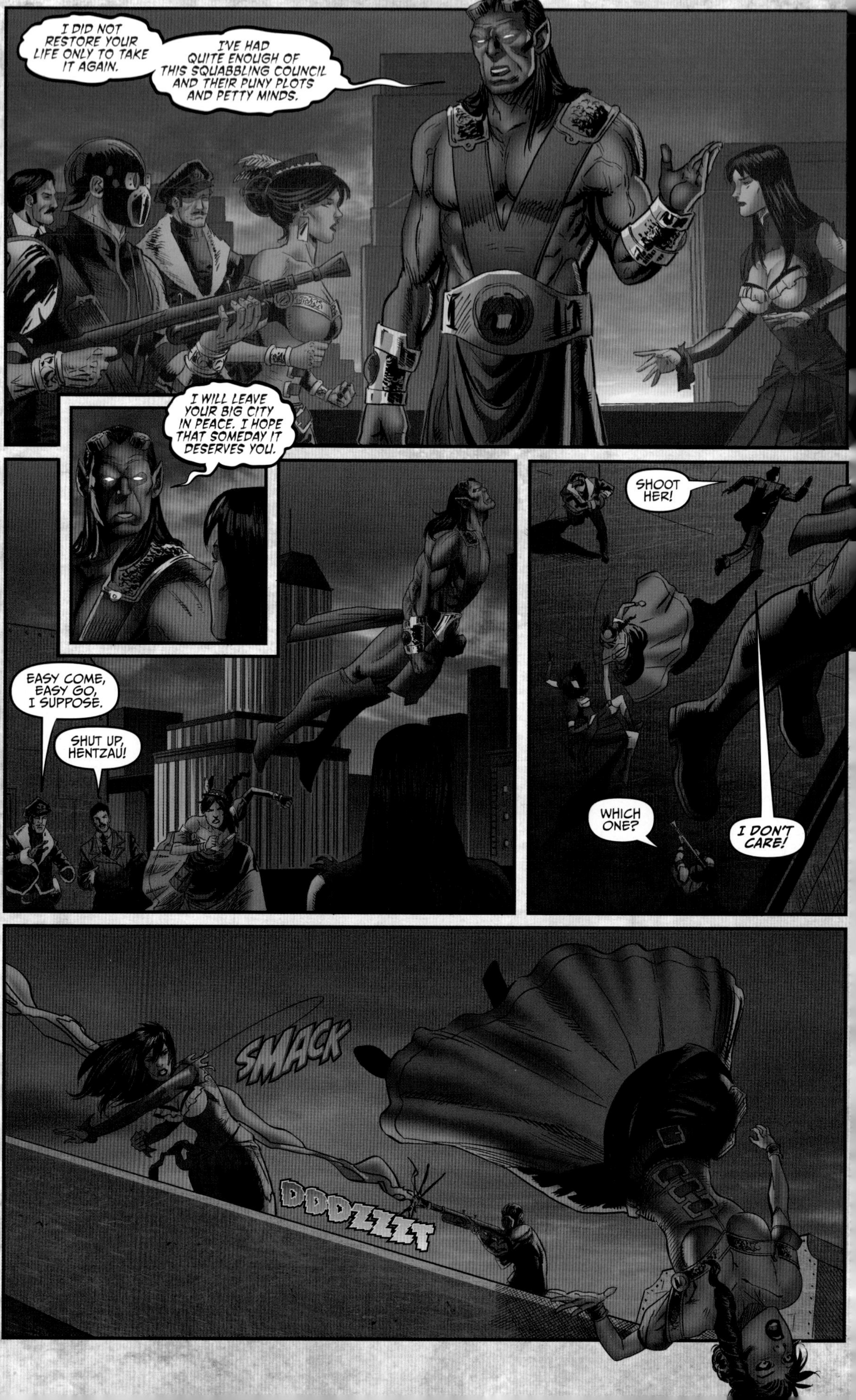
I DID NOT RESTORE YOUR LIFE ONLY TO TAKE IT AGAIN.
I'VE HAD QUITE ENOUGH OF THIS SQUABBLING COUNCIL AND THEIR PUNY PLOTS AND PETTY MINDS.
I WILL LEAVE YOUR BIG CITY IN PEACE. I HOPE THAT SOMEDAY IT DESERVES YOU.
EASY COME, EASY GO, I SUPPOSE.
SHUT UP, HENTZAU!
SHOOT HER!
WHICH ONE?
I DON'T CARE!
SMACK
DDDZZZT

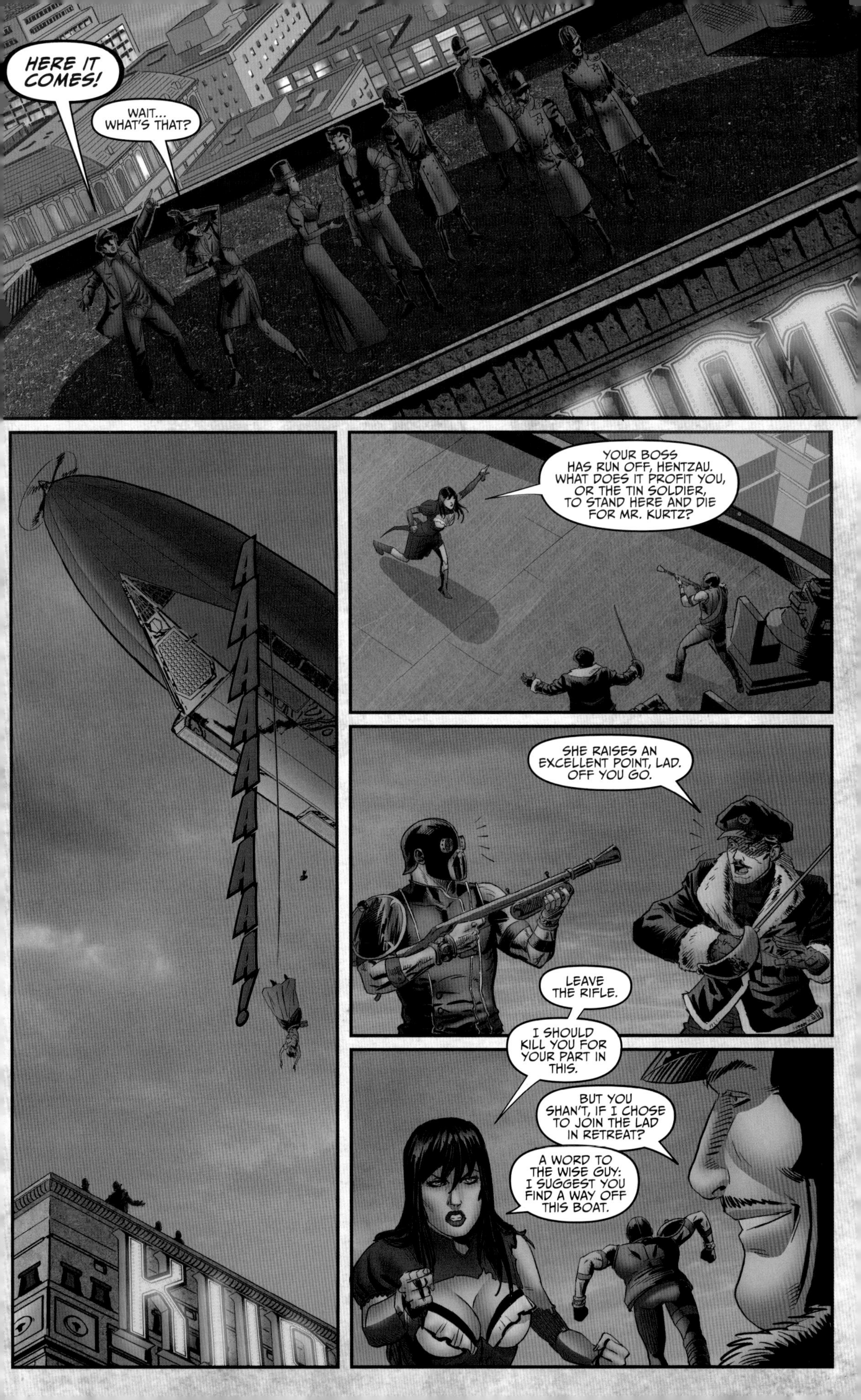
HERE IT COMES!
WAIT... WHAT'S THAT?
AAAAAAAAAAAAAA!
YOUR BOSS HAS RUN OFF, HENTZAU. WHAT DOES IT PROFIT YOU, OR THE TIN SOLDIER, TO STAND HERE AND DIE FOR MR. KURTZ?
SHE RAISES AN EXCELLENT POINT, LAD. OFF YOU GO.
LEAVE THE RIFLE.
I SHOULD KILL YOU FOR YOUR PART IN THIS.
BUT YOU SHAN'T, IF I CHOSE TO JOIN THE LAD IN RETREAT?
A WORD TO THE WISE GUY: I SUGGEST YOU FIND A WAY OFF THIS BOAT.

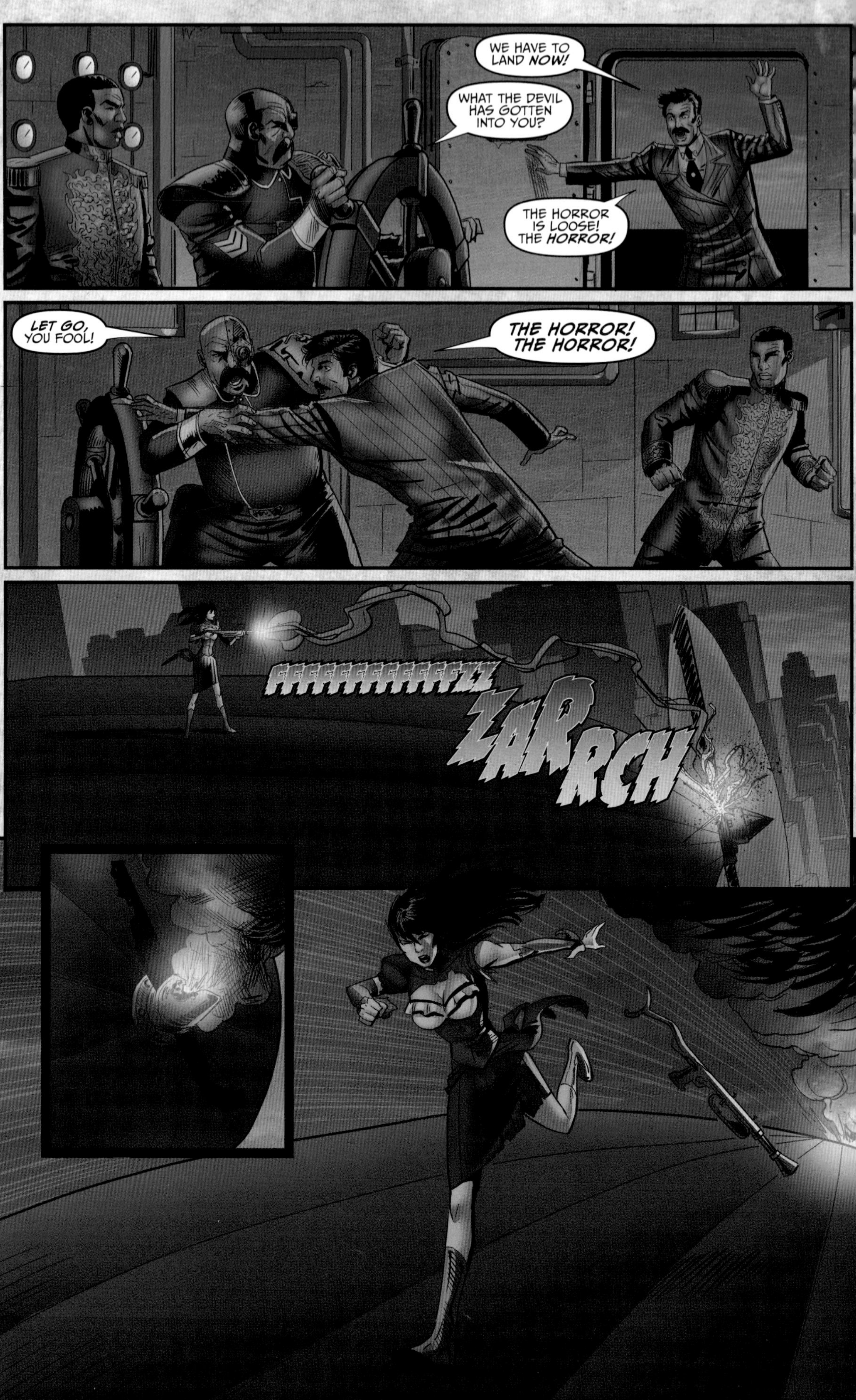
WE HAVE TO LAND NOW!
WHAT THE DEVIL HAS GOTTEN INTO YOU?
THE HORROR IS LOOSE! THE HORROR!
LET GO, YOU FOOL!
THE HORROR! THE HORROR!
FFFFFFFFFFFFZZ
ZARRCH

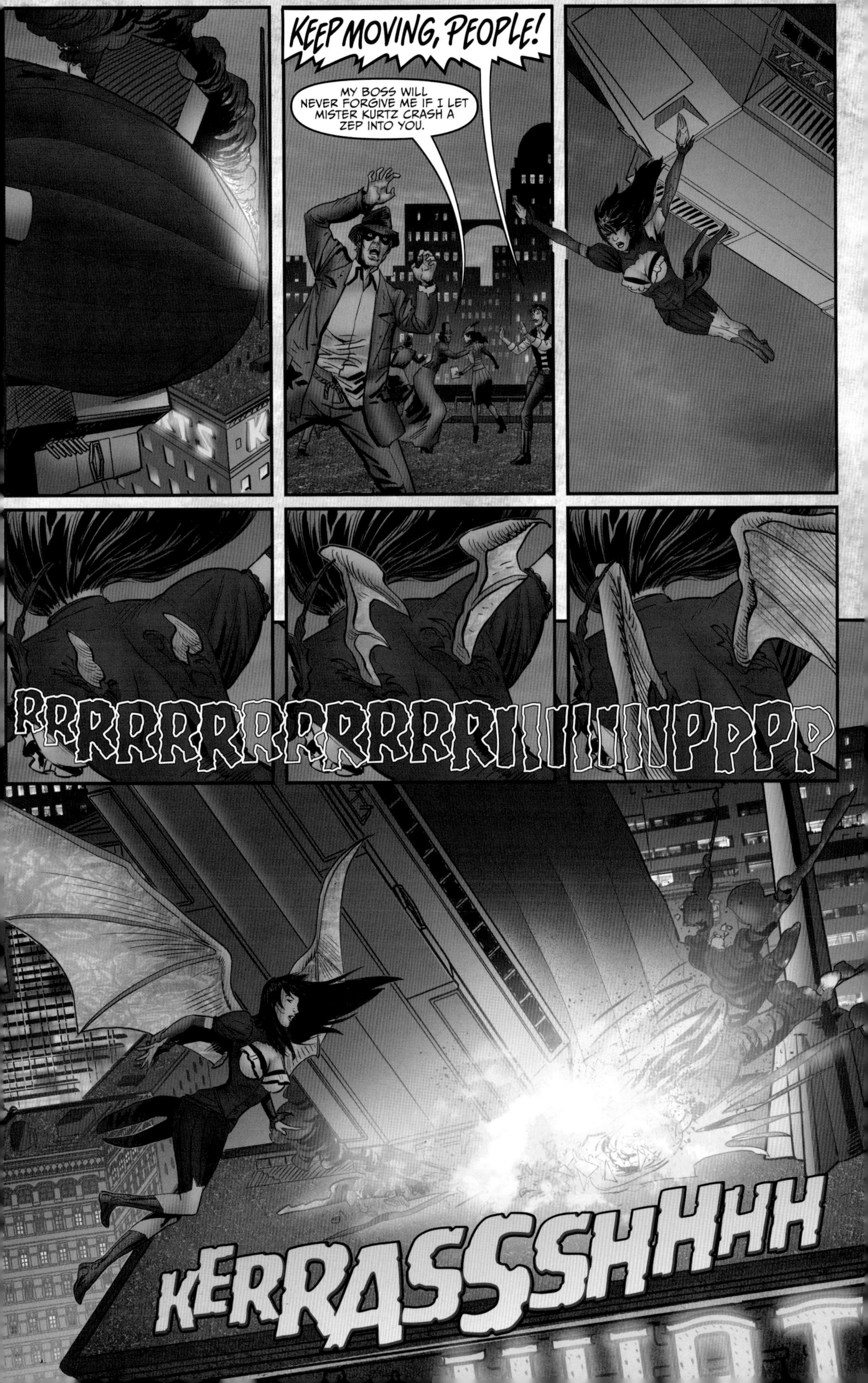
KEEP MOVING, PEOPLE!
MY BOSS WILL NEVER FORGIVE ME IF I LET MISTER KURTZ CRASH A ZEP INTO YOU.
RRRRRRRRRRRRRIIIIIIIIPPPP
KERRASSSHHHH

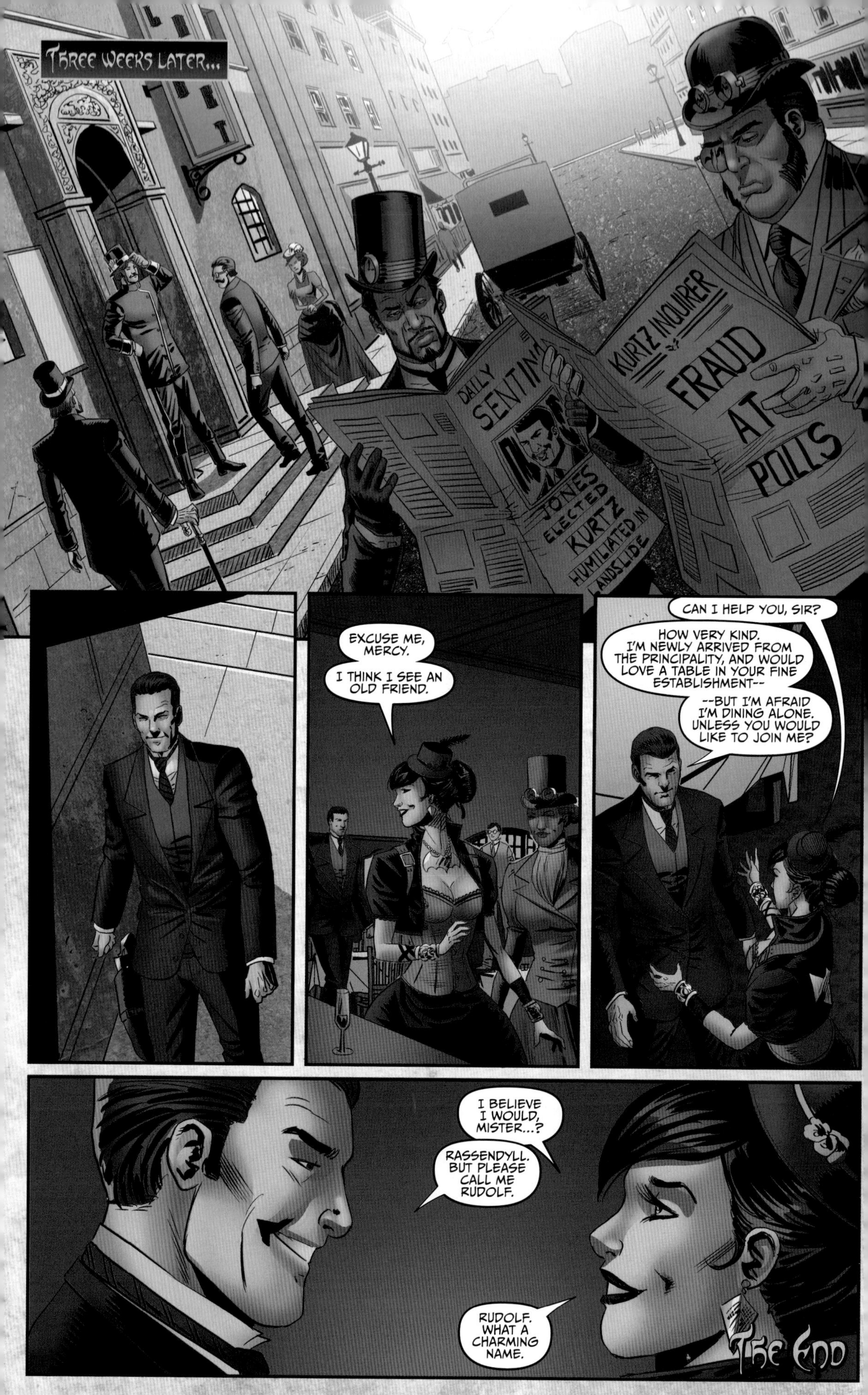
THREE WEEKS LATER...
DAILY SENTIN
JONES ELECTED
KURTZ HUMILIATED IN LANDSLIDE
KURTZ INQUIRER
FRAUD AT POLLS
EXCUSE ME, MERCY.
I THINK I SEE AN OLD FRIEND.
CAN I HELP YOU, SIR?
HOW VERY KIND. I'M NEWLY ARRIVED FROM THE PRINCIPALITY, AND WOULD LOVE A TABLE IN YOUR FINE ESTABLISHMENT--
--BUT I'M AFRAID I'M DINING ALONE. UNLESS YOU WOULD LIKE TO JOIN ME?
I BELIEVE I WOULD, MISTER...?
RASSENDYLL. BUT PLEASE CALL ME RUDOLF.
RUDOLF. WHAT A CHARMING NAME.
THE END

Alternate
Cover
Gallery

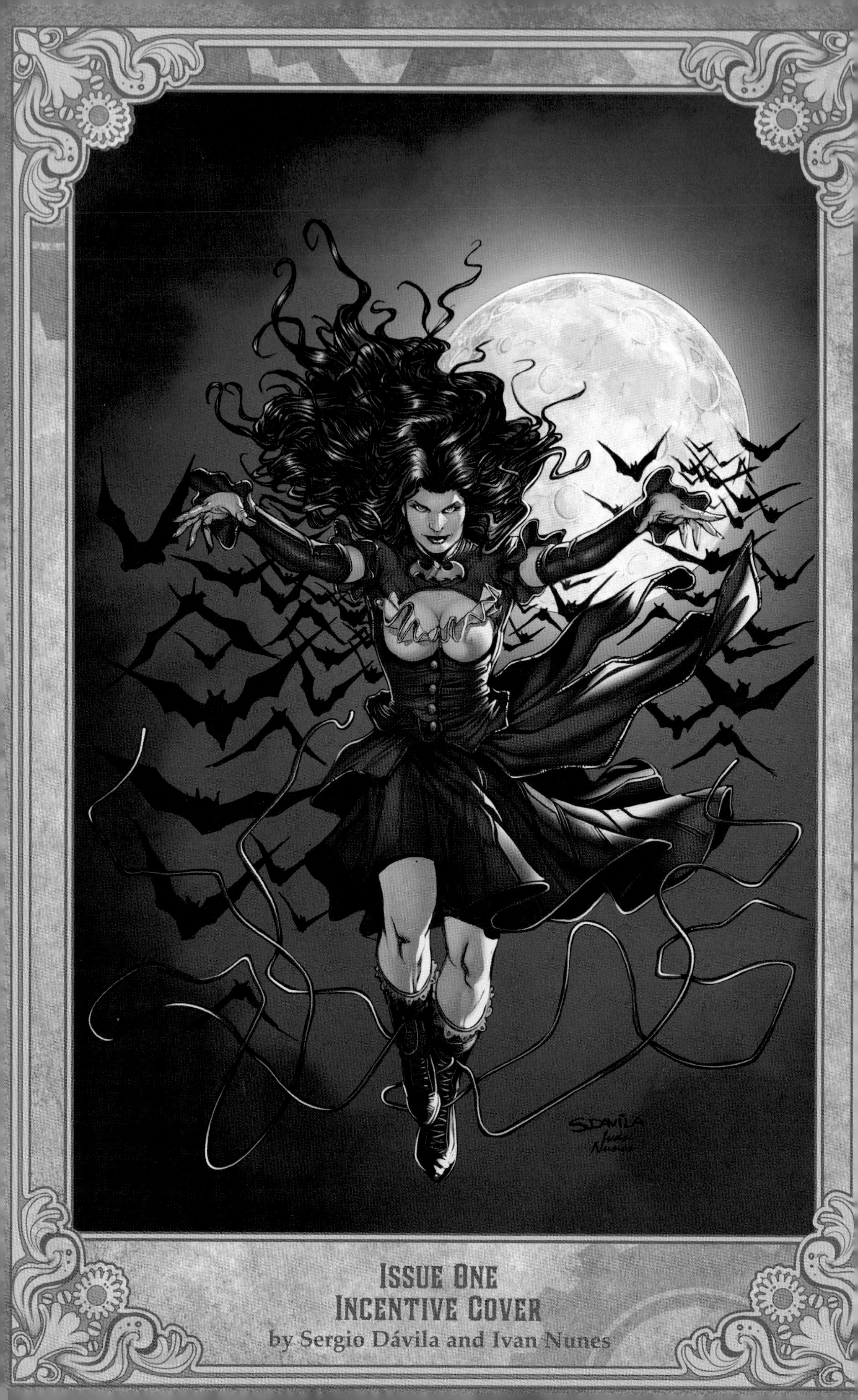

ISSUE ONE
INCENTIVE COVER
by Sergio Dávila and Ivan Nunes

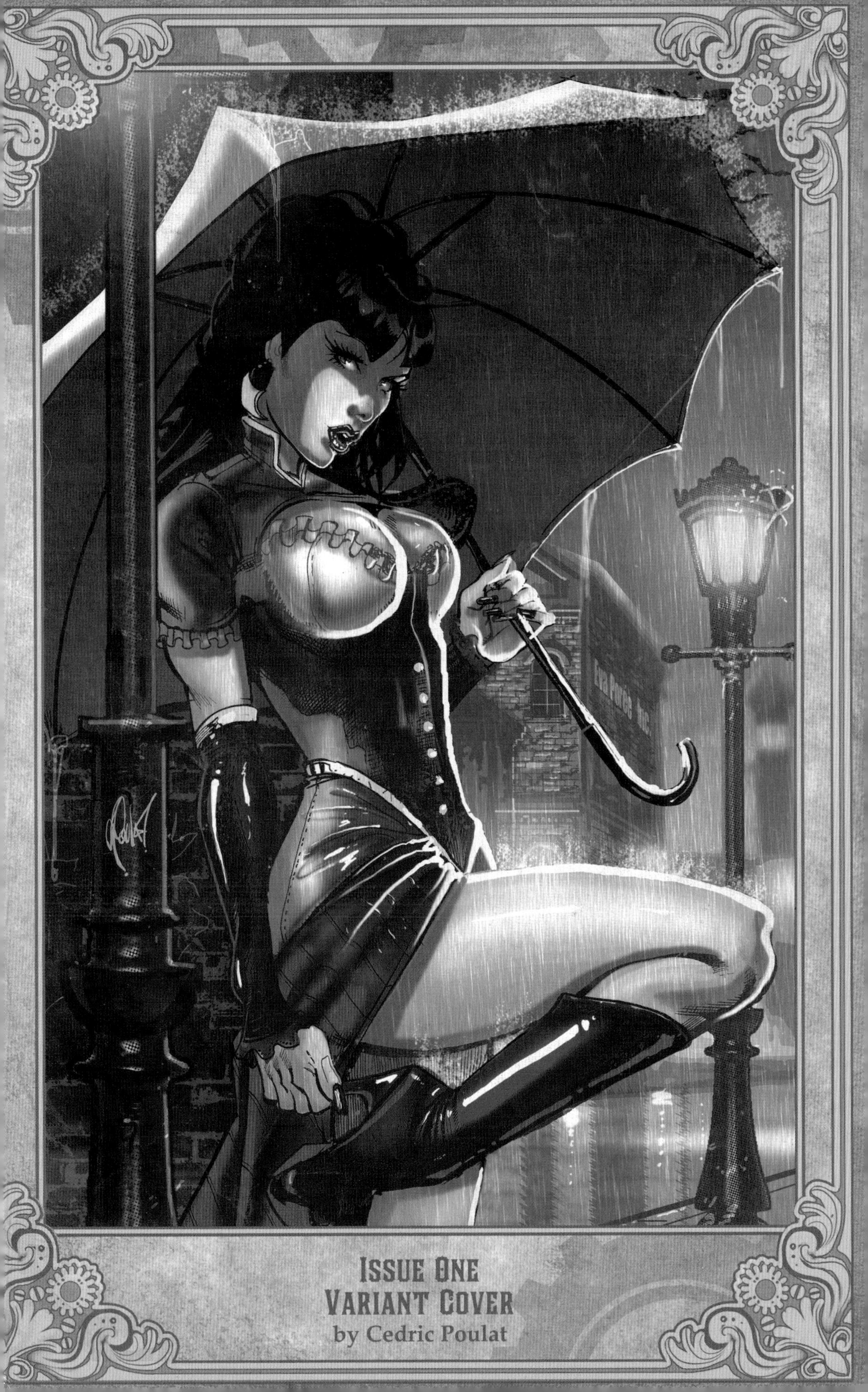

ISSUE ONE
VARIANT COVER
by Cedric Poulat

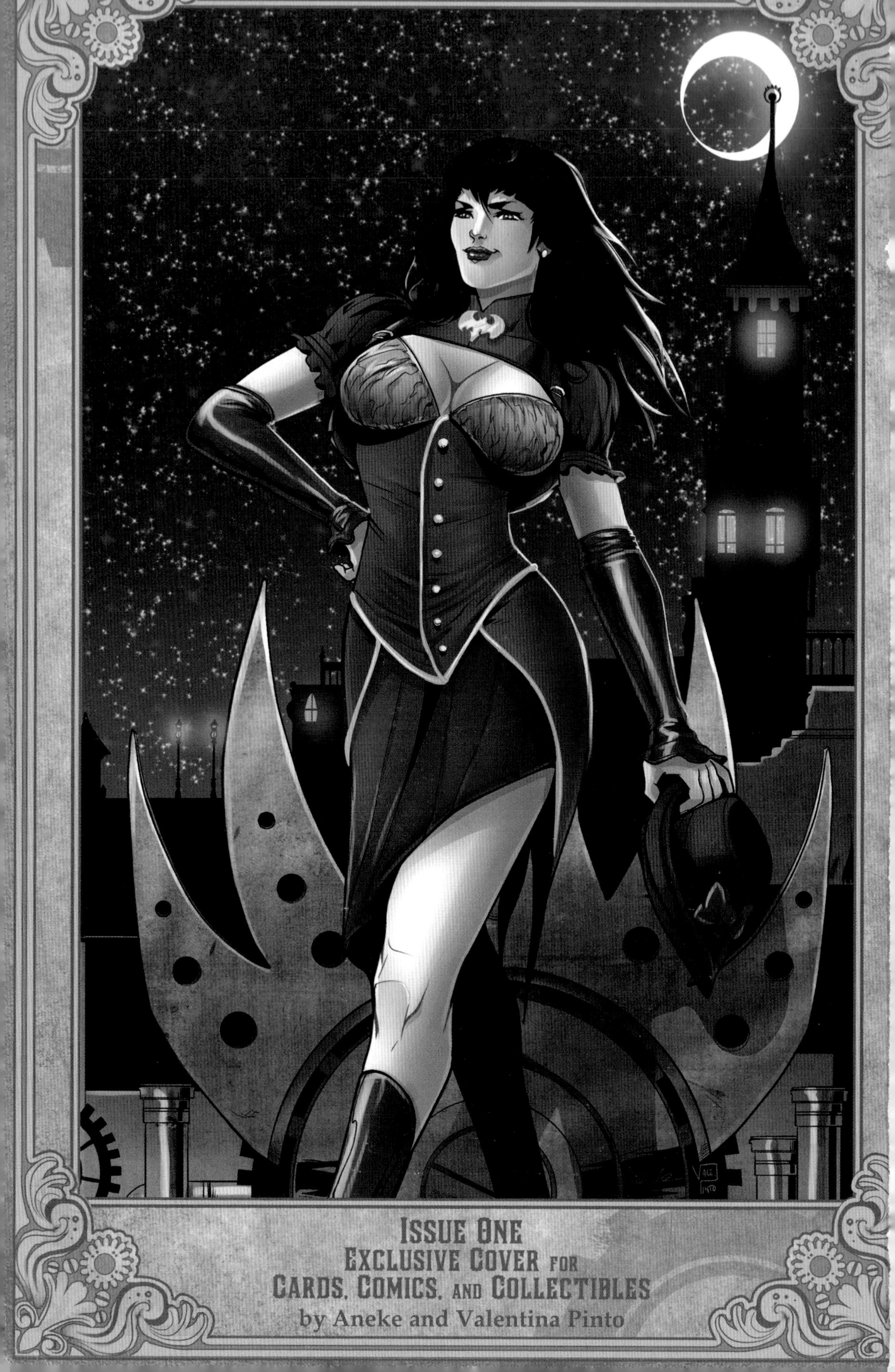

ISSUE ONE
EXCLUSIVE COVER FOR
CARDS, COMICS, AND COLLECTIBLES
by Aneke and Valentina Pinto